SOBER MEN AND TRUE

Christopher McKee

SOBER MEN AND TRUE
Sailor Lives in the Royal Navy
1900–1945

Harvard University Press
Cambridge, Massachusetts
London, England
2002

Library of Congress Cataloging-in-Publication Data

McKee, Christopher.
Sober men and true : sailor lives in the Royal Navy, 1900–1945 / Christopher McKee.
p. cm.
Includes bibliographical references and index.
ISBN 0-674-00736-0 (alk. paper)
1. Great Britain. Royal Navy—Sea life.
2. Sailors—Great Britain—History—20th century.
I. Title.
V737 .M35 2002
359′ .00941′ 0904—dc21   2001051922

For my friends at the Imperial War Museum
and the Royal Naval Museum

Contents

Illustrations follow p.124

⚓

SOBER MEN AND TRUE

Jack's Wrong Image

Since the spring of 1992 it has been my privilege to come to know a remarkable group of men. I encountered them, not as living human beings, but through the diaries they kept, the letters they wrote, the memoirs they prepared, the questionnaires they answered, and the recollections they recorded on audiotape. The men I came to know so well were all former ratings, or enlisted men, who served in Britain's Royal Navy in the first half of the twentieth century, men who fought the two World Wars.

No matter how unromantic the reality of his daily life may have been, the naval sailor is an iconic figure who appeals to historians, fiction writers, and film-makers alike—as witness such novels-become-film as *The Sand Pebbles* and *The Last Detail*. He is a globe-wandering adventurer, dressed in distinctive and attractive costume, short on shoreside personal responsibilities, who flexes the national muscle at enemies, would-be and real, beyond or on the seas. His dark side is a strong part of his appeal; with a prodigious appetite for alcohol and sex, he delights in antisocial behavior which is held in check only by the fear of harsh punishment. Almost certainly because of the appeal of this enduring image, scant historical attention has been devoted to discovering what lies behind the stereotype. I decided to ask those who know naval sailors best—the ratings themselves—What manner of people are sailors, really?

The term *rating* derives from the relative rank a sailor holds in a ship's company. Ratings are men (and today, women) who join the Royal Navy for a fixed period of time as working sailors. Full lists of the different ratings, that is, ranks, to which a sailor could be assigned or promoted in the Royal Navy of 1900–1945 are provided in Appendix 1 and Appendix 2. For present purposes it is sufficient to know that, during the first half of the twentieth century, men in certain of these categories—seamen, signalmen, telegraphists, ship's writers—entered the Royal Navy as boys at age seventeen (sometimes their real age, sometimes one deceitfully inflated with the connivance of the Royal Marine recruiting sergeant) or younger than seventeen with parental consent (real or fraudulent). Other categories of sailors—stokers, sick-berth attendants, and skilled craftsmen—entered directly as men at age eighteen or older. The basic period of enlistment was twelve years—whence the popular sailor expression "Roll on my twelve." That twelve-year clock began to run for those who had entered as boys from the day they turned eighteen; those entering as men began counting with the date of enlistment or *entry*. At the end of twelve years a sailor could re-enter for an additional ten years. Upon completion of twenty-two years of service he became eligible for a lifetime pension. There were many exceptions to this pattern, but the only one important to readers of this book concerns sailors who joined an expanded Royal Navy for the duration of the two World Wars and who intended to return to civilian life ("civvy street") at war's end. Such men were commonly referred to as "HOs" from the designation of their service as "hostilities only."

One HO of the Second World War paints a picture in his diary of a sailor who will be familiar to readers of naval history and sea fiction: "We were put in the forecastle and among a poor crowd of active-service ratings who, I'm afraid, turned me against naval life and both I [and my companion] we[re] morally and physically disgusted with the majority of them . . . [With a few exceptions] the others to us were stupid, thickskulled, ill-mannered gash (rubbish). All the good they were had, I feel, been knocked out of them . . . They seemed solid from the neck up . . . Their only conversation was of women or drink—disgusting!"[1] This particular diarist gradually came to change his mind about his fellow sailors. I hope that readers of *Sober Men and True* will change theirs as well.

In large measure the traditional image of the sailor comes from information historians have collected from elite sources: officers, journalists, and social reformers. All these sources, especially the officers, had a vested interest in portraying naval ratings as the *other*, markedly different from themselves, because in so doing they reinforced their own elite status. Moreover, some of the more accessible primary sources about ratings and enlisted men are colorful disciplinary records of sailors in various kinds of serious trouble—records that have held a hypnotic attraction for naval historians. But just as those who turn up on the police blotter do not represent an accurate cross-section of contemporary society, sailors who encountered the navy's disciplinary system for major infractions were, and are today, a small minority of all who serve. Alas for the image of the naval rating, one drunken sailor ashore calls far more attention to himself than do one hundred men acting more or less in conformity with prevailing community standards.

The sailors I met were no saints, but they deserve a more sensitive and nuanced portrait than the traditional caricature. One rating said best who I think the sailor really was: "The image of 'Jack' was wrong. In the main he was a man who was serious-minded, home-loving, and good-living. However, he was young, healthy, and mostly carefree. Frequently coop[ed] up . . . he had fun when he could."[2]

Is it possible for the historian to recover this "Jack" and present an authentic portrait of him? The sailors themselves call this an impossible task. When asked about their lives in the British navy, the only question to which all the former ratings gave the same response was, *Do you think that the public has ever had a true idea of what it was like to be a naval sailor?* The answer: "Never, if they haven't been one." "No, they *must* live it to know it."[3] But it is impossible to travel back in time to a dreadnought in the North Sea in 1914 or to a cruiser in South American waters in 1939 to experience a rating's life firsthand. That world—and especially its social relationships—has vanished as completely as the world of the bowmen of Agincourt. We can either agree with the old sailors and declare the historical task impossible, or we can attempt to use the imperfect but abundant records that remain to reconstruct, to whatever degree possible, the experience of the naval rating of 1914 or 1939. With a salute of profound respect to the opinion of the old sailors, I have nevertheless chosen the latter.

My interest in British naval ratings of 1900–1945 lies in discovering what they themselves thought about the experience of being a *man of the lower deck*, a phrase rich in symbolic meaning for these sailors. Ratings did not necessarily live on a lower deck of a ship than their officers, though this was sometimes the case. *Man of the lower deck* was, rather, a proud verbal badge indicating that the rating was a member of the navy's working class, with all the rich cultural connotations that the words *working class* held in the first half of the century. I am not particularly interested in what the Royal Navy's officers thought about ratings; nor am I more than passingly concerned by anything Admiralty officials or well-meaning civilian reformers had to say about men of the lower deck. This book is, instead, an exploration, from the ratings' perspective, of what it meant to be a sailor in Britain's Royal Navy during the first half of the twentieth century.

But I had a larger purpose in mind as well as I studied these men: I wished to develop a model of the naval enlisted experience that could be extended to the working sailors of the Royal Navy of the eighteenth and nineteenth centuries. Further, I hoped that this model might illuminate the lives and experiences of enlisted men of the navies that descend from the British tradition—the navies of Australia, Canada, India, New Zealand, the United States, and perhaps even those of Japan and Russia.

The Royal Navy of 1900–1945 makes an excellent foundation for such a model because of the relatively high level of literacy among residents of the British Isles by the beginning of the twentieth century. Unlike their less literate eighteenth- and nineteenth-century counterparts, whose surviving records are often limited, taciturn, enigmatic, and challenging, many of these men of the lower deck maintained detailed and frank diaries and wrote long and frequent letters home. Keen British interest in working-class history has ensured that such contemporary records have been assiduously collected by libraries and archives. Moreover, working-class history has combined with oral history, another powerful British interest. The result is that these contemporary written records have been richly supplemented by taped interviews with, and questionnaires answered by, veterans of the Royal Navy's lower deck. I am aware of no other English-speaking country in which sailors' firsthand experience is so well recorded as it is in Great Britain.

The model derived from the twentieth-century British experience can help historians understand enlisted men of the eighteenth and nineteenth centuries because—despite enormous material changes in naval technology—at least until after the Second World War the traditions, culture, daily routines, and fundamental conditions of lower-deck life displayed a remarkable continuity over some two hundred years of naval warfare. This situation was captured in the half-truth of a popular naval saying: "Nothing very much has altered since Nelson's days."[4] Indeed, I will even go so far as to assert that if an intelligent, skilled, and experienced nineteenth-century American sailor of 1850 could somehow have been transported to a British warship in 1914 or 1939, weapons technology aside, that nineteenth-century American sailor would have been able to fit in and be up to speed with his new British messmates in a matter of days.[5]

Equally important for the model I am formulating is the complex relationship that persists between the Royal Navy and its descendant navies. Some of the latter consciously, if grudgingly, express admiration of Britain's navy as the preeminent sea-fighting force of the post-1500 world. Others have so internalized the British prototype that they do not even recognize its influence in many of their own practices and doctrines. In examining the experience of British ratings, the historian explores tradition at its point of origin.

⚓

As I came to know British sailors of 1900–1945 through their writings, I encountered some topics, important in themselves, which I have omitted or mentioned only in passing. These include the role of Freemasonry in lower-deck life;[6] training ships for boy seamen;[7] organized competitive sport; life in the naval barracks ashore; Dame Agnes Weston, the founder of the Royal Sailors' Rests, and counterpart efforts such as those of the Salvation Army. Each of these subjects is well worth investigating—Miss Aggie provides a major temptation to wander off down a fascinating side trail—but I have not pursued them because I think they are aspects of the twentieth-century British experience which cannot be generalized to naval enlisted life in another country or a different century. Neither is this book intended to be a comprehensive history of the British lower deck during the years 1900 to 1945. Those in search of that more inclusive perspective should turn foremost to Anthony Carew's superlative book *The Lower Deck of the Royal Navy, 1900–39: The Invergordon Mutiny in Perspective*.[8] If my view of conditions for sailors in the Royal Navy in the first half of the twentieth century seems more upbeat than Carew's, that implies no lack of keen appreciation for his pioneering and remarkable achievement. Carew went looking for the conditions that demanded change, the people and the organizations working for (and against) these changes, and the successes and failures of those efforts. I have been in search of the continuities of the lower-deck experience. We both looked at the same navy, but chose sometimes to emphasize different facets of lower-deck life.

⚓

Not all aspects of the British lower-deck experience are equally well recorded. Some major holes exist in the story. So far as I am aware no former rating has recorded in detail his incarceration in naval detention barracks, an experience said to make one of His Majesty's prisons seem like a spa by comparison. Although ex-ratings were asked about their experiences with prostitutes, no one ever interviewed women who once worked as members of the world's oldest profession in Chatham, Devonport, or Portsmouth to get their perspective on naval men. The information that is available clusters around specific aspects of naval life, including battle, discipline, alcohol, messdeck living, as well as sailors' childhoods and their return to civvy street at the end of their careers. One can think of these facets of sailor life about which much is known as passages into the minds and hearts of men of the lower deck. Once inside those minds and hearts the inquisitive historian may be able to explore other psychic terrain.

The relative reliability of letters and diaries as historical sources has long been recognized by historians. But if the historian of the lower deck depended only on such diaries and letters, much of that story would remain unknown. *Sober Men and True* hangs heavily on oral histories contributed, questionnaires answered, and memoirs written by former sailors in the later years of their lives. Certainly they are interesting, but how reliable are they as historical sources? Discoveries by experimental psychologists who study memory can help answer that question. The autobiographical narratives—memories—which we humans construct of our lives enable us to define ourselves. These memories are not photographically accurate videotapes of experienced events but rather selected pieces of that past woven together and enabling us to understand the meaning of our lives: who we have been and (consequently) who we are. As such they are subject to decay and distortion. So much by way of a large *Caution* sign. Experimental psychologists also have two pieces of good news for historians.

For one, psychologists distinguish among three levels of memories: lifetime periods ("when I served in the navy"); general events, that is, composite happenings that are repeated or extended in time ("how we handled cooking in my mess"); and specific events ("my participation in the battle of the Falkland Islands in 1914"). Strong experimental evidence exists that typical human memories of the broad contours of our lives (lifetime periods) are fundamentally accurate. Similarly, when adults draw on the second level of memory, general-event knowledge, our recollections are substantially reliable. It is primarily at the level of event-specific knowledge that memories are most subject to distortion and decay.

Moreover, as adults age, we remember fewer and fewer events from the more distant past—with one key exception: memories of late adolescence and early adulthood remain vivid ones.[9] This is directly relevant to the informants whose memories have shaped *Sober Men and True*. The period of their lives about which these old sailors were being questioned—or about which they wrote—coincides closely with their late adolescence and their early adulthood. When these insights from experimental psychology are combined with the historian's ability to verify many of the objective facts mentioned in the oral histories, questionnaires, and memoirs—the name of a chaplain, the whereabouts of a particular ship on a certain Christmas day—the historian has the tools with which to assess the accuracy of the memories of, say, an eighty-nine-year-old Edward Pullen, a man who, in fact, I find to be a highly reliable informant.

All that granted, in my attempt to get inside the heads of sailors there is one class of sources I have used sparingly and with caution. These are lower-deck memoirs and autobiographies. A number have been commercially published, more were printed privately, and many still exist as unpublished manuscripts in libraries, archives, and the hands of family. As sources they are, in my opinion, open to a number of challenges. Most obviously, they lack the immediacy and accuracy of diaries and letters written in close proximity to the events described. The longer the elapsed years, the more likely the memoir writer is to edit (perhaps unconsciously) events as they actually took place to meet a variety of personal needs. Unlike interviews and questionnaires, whose content is determined by the person asking the questions, memoirs often focus on major happenings which the old sailor thinks were important at the expense of mundane, everyday naval life, where his contribution might be unusually valuable. Most objectionable of all, the majority of the sailors who wrote memoirs seem to have internalized what they perceived to be the demands of the naval-memoir genre—the expectation of what a sailor's autobiography ought to be: one continuous fabric of supposedly hilarious pranks and misadventures, laundered of the waiting, the boredom, the deprivations, the debilitating illnesses, and the occasional terror that are much of the naval sailor's reality. There are some notable exceptions, but in reading the memoirs I did not feel the texture of naval life with the same fidelity and authenticity I discovered in the diaries, the letters, the questionnaires, and the interviews.[10]

⚓

I can make no claim that the eighty-odd former sailors whose written and recorded words are the foundation of *Sober Men and True* constitute a statistically valid sample of the hundreds of thousands of men who served as ratings in the Royal Navy between 1900 and 1945. Although some of them are still alive, there is no way to raise the greater number of those sailors from their graves and draw such a sample. Instead, the historian must work with the sources which survive, be they biased or not. In 1919 the Royal Navy had a lower-deck strength of approximately 106,750 men. Of these, signalmen, telegraphists, and writers—typically (but not universally) the most literate members of the enlisted force—numbered approximately 9,500, or something like 9 percent of the navy's lower deck.[11] The relative proportions were typical of other years as well, but signalmen, telegraphists, and writers are a larger share of the men who serve as informants for this book than they were in the navy in which they sailed. One attempts to fight against such biases—I have, for example, been especially attentive to stoker voices—but they cannot be entirely avoided.

Rather than depending on the seemingly comfortable objectivity of the familiar statistical sample, the historian of the inner sailor must employ a more subjective plan, known to anthropologists and other social scientists as *qualitative research*. I read as widely as I could in the types of autobiographical sources which I have described in earlier paragraphs, and I explicitly sought as many different perspectives—loved the navy, hated the navy, somewhere in between—as I could discover. I kept searching and reading until I decided that I was only encountering similar incidents and reflections parallel to those I had met before. Further reading would, I thought, neither tell me more nor deepen my insights. There I chose to stop.

If I tell the story of this seaman's childhood or quote that stoker's opinion about chaplains, it is because that story or that opinion is typical of the group of men whose self-narratives I studied. When there are conflicting perspectives I try to give each equal time on stage. Should one sailor's opinion appear to stand far apart from the crowd, I have tagged it as such. I think that the life-stories that I have told and the opinion-reflections which I have highlighted are an accurate portrait of Royal Navy lower-deck life in the first half of the twentieth century as that life was experienced by the men who were there, but this book is not meant to be the final word on the mentality of naval sailors. I would be sadly disappointed if it were.

Throughout *Sober Men and True* I make ample use of the actual words, written or spoken, of the sailors themselves. They lived these lives, and they should be allowed to describe them directly. They are, after all, the most reliable source available on what they thought and felt. For this reason I have been reluctant, except for reasons of clarity, to rewrite the sailors' words into my own. Rather, I saw my task as one of discovering and weaving the shared threads of lower-deck life in order to bring out patterns perhaps obscured by the sheer mass of diaries, letters, memoirs, and interviews. Whenever I could find a sailor who expressed his thoughts in an articulate manner, I have chosen his words over my own. Especially in the case of the oral interviews, I have resisted the temptation to clean up my informants' words editorially. The ubiquity of *you know* or *I mean*, the sentences that trail off unfinished, and the abrupt changes of thought convey an immediacy and authenticity which would be lost if those words were edited into smooth, unambiguous prose. In attempting to make the sailors' actual voices and thoughts heard, I have sought to stand out of the way.

In the case of written texts I have (with one or two exceptions) silently corrected misspelled words and punctuated according to contemporary rules. Misspelled words and idiosyncratic punctuation are an obstacle, not a facilitator, to understanding the ratings' thoughts. For consistency British spelling has been Americanized throughout.

⚓

No dreadnought-era British battleship remains afloat to enable us to experience today the physical surroundings of the sailor of 1900–1945 with the same immediacy that visitors to HMS *Warrior* at Portsmouth experience the sailors' world of the 1860s. Old photographs and postcards can assist the leap of understanding, as can divers' explorations of sunken wrecks.[12] But ashore at Chatham, Portsmouth, and Devonport—the three great home bases of the fleet—chances of glimpsing the sailors' physical world are marginally better. Armed with a clutch of vintage photographs, notes from old city directories, and the historical imagination, it is almost possible to visualize the home ports as they were on the eve of the First World War or in the years between the wars, when their streets swarmed with uniformed off-duty sailors in search of recreation.

At Chatham the sailors' historian can part company with the tourists heading toward The Historic Dockyard, cross to the other side of Dock Road at the roundabout, pass an old gatehouse no longer manned by intimidating naval police, skirt St. George's naval church (now a community center) with its eloquent memorials to men and ships long lost, and arrive at the orange-brick and cut-stone buildings of HMS *Pembroke*, the former naval barracks. It is now a campus of the University of Greenwich, but on a bright Saturday afternoon in late spring one can stand in the shade of a big tree and, without too much difficulty, imagine the buildings and grounds alive with sailors. Marching here. A work party there. At sport on the playing fields. A gun crew training to perform at Olympia. Naval police checking passes and papers. Cooks struggling to prepare food for hundreds and hundreds of hungry men, all of whom expected to eat at the same time.

Back in the town of Chatham itself the task of the historical imagination is more difficult. The disused Royal Sailors' Home sits forlornly on a hill overlooking the city center. Along High Street and Military Road the notorious old sailor pubs—Mother Knott's (the Crown and Thistle), the Red Lion, and the Dover Castle—have either become the homes of other businesses, meccas for crowds of Saturday shoppers, or have fallen victim to new motorways and urban redevelopment. It is almost impossible to visualize this sedate High Street furniture store as the Bull Inn, a pub and favorite hangout of sailors, homosexuals, and chorus girls from the long-gone Barnard's Palace of Varieties, a door or two farther west, or the still-standing Theatre Royal down at the corner of High Street and Manor Road.

Relatively few German bombs appear to have made it to Chatham, but Portsmouth is a different story. Fifties-style naval barracks have replaced the rubble to which aerial attacks reduced their predecessors. City-center Portsmouth is even more challenging terrain for the time-traveling imagination. What the Germans failed to get the urban redevelopers did. One can see where Dame Agnes Weston's Royal Sailors' Rest stood before it was destroyed during a German air raid in January 1941, but the historian-tourist cannot conjure the feel of that Edwardian pile and its adjacent streets from the rows of shops that line the pedestrian mall of Commercial Road. The Trafalgar Church of England Soldiers' and Sailors' Institute in Edinburgh Road and the Salvation Army Naval and Military Home at 32 Queen Street, both less popular with sailors than was Miss Aggie's place, have survived time's ravages more or less intact. The Trafalgar is now a residence hall for the University of Portsmouth; the Salvation Army is still the Salvation Army.

Portsmouth and Southsea railway station is relatively unchanged from the facility which battleship-era ratings used. So, too, is Fratton station, one stop farther along the line, where sailors caught the train when they wanted to avoid the naval police at Portsmouth and Southsea. Here and there a few of the old sailor pubs survive, but they have been so transmuted as sports bars or fake Irish pubs that it is difficult to imagine them populated with thirsty, noisy ratings. Even the Albany, according to sailors the roughest pub in Portsmouth, seems tame now. A few regulars nurse pints at the bar or play a quiet game of billiards in the back room of an afternoon. The Albany is livelier in the early evening, but today the patrons are young, friendly men and women—not foreign seamen in search of a fight. Only the urinals seem old enough to be authentic relics of that earlier day.

Urban redevelopment has laid its insensitive hand on Plymouth and Devonport as well, and its works continue. Once there was a pub called the Chester Cup near the west end of Union Street where newly made ordinary seamen—"You know, Jack-me-hearty sort of thing, he'd just joined up and got [his] uniform"—liked to go to bait "these here fairies ... they used to congregate there ... Now any old sailor that was in at my time [said Stoker First Class James Leary], you mention the Chester Cup, he'd know it, because all the riff-raff and all the—you know—the fancy girls and all that, they used to make [for] there to catch the sailor that had a few bob to spare and was wanting a night out sort of thing." Today the Chester Cup is gone, closed in 1957 and demolished by urban redevelopment in the 1970s.[13]

But if the historical tourist hurries and gets there ahead of the wreckers, a piece of the sailors' Plymouth survives—authentic, seedy, partly boarded-up, ungentrified: Union Street from the old Grand Theatre east to the roundabout at the intersection with the Western Approach. Here is a sailor street one can walk, past the pubs—some closed, some still pulling pints—past the United Service Men's YMCA Institute (disused, empty, and in search of a tenant), past the gloriously elaborate New Palace Theatre with its exterior mural depicting the defeat of the Spanish Armada, past the Gaumont Palace cinema, now descended to shabbier days and uses, past seedy businesses, gaudily painted discos, massage parlors, and shopfronts selling southern fried chicken. Here it is much less of a challenge for the visitor to travel back to the Union Street the sailors remembered, one tough place swarming with prostitutes. There is even the occasional young woman, wandering with no apparent destination, whose manner and clothing hint that she just might be today's counterpart to the old sailors' female companions.

I Went Away to Join the Navy

With one exception, all the ratings whose life-narratives are the basis of *Sober Men and True* identified themselves as working class.[1] Several of these sailors achieved significant upward social mobility as a result of their naval service. Often their children climbed higher still. But in every case the class into which a future sailor was born set limits on how far even the most able could go. One rating said it best: "If Winston Churchill had been born in the house next door to the one where I was born and lived in there, with a great deal of hard work he might have attained the lofty position of a chief p[etty] o[fficer] telegraphist."[2]

Within the broad term *working class*—as much a mindset as an economic category—there was ample variation of individual circumstance. Paul Thompson's analysis of the social classes in early-twentieth-century Britain can help illuminate the rich fabric of this broad social category.[3] In 1911 manual workers, eight of every ten employed men and women, numbered approximately fourteen and a half million persons in a total population of nearly forty-one million in England, Scotland, and Wales. At the bottom of this large mass, and constituting perhaps one-tenth of the employed population, were unskilled manual workers: laborers of various sorts, scavengers, and the like. (The unskilled were not at the absolute bottom of the social ladder. Below them were the truly poor—the unemployable, the chronically ill.) One rung above the unskilled manual workers on the Edwardian occupational ladder was that portion of the working population (approximately four out of ten people) who can be classified as semi-skilled. Here Thompson places domestic servants, agricultural laborers, horse drivers, and shop assistants. On the next rung, amounting to roughly three out of every ten employed people, were the men and women classified as skilled manual workers: coal miners, carpenters, painters, and weavers. Above the population described thus far (80 percent of all employed people) was a gray area in which the working class gradually shaded into the lower middle class. Here were to be found the clerks, the shopkeepers, and the small-scale self-employed entrepreneurs. Although their aspirations and their efforts might be moving such workers and their families toward a middle-class way of life, many still thought of themselves as working class. One factor contributing to this self-definition was surely an awareness of the fragility of their economic and social achievement, which was constantly threatened by forces—a downturn in the economy or the illness or death of the primary earner—over which they had no control.

To understand the working class's self-perception it is important to note that its members further distinguished themselves as either *respectable* or *rough*. The respectable saw themselves as thrifty, hard-working, law-abiding people, committed to cleanliness, conventional standards in clothing (especially on Sundays), sexual fidelity, nuclear families, church or chapel membership (if not attendance), and whatever degree of education and culture their limited means could afford. In short, they aspired to what are conventionally characterized as middle-class values and a middle-class way of life. Those living rough shared no such aspirations. The few material possessions they owned were of the crudest sort, and they gave allegiance, not to upwardly aspiring respectability, but to a contrary culture: sexual gratification however it could be found; defiance of the law and its representatives, the police; coexistence with dirt and tattered clothing; and avoidance of education or disruptive behavior when school could not be avoided.

It is not possible to identify with certainty the segment of the working class in which every sailor in this book began his life. But it appears that the majority of them were from families that ranked with the semi-skilled or skilled manual workers or from upwardly mobile working-class families which had edged their way into the gray area between working class and lower middle class—even if they still thought of themselves as members of the former group. No sailor whose origins were rough can be positively identified among the more than eighty men whose life stories inform *Sober Men and True*. Certainly such individuals were to be found in the Royal Navy in the first half of the twentieth century; indeed, here and there in the sources the informants can be found peering down their respectable noses at them. But the navy's recruiting methods—its testing for literacy and basic computational skills, its requirement of a character reference from clergyman or constable upon joining—make it clear that it preferred to recruit from the upper, respectable end of the working class. For much of the first four decades of the twentieth century Britain had more people than there were jobs for them. Its sea service enjoyed a better public image than its army. The Royal Navy could afford to be choosy in the young men it recruited.

Leading Signalman Reginald Ashley's family was typical of those living in the hazy area between working class and middle class. His mother ran a shop and post office in the small Wiltshire village of Edington, where Reginald's father was the postman and his uncles were farmers.[4] But the kind of self-propelled upward mobility it took to get to that horizonland between the classes is perhaps better seen in the story of Chief Petty Officer James George Cox, who came from a family of sixteen in London's east end. Introduced that way—big family, poor neighborhood—the Cox family's story sounds like a recipe for grinding poverty. And perhaps it would have been but for the energy, business cunning, and entrepreneurship of James's father, George Cox. He was a man with a lot of pots boiling on the stove—and all of them productively. The Cox family was living in Hoxton and the father was employed as a journeyman carman when James was born in 1892, but by James's teenage years they had relocated to Number 167 Turner's Road, Bow Common, in a large house that George had purchased for about £380. By then the senior Cox had risen to greengrocer and coal merchant. He dedicated himself to making the members of his big family hard-working individuals, and profit-making ones as well, setting up each of his older sons with a little shed in which to sell coal. George imported the coal in his own lorries directly from the Midland collieries and sold it to his sons in their little sheds at 18 shillings a ton. The boys in turn retailed the coal at 22 shillings a ton, pocketing the profits themselves and, father hoped, developing a good business sense from the experience. Meanwhile, James's mother, Annie Cox, was busy minding the greengrocery business, 6 A.M. to midnight, in the shop on the ground floor of the house in Turner's Road. But George Cox was always on the lookout for other ways to make a shilling or two. When old houses were being demolished he would buy the lumber they contained, lice, bugs, and all, and he kept an old man employed sawing and chopping it into firewood at fourpence a hundredweight for eventual resale in penny and half-penny bundles. And then there was the drayage business. George or his employees would go down to the docks, remove goods, and transport them wherever they had to go. It was a business brisk enough that George stabled three horses behind the Cox home—perhaps in the arch of the railway viaduct—and still other horses at two different stables which he owned or rented.[5]

Even for families whose primary wage earner was a skilled manual worker, economic survival was a constant struggle, as the Bristol childhood of Petty Officer Edward Pullen attests. Edward's father, Abraham Pullen, a carpenter and joiner who built spiral staircases, had trouble finding and keeping work. "Hard times it was at home at times," Edward Pullen remembered. "Food was scarce. I've known my old mother to go out and do a day's washing for 18 pence, come home with two loaves of bread and a half a pound of margarine. We could only have one round of bread and go to bed."

Things took a turn for the better when Abraham Pullen landed a contract to build the staircases for approximately sixty houses under construction in Roseberry Park, a new street being developed in Bristol. "I used to go there sometimes [as] a boy," said Edward. "They used to make their staircases out in the road when it was a nice day or in the houses that they were—you know, that was still partly built. And many times the men used to say to me: 'There's a apple in my coat pocket, son. You can have it.' And I used to take their bottle up the Fire Engine, a public house, and get their beer, bring it back to—you know."

But even before the sixty-staircase contract was finished, Abraham Pullen began to fall apart. The Pullen family slid down the economic scale: "We went back to a place called Bloy Street [Number 90] to live, rent five shillings a week, no bathroom, just the kitchen sink. And we all used to wash in the kitchen sink. And so that my father shouldn't see our [two] girls half undressed, he knocked the glass out and put wood in the panels of the doors. So if [any of] us [eight] boys looked in, we couldn't see our sisters, you know.

"And we used to get a woman come down the street of a Saturday with a box on wheels. And she'd go round during the week collecting up old clothes, see? And she'd tip the clothes up in the road if it was a fine day. And each woman would pick up something. My mother picked up a nice Norfolk coat, threepence. Just fit me, you see? But it had no belt round it—you know, it had the belt there—threepence. And then she bought me a pair of corduroy trousers for half a crown, and I was nicely rigged out.

"Headmaster [at school] used to say every evening: 'Any boys whose father's out of work?' We put our hand up and he'd give us a ticket. Then I used to go in the morning at 8 o'clock in the Bethesda Chapel in Bristol. And they used to give us a big tin cup of cocoa, half sweetened and half milk, and a lump of bread and treacle. That had to last us all day to do our schooling.

"So you see how life was in those really hard times. Almost Dickens's days, wasn't it? But we survived all right. We got along."

There was more to the Pullen family's financial problems than the difficult economic times of the 1890s, bad as those may have been. Edward Pullen put it in one sentence and said no more: "And then my father went on the drink a lot during that time, during the [sixty-staircase] contract business."[6] Parental drinking is a theme that runs through several of the former ratings' childhood memories. Consuming alcoholic beverages through the workday and drinking alcohol at an early age were widely practiced when these future sailors were children and young adults. Deplored by reformers though it might be, alcohol was a deeply embedded part of Edwardian working-class life: "I had a good father," recalled Stoker First Class Henry Boin. "He looked after me and I had nothing against my parents, although they used to like their drop of beer and all that kind of—everybody did in those days. I used to have my little glass of beer. Although I was only a wee boy, I always had my little glass of beer with them. But, although we was poor, we was happy, just standard to today."[7]

Even for as successful and entrepreneurial a figure as George Cox, alcohol was an integral part of the fabric of daily life and work. According to his son James: "In those days us kids used to go in the pub and have half a pint of beer the same as what the old man did, you see. I mean, if we went out on a moving job after coming home from school of an evening, we used to go in and have a drink with 'em, see? The man who you'd moved would always take the carmen into the pub and have a pint of beer, and 'What are you going to have, boy?'—you know. 'Well, I'll have a shandy.' Or 'I'll have a half a pint.' They never stopped it in those days. We drank it. We always had beer at home. My father always had a cask of beer every Sunday morning in the stables for the men to drink while they was cleaning the horses, you see. And they'd drink this nine-gallon cask of a Sunday morning. And then they'd go over the pub [the Prince Arthur, down the block at the corner of Bow Common Road] about one o'clock to have a drink, you see. That was only a snack. And then they'd come out of the pub about three o'clock when the pubs closed to dinner, go home."[8]

But other sailors, men like Edward Pullen, remembered the damaging effect of alcohol on the families in which they grew up. Chief Stoker James Dunn's parents had a greengrocery business in east London that should have provided enough income to keep the family modestly comfortable. "I've seen after twelve o'clock at night on a Saturday night [after the store closed], I've seen our table, piles of money on it, all counting, counting, right till one or two o'clock in the morning. And I've seen us, well, down where we never knew where to get the last loaf of bread from."

Why these dramatic changes of family fortunes, Mr. Dunn? "I had a father who done a bit of boozing, that was our trouble. He was a good friend of the publican, you see, and him and a whiskey traveler, they all used to get together. Well, that's where we were up and down a lot."[9]

Pence-watching and austere as most of these childhoods may have been, many of them were still recalled as happy times. The critical factor in creating what was remembered as a happy childhood was the personality, integrity, and strength of character of the parents—their attitudes toward life and life's hardships. "Did you join the navy to get away from home?" a questioner asked Leading Stoker Richard Rose, whose father had been a plumber in Bognor Regis. "No," came Rose's emphatic reply: "It was a wonderful family circle. We often talk about it. We look back over the wonderful time that we had even as children. We weren't rich and we weren't poor, as the saying is, but we had things that were necessary to us in those days . . . We had a wonderful life. We were well brought up, religiously and scholastically, too, in school, and none of us were dunces and we felt that we could face a world, you know, with some strength of purpose with what we'd gained at home."

Rose's questioner pressed on: "You weren't exactly a poor family, but you weren't a wealthy one. You were above the poor, though?" "Just a normal—well, at that time Edwardian family, working family . . . If ever I had to live my life over again, I only hope it would be the same conditions."[10]

Not all the future ratings came from the kind of happy home that Richard Rose remembered. When childhood memories were bitter ones, the critical factor was often the death of a parent, the remarriage of the surviving parent, and the resulting presence in the home of a stepparent with whom the basic relationship was one of hostility.[11] The danger here lies in succumbing to fairytale stereotypes and scapegoating the new parent. In more than one sailor childhood the biological mother's death left a wound that the stepmother simply could not heal no matter how hard she may have tried: "I didn't never call her *Mum*," said Leading Seaman Arthur Ford of the family's new mother-figure. "I just called her *Mrs. Steigal*. I don't know why, but I just couldn't call her *Mum*." When pushed, Ford admitted that he had a good and loving home life with his father and stepmother, although—like most of the ratings who told stories of their childhoods—Arthur Ford's memories were of strict parental authority enforced by physical punishment: "Yes, we were looked after, yes. Of course they were very strict, you know. My father, of course, he was a good man. But he was very strict you know. I mean, if you didn't do as you were told, you got a hiding, you know. Oh yes, there's no doubt about that. But I always had a love for me father right up till he died, oh yes. Oh, he was a humorous man, one of the old dry characters, you know . . . He got that dry country humor, you know, what they live on, really."[12]

Fairytales to the contrary notwithstanding, the new and difficult stepparent was not always the step*mother*. Although stepfathers appeared less frequently in the future ratings' stories than stepmothers, a male stepparent could create an unhappy home just as adeptly as a female one. Why was Chief Yeoman of Signals Thomas Wallace so keen to leave home? "Well, because of stepfather. The stepfather had no room for us at all. He hated the sight of us." What sort of fellow was he? "Oh, great big rough navvy . . . He always found fault. We could never do anything right. But his own son—he had a son and daughter from his first marriage—and he treated them all right."[13]

Edwardian demography fueled the legend of the cruel stepmother. Because more future sailors' mothers died at a young age than did their fathers (at least in the group whose life stories are the basis for this book), the hostile foster parent was commonly the stepmother. Joiner First Class George Michael Clarkson's father, George, was an enlisted soldier in the army pay corps when his wife (and George Michael's mother), Mary, died, leaving George Clarkson with seven motherless children. He apparently decided that there was no way he could remain in the army and be a responsible parent for seven children, so he applied for a discharge. It was granted, but—most unfortunately for the family's future welfare—two or three years before George Clarkson would have been entitled to an army pension. And he was discharged right into the middle of a depression. Now came grim days for the Clarkson family. "Everybody was out of work," George Michael remembered. "And we were in a very, very bad state . . . We did know what it was to wake up in the morning and have nothing to eat *all day* at times and sit with the sun coming through the window on our feet to warm them, not having any fuel."

Eventually, perhaps three years after his wife's death, George Clarkson got a post as chief clerk at the Royal Engineers establishment at Aldershot. About that same time he formed a relationship with a woman named Jane. (Although George and Jane always represented themselves as man and wife, no one has ever been able to locate a record of their marriage.) Jane had no children herself and no skill at managing her newly acquired stepfamily. "She was always telling us what would happen if she did" have children of her own, said George Michael. "If she had a child, that would take preference over us."

By this time only the two oldest boys, George Michael and John, were left at home. The eldest girl had been "taken away"—by whom is not recorded—and put into service; her two younger sisters were dispatched to a convent (the Clarkson family were Roman Catholic) and the two younger boys sent to Lord Mayor Treloar Cripples' Home and College at nearby Alton. Jane Clarkson's side of the story is not on record, leaving us to rely solely on George Michael's account. This makes no allowance for what it must have been like for Jane to assume the role of mother-substitute for two boys, twelve to fourteen years of age, who had been used to running their own lives, "look[ing] after father and do[ing] the cooking and all that sort of thing." Almost certainly George Michael and John greeted the intruder into their fragile world with an air of protective hostility, which the new Mrs. Clarkson chose to attribute to their father's lenient approach to discipline. The antidote, she decided, was a regime of hard work around the house after school and harsh punishments for perceived transgressions—typically a cup of water and a slice of bread as the meal of the day. "She was really cruel to us," was George Michael's simple summation.

To make a bad situation worse, George Michael perceived a double-standard favoritism: "She worshiped my father. She'd do everything for him. But she seemed to have a hatred of us . . . They used to have butter. We had margarine. Anything that was good that was going, that wasn't for us. It was for them two." From these stories one can surmise that George Clarkson, for all the ramrod posture and fierce mustache he displays in family photographs, was the weaker and more compliant of the couple, inclined to avoid quarrels and let Jane, for whatever reason—a fear of the teenage boys, or perhaps a desire to get the old family out of the way so that she could keep her new husband and any children they might have (but never did) entirely to herself—have things her way.

Fortunately for the Clarkson boys, they had an unlikely protector in their fifteen-year-old sister, Margaret, who had gone into domestic service and would eventually rise to the post of matron in a psychiatric hospital. On big sister's visits home it was clear that she had the psychological upper hand over her new stepmother. But then Margaret was clearly a formidable person. Her nephew remembers that she "never married . . . never stopped talking . . . and spent her life running around the country seeing to anyone in the family who was in need—or perhaps she felt was in need." Jane Clarkson was definitely frightened of the hostile (and perhaps possessive) Margaret, who always came to John and George Michael's defense, warning, "If you lay a hand on any of them, I'll tear your eyes out." "And she would have done [it], too," said George Michael.[14]

Stepmothers aside, the parent the future sailors seemed to identify with and remember most vividly was their father. Is it too hazardous a speculation to connect this with the enthusiasm they felt for, and the comfort most of them came to find in, the all-male worlds of the navy and the ship? The mothers they remember often resemble the bland, self-effacing woman who appears in James Cox's end-of-life recollections. When asked to describe his mother's relationship with his dynamic, controlling father, Cox did not mince words: "Oh, my mother didn't ever have much to say where my father was concerned. My mother done what my father told her. All she done was breed and work. She worked in the shop from, I suppose, six in the morning—five or six in the morning. Father'd go down to the market, bring in the vegetables and stuff like that. My mother would be in the shop. We'd open about six. And people would come in for pennyworth's of coal, half-pennyworth's of wood, pound of potatoes and so on; a pound of apples, if we had them, and all that kind of business, see. And she'd keep going in that shop *and* her domestic work, look after the kids and cook and help all us kids and work till eleven or twelve o'clock at night. And I can see her now standing at her washtub washing for us *every* day—always done a couple of hours washing every day, you see. It was a terrible life for a woman. When I look back I think to myself, 'My God, my mother had a terrible life.' And yet she was very happy."[15]

Several of the sailors were superior students and were eager to continue their educations beyond the mandatory school attendance age of fourteen. Some won scholarships that would have permitted them to go on to secondary school and prepare for higher-status lives than their parents had known. In every case but one the boy's parents, driven by the family's economic needs—and perhaps by other, unspoken motivations, such as jealousy that a child should rise out of the class in which they felt trapped—demanded that their sons leave school at the permitted age, go to work, and contribute to the family income.[16]

George Michael Clarkson was the top boy academically at Newport Road Elementary School in Aldershot. His headmaster told him that he was almost assured of a scholarship at Farnham Grammar School. "I was highly delighted. I liked school," Clarkson admitted. "I was always interested in study." His joy was short-lived. When George Michael went home to report the good news, stepmother Jane squashed his hopes: "Oh no you don't. We've got a job for you. You're going to bring some money in." If George Michael's father had a different idea, he kept his mouth shut and let Jane do all the talking. As an old man, one whose own son had received a university education, George Michael Clarkson was still deeply bitter toward his father and stepmother about his lost opportunity.[17]

Edward Pullen was less bitter toward his parents than was George Michael Clarkson, yet he was still keenly disappointed when, after having passed the entrance examination for Colston's Hospital, which provided a free secondary education for one hundred boys from impoverished backgrounds, his parents turned down the offer, citing their son's need to contribute to the family's income. Edward always wondered whether, if he had been able to attend Colston's Hospital, he might not one day have finished up as a Labour Member of Parliament.[18] Even James Cox's entrepreneurial father failed to appreciate the opportunity a grammar school scholarship presented to his son. He did say that James could accept, but there was an impossible catch: he would also have to work full time in the family business. "We want no Gentlemen Jims in our family," said his father. "We don't want no gentlemen in our family. We want working people."[19]

The sailors imagined vividly how different their lives might have been if they had been able to attend the forbidden grammar schools. But even if they had made it to grammar school, the psychological obstacles to success would have required great determination. Chief Petty Officer Albert Heron's father, a brewer at the New London Brewery in Durham Street, Vauxhall, died when Albert was about eight years old. Between his mother's small pension from the brewery and her part-time job as a lady's maid, Albert's life, although markedly less comfortable than when his father was living, stayed well above real poverty, and he was actually able to attend a grammar school on a scholarship. But just getting to go to grammar school was not enough. Once there, he had fresh psychological hurdles to overcome. Perhaps Albert was simply less intensely committed to education and a potentially better life than George Michael Clarkson or Edward Pullen would have been. "I went to grammar school," he recalled, "but didn't like it, for a few months . . . I wasn't in that sort of class dresswise and that sort of thing, you know. I felt that I was a little below their standard. They were more semi-middle-class boys . . . I couldn't sort of keep up. I mean, if they went to buy sweets, I didn't have the money to buy sweets and that sort of thing. And then I used to have to walk home. These boys had bicycles and that. I didn't have a bike and things like that. I didn't feel that I was with that class and it was hurting my pride. And I left."[20]

In reading story after story of smart boys with frustrated academic ambitions who eventually made their way to the navy's lower deck, one should keep two possible correctives in mind, because such boys may be over-represented in the surviving autobiographical narratives of childhood. For one, it is possible, and perhaps likely, that the former sailors who had been good in school—the book and newspaper readers, the literate keepers of diaries, the thinkers who reflected on their lives and on the times—would also be the elderly men most likely to respond to newspaper notices by historians eager to meet and interview former sailors.[21] If so, such a self-selected group might present a skewed picture of the academic talents of the navy's sailors. For another, if a boy's parents envisioned a better life for their son and were willing to endure the intense deprivation that educating him would demand, the likelihood that their grammar school–educated son would ever choose to serve on the navy's lower deck was small. This leaves the parents who, like George Michael Clarkson's self-centered father and stepmother, refused to support additional education for their sons as the only parents who appear in the former sailors' stories.

Unable, or in many cases unwilling, to continue in school, the future sailors terminated their formal educations at fourteen (in a few cases a year or two earlier) and went to work. On the surface each story of early work experiences appears different, but in reality they are almost all the same tale: a series of low-paying, dead-end jobs is followed by a decision to join the navy.

Edward Pullen's story was as typical as any. When he left school at fourteen he went to work for a Bristol baker at five shillings a week. The hours were long—6 A.M. till midnight (1 A.M. on Saturdays), six days a week—but they were not unusual for the kinds of first jobs the future sailors could find. For the initial three hours of the workday young Ted Pullen scrubbed out the dough pans. At 9 A.M. he teamed up with an adult employee in a four-wheel horse-drawn van and delivered bread until noon, when he had a dinner break. His meal finished, Ted set off with a wheelbarrow to make bread deliveries to customers living nearby, a task he finished up by half-past two or so. At this point he reported to the stables, where he took the bakery's horses from the carts and van, fed them, cleaned them, and bedded them down for the night. This stable work kept Pullen occupied until about ten at night, at which point he and another boy employee had coffee, bread, and cheese.

What Ted did between 10 P.M. and midnight is not recorded—and that perhaps makes an important point. Although the hours were long, the work was not necessarily onerous, and the day was punctuated with periods of slack time. As another future sailor who apprenticed in a foundry explained, "Half your time when you go in these places you spend skylarking." In his case a major part of the duties, at least as he re-called them, was to collect the older men's beer and tea from a nearby coffee shop at lunch and to go around the adjacent streets in search of the bookie's runner—who was himself on the move to evade the po-lice—to place his co-workers' daily wagers.[22]

For young Ted Pullen, all went well at the bakery until the day he was trusted to drive the van by himself. Out of a side street Ted pulled—and straight in front of a tram car that was coming down the main road. Smash! Over went the van, badly damaged. The horses were down, too, but luckily unhurt. Into Bristol's Royal Infirmary went the novice van-driver for a couple of days of observation. Understandably, and perhaps leniently, the baker cut Ted Pullen's wages for the week to two shillings. Thereupon Ted's father—perhaps somewhat the worse for a visit to the pub—showed up at the bakery and roundly cursed his son's boss over the wage cut. End of Ted Pullen's bakery job.

It was Ted's responsibility to find a new one, so off he set on foot through downtown Bristol until he came to the W. H. Vowles & Sons brush factory, which displayed a sign: "A Strong Boy Wanted." Ted stepped in and found the boss sitting in a chair just inside the entrance. He quizzed young Pullen for a bit, then told him to go into the office where a Mr. Maitland would sign him up. The pay was better than at the baker's: six shillings a week, most of which went into the Pullen family's collective finances, not Ted's pocket. The hours were shorter, too: eight A.M. to six P.M., with an hour for dinner.

But the work was monotonous: "I used to have twenty-six girls there to supply them with what they called the *bass*, you know, for pushing into the stock of the broom. They used to all sit round pitch pans, look see, red-hot pitch pans. They'd get so much on their oar, see, dip it into the pitch, put a bit of twine around it and stick it into the stock of the brush. That was my job, to keep those pans going and these women supplied with the pitch and the material, you know, for working." After he had been on the job a while Edward Pullen, now seventeen years old or almost so, began to think about using his dinner hour to go down to the Royal Navy's Bristol recruiting station at 17 Bath Street and inquire about joining.[23]

The few exceptions to this pattern of dead-end (and deadening) shoreside jobs were the young men who were just launched on what looked to be promising career paths when the First World War ruptured their lives. George Michael Clarkson—he of the mean-hearted stepmother, Jane—was one such young man. Through the help of his headmaster, who was keenly disappointed that George Michael's father and stepmother had thwarted the further education of so bright a student, young Clarkson landed a job with a builder. (The headmaster moonlighted by keeping the builder's books.) "I was there eighteen months. And then again my stepmother stepped in. I used to have to walk—we lived at Ash then. And it was—what?—two or three miles, I suppose, from where I was working in Aldershot. And she'd bought me a brand-new pair of hobnail boots, couple of sizes too small for me. And I used to have to be at work at six. So I had to get up at four, and it used to take me half an hour to struggle into these boots. And I told her they were crucifying me, but she said, 'You'll wear them.'

"And the result was I used to walk to work these three miles, work till half-past five at night, then walk back. And I used to take these shoes off and walk in my socks, then put 'em on just before I got indoors. Of course I used to get a cuff around the ear and [she'd] say that I was putting it on, and there was nothing wrong with 'em, and that sort of thing.

"Anyhow, one day the boss's wife said to me, 'Is there anything wrong with your feet, George?' Because I was hobbling a bit, I suppose. And I said, 'No.' So she said, 'Take your shoes off.' So these hobnail boots, I took them off. And the stockings that I wore, the ribs of 'em were planted right into the skin. So she said, 'Now go home and tell your father that he's not to send you back until he's got a bigger pair of shoes for you.' So I went home and she created hell. And she gee'd father up, you know, and he said . . . 'You're not learning anything there' and 'take you away from there.' He was annoyed to think that, see, I'd been sent home. So I didn't go back and then I had to look for a job."

The employment George Michael could find was with a pimp merchant, a man who sold bundles of kindling (pimps) for starting fires. "He
was quite a crude sort of a fellow. And I remember he had a wife and a
baby. He had an old mare and he had a dogcart. And every morning used
to go up there six o'clock, drive out in the country and he used to buy up
branches of trees and all that that had been cut up. We used to take them
back, saw them up into lengths nine inches long—all by hand, of course,
no machinery—and then chop them up into sticks, put them into this
little machine of his, tie 'em up into bundles. And then I was the traveler.
I had to go out and go round all the shops, Farnborough, Frimley,
Aldershot, with this old mare and dogcart, of course, and then go in the
shops: 'Could you do with some pimps? So-much a dozen.' And I used
to get all the orders, come back again, fill the dogcart up and go out and
deliver 'em."

Other days George Michael had to look after his employer's baby.
"Something happened there," Clarkson recalled, with perhaps deliber-
ate opaqueness about the unexplained *something*. "Father went up"—at
stepmother Jane's instigation?—"and had a row with him, and I had to
pack that in."

Almost immediately George Michael heard that the boy who worked
in the local blacksmith's shop had joined the army. Off George Michael
went to apply for the boy's job, which he got. The shop was owned by a
Canadian who did blacksmithing, wheelwrighting, and painting. "That
was a very good job, hard work . . . five bob a week," George Michael recalled. "I used to do a week in the blacksmith shop, a week in the wheel-
wright shop, and a week in the paint shop. Well, he used to buy all this
old iron. He used to shoe horses, make traps, and that sort of thing . . .
And all this iron that we used to make shoes of was secondhand stuff that
he'd bought. And you had to cut it down into strips. And then used to
fashion the shoes, anything from ponies up to hunters and great big
farm horses. And they used to work from six in the morning and overtime till ten o'clock at night. And I used to get three halfpence an hour
overtime. And I'd been promoted then to taking shoes off. And you can
imagine me, a little fellow though I was then, pulling the shoes off a
great big farm horse and [the horse] shooting its back legs out . . . all
over the place."

But the blacksmith went bankrupt. For the third time George Michael Clarkson was out of work. And once more it was not for long. He was laid off in the morning, and that evening two brothers, builders, came to see his father. They passed the blacksmith shop every day, had seen George Michael at work there, and decided that he was the sort of lad they wished they had working for them—and here he was in need of a job. Much as he had liked the blacksmith and his wife ("She was a real ladylike woman, a nice person"), George Michael liked the builder-brothers just as well. The feeling was mutual, and the brothers tried to fill in some of the voids in George Michael's home environment. "I was the only apprentice they ever had. And they used to lend me books and look after my moral welfare. They were great church-goers and that sort of thing." At last it looked as though George Michael Clarkson had an assured future. Eventually the brothers were sure to make him a partner in the building business. Then bigger events, in the shape of the First World War, intervened. Late Saturday afternoon, September 5, 1914, George Michael and his employers were hanging gates at a big country home in Ash Green when someone came by saying, "The [scout cruiser] *Pathfinder*'s been sunk!"—by U-21, though the enemy's identity was not immediately known. "That decided me," Clarkson remembered. "I went away to join the navy."[24]

⚓

All this information about sailors' childhoods prepares us well to ask and answer the crucial question: Why did young men join the Royal Navy as ratings? But to start talking about motivation is to sail into fog-shrouded and dangerous waters. Individuals will often do things for reasons they themselves do not consciously understand. Or they may deliberately conceal the real reasons for their actions and substitute others thought more acceptable to the perceived audience. Or time may have obscured the memory of exactly why they did certain things, and some plausible and flattering conjecture is inserted into the memory void. The historian must recognize all these dangers, but the hard fact remains that the only information available about why men joined the Royal Navy in the first four decades of the twentieth century comes from the sailors themselves.

On the basis of what has already been said about sailors' early years, it stands out starkly that the most obvious reasons to enlist were the economic ones: escape from austerity (if not poverty) and a sure supply of food and clothing. Many young men did join for just these benefits. Chief Petty Officer Ronald Watts remembered that he signed up in "the year of the infamous General Strike [1926]. I was 15 years, 9 months [old]—cold—hungry and hardly a rag to my back—18 inches [of] snow on the ground and absolutely no hopes of a job." By joining the navy, Richard Rose remembered, "you knew where your next meal was coming from and your next wages, and also you didn't have to worry about buying clothes, which was a big problem in those days."[25]

Beyond the immediate motivators of clothes, food, and guaranteed money every month, some young men thought ahead to the pension to which they would be entitled at the end of twenty-two years of active-duty service. George Michael Clarkson remembered the days after his mother's death and his father's premature discharge from the army without a pension, days when they had no fuel for heat and he had to sit where the sun came through the window glass to warm his feet. "And that was the time when I decided—I'd have been nine, ten—then I decided, if ever I had a job, that it would be one where there was a pension attached to it to keep me out of the workhouse."[26]

From what we already have learned about these young men's dead-end civvy street jobs, the navy's appeal as a potential employer is easily understood. James Dunn's job as an apprentice in a foundry was, for a teenager, a fairly good one. He landed it through a neighbor who happened to be a foreman at the plant—and it came only at the end of a chain of long, discouraging days of walking from one London factory to another, only to be greeted by the same placard: "No Hands Required." Now he had the job, but there was no future in it. Dunn knew that, as soon as he turned twenty-one and the foundry had to pay him union wages as a man, management would let him go and he would be back out on the street. Then, in the summer of 1909, the Home Fleet made an elaborate visit to the River Thames and London. Dunn particularly remembered three destroyers that came up the river and anchored between London Bridge and Tower Bridge. Here was an alternative far more appealing than the foundry! Not too long thereafter James Dunn and a fellow apprentice were on their way to the naval recruiting station at Number 7 Whitehall Place, Westminster.[27]

A few young men went to the nearest recruiting office to escape unhappy homes. "Why did you join the navy?" a questioner asked Petty

Officer Raymond Blowers. "To get away from stepmother. Her discipline was worse than any navy." Other young men—more than those in flight from dysfunctional homes but still not a large proportion of all recruits—joined the navy because of family tradition. "My itch to go to sea came about at a very early age," recollected a former yeoman of signals, "probably because Dad had been in the navy. He had joined as a boy in 1896 . . . I was greatly influenced by the stories my dad had told, and it never occurred to me that his personality was greatly different from mine." The consequences of this youthful failure in self-awareness will be reported in a later chapter.[28]

Thomas William Bunter knew himself better. His father, too, was a navy man, a chief petty officer armorer, and he also had an uncle in the navy. "Seeing that I was born in a naval port [the Stonehouse section of Plymouth]," he recalled, "I lived with the navy, and my father used to reminisce about his adventures, and I was very interested in it, and certainly I thought, 'Now I think I would like to join the service.' [But as an armorer my father] was in charge of the destructive element of life, which didn't appeal to me. He was a tradesman, of course. But I took the opposite view. I didn't want to destroy life. I wanted to save life. I always had a principle of helping others, and the only way I thought I could do that . . . by joining the navy was to join the medical branch so I could serve others who were sick and ill." So Thomas Bunter became a sick-berth attendant.[29]

Being young men at a pivotal juncture in history gave many of the future sailors a strong push toward naval careers they might not otherwise have considered or embraced. For those who were not already in the navy when the war with Germany commenced in August 1914, the sea service was perceived as a better alternative to the army and (especially) to possible conscription. A subjective assessment that one's chances of staying alive were greater in the navy than in the army or that living conditions were likely to be better in a ship than in a trench played a big role in these wartime decisions. There were other factors, too.

"The navy was always held in, by everybody's estimation—they always felt a certain respect for the navy, where they didn't [have it] for the army," George Michael Clarkson declared. "Living where we did in Aldershot you rarely found a boy joining the army. They'd seen too much of it. But they're all little heroes that went in the navy.

"I can always remember when my brother [John] joined the navy . . . He was on a little destroyer, the *Waveney*. And at that time he was a stoker. And having done a watch in the stokehold, he used to come up and have to do a watch on a gun at night in those wintertimes . . . The end of '14 that would be, practically. And I saw him coming along from the station, coming home on leave. They'd been into Immingham to clean boilers or something. And he came home and you could still see the dark rings of coal dust round his eyes. And he'd had a few pints on the way. And he was tired and sleepy. And as we came down from the station he staggered a bit. And I remember some women there saying, 'Oh, poor Jack.' If that had been a soldier, he would have been a drunken slut, wouldn't he?

"The navy was much more appreciated in military circles down there than the army . . . because anybody could join the army. But to join the navy then, even in wartime, you had to have a reference from the local clergyman, from the sergeant of police, and it's a well-known fact that there was no criminals in the navy then."

But there were other, even harder to pin down, reasons that George Michael Clarkson chose the Royal Navy: "Actually, I . . . always liked the navy. I think that must have been dated back from the time that we lived in Holywood, you know, near Belfast [before his mother's death]. And when we were coming over to England we seemed to be right out in the sea. And I saw a naval picket boat pass right close to us. And to see them standing up there looking so smart and efficient—always had a liking for the navy. I've never had any—none of my relations had ever been in the navy before."[30]

Economic deprivation, unhappy homes, an inability to continue in school, poor job prospects ashore, and the threat of army conscription all narrowed young men's options and made the Royal Navy an attractive choice. But the single most common reason cited by former ratings for joining the navy was the opportunity for travel and for what they perceived as adventure. These old sailors were clear about the economic and social forces that helped to shape their decisions to join, and yet many of them affirmed again and again that it was the opportunity to see the world, to widen their personal and cultural horizons, and to have some fun and excitement along the way, that were the decisive components in their decisions to choose the navy.

To understand this motivating factor, one needs to remember that opportunities for foreign travel were far more limited in the first half of the twentieth century than they were to become in the second half. Foreign places were much farther away, in time and psychic distance alike, when the swiftest means of travel commonly available was steamship or railroad train. Long-distance recreational travel was restricted to members of the upper middle class and their betters. For a working-class boy of the 1920s or 1930s with a desire to see foreign lands and different customs, the navy was his best choice.

"I can tell you why I joined the navy," said Reginald Ashley. "It was because a pal of mine came home, and he was spinning me yarns about his experience aboard, especially in China, and I immediately said to my father, 'Well, I'm going to join the navy.' He says, 'You're not.' 'Well,' I said, 'I am.' And I pushed off to Southampton and joined . . . Blandford [where I was living] was [a] very small place; there was nothing there to do, you know, of my age, about fifteen. All we used to do was congregate on the street corners and get up to mischief . . . Oh yes, I wanted to get out of Blandford, because Blandford was one of these one-eyed towns, you know."[31]

Arthur Ford was a farm boy who had no personal or geographic bond to the sea, but the navy and the sea were where he wanted to be. After leaving school, Ford remembered, "I went to plowing and all that. So now I got fed up with just walking up and seeing one hedge and walking back and looking at the other hedge all day long. You know, if you got any brain at all, you know, if you got a moderate intelligence, ordinary intelligence, it gets boring, you see.

"But apart from that I always . . . wanted adventure, you know. I used to look right up this long Roman road and I used to think: 'What's up there? What's over the other side of there?' . . . I wouldn't never have settled down [in farm life] although I'm a lover of the country and still am. But I wouldn't have settled down.

"I can explain it. I've got a very vivid imagination, you see . . . I think that would be the word, *restless*. I think that would be the word. Even though you don't get many newspapers to read [in the country], you do get smatterings of what's going on outside a bit, you know, you see. And you begin to want to spread your wings a bit, you know. Oh yes, I did want to see something . . .

"I don't know where it came, the navy, really. I'm never in contact with any sailors or anything like that. But I was mad on it."[32]

Ford, one of the former ratings who was most candid about his sex life, added another reason motivating his desire to join the navy: access to women. "I was very fond of the opposite sex. And I did know that it was a better chance [in the navy] of mixing with—well, of course, you hear these things, don't you? [In the country] they're scattered, you see. One or two on this farm, youngsters, and one or two long way away. There wasn't much connection, no, no."

When asked if young men really joined the navy for girls and sex, Ford replied, "I would say, what I know about it and what I hear . . . that would be [the] predominating thing, because, you know, [sailors] used to talk so much about it, you see, where they'd been with the girl they'd been out with last night or they was going out with tonight. It was a great topic."

The interviewer pressed further: But how could you get a greater chance to meet women in the navy when you spend most of your time on shipboard with other men? "Well, you'd travel to foreign ports, you see. And, of course, as you know, there are places out there for women. And a lot of 'em used to gravitate to those when they went ashore. I won't say all of 'em. That wouldn't be right to say all of them. But a lot of them, you know, it's the first thing they make for, you know. Oh yes, they did."

And the opportunity to meet women was the reason Ford joined up? "I would say so, yes. I would say they just wanted to see the world and have a good time . . . Looking forward to a pension perhaps, but not so much when you're young. You don't look so far ahead as that when you're young, do you?"[33]

Join the navy and see the world. This may seem a trite recruiters' slogan, but it expresses a powerful and real motivation that brought men into naval life. The desire to travel, to see what is over the hill or across the river—and perhaps to experience some excitement in finding out—is a fundamental facet of human nature that sent prehistoric traders across the Sahara Desert, medieval Europeans on pilgrimages and crusades, and Edwardian and interwar working-class boys into the Royal Navy as much, or perhaps more, than self-interested economic motives.

2

They Were Officers and You Were Not

One November day in 1912 future leading stoker Richard Frank Rose went to join up at the Royal Navy's recruiting office on The Hard, just outside the dockyard gate in Portsmouth. He took the written examinations in the morning, then had a dinner break before his afternoon physical with the doctor. Rose did not have enough money to buy dinner, so he purchased a cup of tea and a couple of cakes, then he "had a walk around the harbor and looked at the ships coming in, and in those days it was not an unusual sight to see a huge battleship coming in. I remember the first one I saw was the *Bulwark*, an *enormous* great thing it looked coming in harbor with all the sailors standing up, you know. It gave you a certain glow of pride. And then I thought . . . 'I shall be one of those one of these days.'" Rose chuckled. "Not much glamour when you do do it, really."[1]

The aspect of naval life most responsible for shattering the illusion of glamour was the encounter with barracks and shipboard discipline. "I didn't realize that the navy was going to be so hard as what it was at that time," recalled Chief Stoker James Dunn. "When I got down to Devonport that first night, if I could have gone home . . . I would have done. I think everybody else would have done, but it being in, you were in and that was that."[2] Is it possible to recapture something of the feel of this initially terrifying and thereafter relentless discipline?

Among the six or seven possible meanings of the word *discipline* three are helpful to keep in mind when thinking about sailors and discipline. For one, the word *discipline* can refer to the control gained by enforcing obedience or order—strict government aimed at achieving effective action for a particular purpose or purposes. Here is a definition that easily and clearly applies to the life of military forces. For another, *discipline* can refer to a system of sanctions used to correct those who fail to maintain (or who are perceived as having failed to maintain) the standard of obedience and orderliness set by those in authority. Again, this is a well-known aspect of military life. Finally, *discipline* may mean training and experience that corrects, molds, strengthens, or perfects—especially one's character. This definition leads into the realm of *self-discipline*, the state of control over the would-be dysfunctional forces in oneself. When ratings used the word *discipline*, they used it in all three of these senses, and they slid seamlessly from using the word in one of its meanings to employing the word with a different connotation. That they did this is a clear marker of the complex manner in which the three meanings are intertwined in everyday military and naval life.

In discipline, as in all other matters, the captain was the supreme authority within a warship of the Royal Navy. Under the captain the officer responsible for directing all aspects of the ship's daily life was his second-in-command. In big ships—battleships, cruisers, aircraft carriers—this man was the *commander*. For smaller ships—destroyers, submarines, and the like—it was the *first lieutenant*. To those unfamiliar with naval organization and to American readers, it may not be immediately evident that an officer called the *commander* in a British battleship or cruiser is actually subordinate to the captain. They will perhaps be more familiar with the term *executive officer* when describing the person who fills this role.

In enforcing discipline in the big ships of the pre-1945 Royal Navy but not in the smaller vessels, the captain and the commander depended on a group of senior ratings known as *ship's police* or the *regulating branch*. This branch of the navy was reputed to attract men of mean and bullying dispositions who were not competent to make petty officer in another (and supposedly more demanding) career line within the service. These much disliked and perhaps maligned functionaries were commanded by a chief petty officer called the *master-at-arms* (the MA). The MA—in effect the chief of the ship's police—was more commonly known to sailors as the *jaunty*, although as one rating cautioned, it was "unwise to use this [term] in his presence."[3] The master-at-arms was, in turn, supported by petty officers known early in the century as *ship's cor-*

porals but later as *regulating petty officers* (RPOs). At least those were the official designations. To sailors, ship's corporals or RPOs were always *crushers*—when out of earshot.

The MA and the RPOs did not actually punish sailors. Instead, they issued citations—in naval language, *put a man on report*—that required the accused rating to appear before the commander *(commander's report)* or the captain *(captain's report)*, depending on the severity of the alleged offense and the punishment to be meted out. At these daily rituals, signaled by the call "Defaulters" blown on a boatswain's pipe (or whistle), the sailor charged with misconduct was marched before the commander or the captain by a ship's corporal, who sang out the charge against the accused: "Four hours late returning from leave, Sir!" The sailor was given an opportunity to justify his conduct to the commander or the captain: "What have you got to say for yourself, Seaman Watson?" The rating offered his best excuse, real or concocted, which the commander or the captain typically dismissed—"A man of your experience certainly ought to know better"—and sentenced the sailor to his punishment.

The offenses for which sailors were put on report differed significantly from crimes as they are understood in civilian life. The "Index of Offences" in the 1906 edition of *The King's Regulations and Admiralty Instructions for the Government of His Majesty's Naval Service* listed seventy possible charges against ratings but noted ominously: "This Table is not exhaustive as to offences . . . it is intended to be merely suggestive."[4] Although a number of these offenses would have been regarded as true crimes, whether committed in shoreside or shipboard society—violent assault; theft; making false charges; indecent acts of a grossly immoral character—many more are properly characterized as disciplinary infractions, some of which it would be impossible to commit anywhere but in a ship: smuggling liquor on board; smoking (if under eighteen); misbehaving at Divine Service; desertion; examining another man's bag or locker; spitting on the deck; skulking from, or neglect of, duty; negligently throwing or lowering anything from aloft; drunkenness; sleeping in another man's hammock; insolence or contempt to superiors; and not being in proper dress or being slovenly in person or dress.

The sailor unlucky enough to be hauled up on commander's or captain's report was subject to a number of low-level or *summary* punishments which could be served out at the commander's or the captain's discretion and which had to be performed during what would normally be the sailor's free time at the end of the workday. Of these the most infamous and resented, at least to judge by the frequency with which it was mentioned or denounced by former sailors, was the punishment known as *10A*. This took its name from punishment number 10A in the "Description of Summary Punishments allowed by the Admiralty to be awarded to Persons subject to the Naval Discipline Act, of and below the Grade of Chief Petty Officer or Non-Commissioned Officer" in the 1906 edition of *The King's Regulations and Admiralty Instructions.* The punishment specified: "Grog to be stopped; eat meals under Sentry's charge; after half an hour for dinner to stand for the remainder of the dinner time on the upper deck in the place appointed; extra work in watch below; to be deprived of smoking, and to be under the Sentry's charge during smoking hours. If in harbor or an idler at sea, to stand on the upper deck in the place appointed from 8 to 10 P.M. *Not to exceed Fourteen Days.*"[5]

First Class Blacksmith Sidney Knock told of the extreme to which this regulation could be taken by a sundowner commander or captain: "An offender was roused at 4 A.M., an hour before the ship's company. Having lashed up his hammock and performed his toilet, he would proceed with his half-pint of cocoa to an exposed part of the upper deck. There, under the eye of the duty ship's corporal, he would drink his cocoa; then, armed with the orthodox holystones, apply them to a portion of the deck allotted until the hands mustered at 5:30 A.M. to begin the day's routine by scrubbing decks.

"At 'stand easy'—8 A.M.—he breakfasted, taking his meal standing exposed to the weather. After the meal he was granted time for a hurried shave and to dress in the 'rig of the day,' as ordered. He then attended the daily inspection and prayers, thereafter doing the usual duties in the part of the ship to which he belonged.

"At eight bells, midday, he had his dinner under the same conditions. At 12:30—one bell—and until the conclusion of the dinner-hour he was led to an isolated part of the upper deck and stood facing the bulkhead as a child in disgrace in a school classroom. It is known as 'keeping the flies off the paintwork.'

"The remainder of the day was occupied in work about the ship. During the dog watches he was employed at special tasks or with the watch on deck. At 8:30 P.M.—one bell—until 10 P.M.—four bells—he again stood 'watching the paintwork.' This being the hour to 'pipe down,' he was free to turn into his hammock. This was the routine, with the exception of Sunday, when he was allowed certain time for washing his clothes during the punishment."[6]

No informant for this book described so draconian an application of 10A as Knock reported, but Petty Officer Edward Pullen, who joined the navy in the earliest years of the twentieth century and who himself had some memorable encounters with naval discipline during nearly twenty-three years of active service, described two punishments that had survived from an older navy: "If you was a bit late falling in when they piped the watch to fall in, you was put in what they called the *half-speed party*. And then every so often they'd say, 'Half-speed party fall in,' see? Up you'd rush and fall in. Just as you was walking away, 'Half-speed party fall in,' see? Keep on like that, harassing you all the time, see?"

Then there was the time Pullen was ordered to worship his kit bag: "They piped 'Starboard watch fall in.' And of course when anything is piped you always had to rush straight up to the quarterdeck. Consequence was that I pulled my bag out and just as they piped 'Starboard watch fall in.' . . . I run up on deck and left my bag out. When I came back the ship's corporal said, 'Your bag, Pullen?' I said, 'Yes, that's mine, Corporal.' 'Answer the bugle tomorrow.' That's, you know, like going to court. So the next day when I answered the bugle, commander said, 'You got anything to say?' I had to explain to him, you know. He said, 'All right, seven days worship your bag.' So now, from that time onwards, when the ship's company was having a quiet time, I had to get my bag out and kneel down and say to that bag and my clothes all in it: 'I'm sorry I left you out. I'm sorry I left you out.' And I had to keep on saying 'I'm sorry I left you out' till it was time to turn to work again, see? And that went on for seven days now."[7]

If the offenses were more serious—perhaps an irritated ordinary seaman told a petty officer where to get off—the captain could send a man to the ship's cells for up to fourteen days. Several ratings recounted the experience of being confined to cells, but once again Edward Pullen is the best informant. Pullen's confinement came during his 1907–1909 service in the armored cruiser *Drake*, then under the command of Captain Charles M. de Bartolomé. Pullen and a shipmate, "Nancy" Lee, were aloft in *Drake* putting grease on the turnbuckles that secured the stays to the mast. "Nancy" disappeared into the fighting top for a clandestine cigarette, leaving Ted Pullen to carry on alone. *Drake* was tied up to the Farewell Jetty at Portsmouth, and who should Ted spy standing on the jetty, more or less directly below, but a city policeman talking to a woman. In Pullen's hand was a tin, and in that tin was a lump of tallow. The temptation was not to be resisted. Pullen took aim at the policeman, threw the lump of tallow "and hit him right on the helmet. You couldn't have done it in ninety times over, I don't suppose, eh? Now when we came down from aloft at twelve o'clock, they were piping dinner [and] the master-at-arms said, 'What have you been doing, Pullen?' 'Oh,' I said, 'aloft doing bottle screws,' putting the grease in, putting canvas round, keep 'em from rusting, see? 'Jump aft.' . . . And there was the policeman wiping the grease off his helmet, see? He looked at me with a nasty look, see? So de Bartolomé said, 'Did you do that?' I said, 'No, Sir.' He said, 'I believe you did. Therefore,' he said, 'I'm going to punish you, not for the grease, but spoiling the uniform of the policeman.' So he said, 'You have seven days cells.'

"So at four o'clock they took me down the cells. And the ship's corporal said, 'Have you ever picked oakum before, Ted?' I said, 'No.' So he showed me how to pick the first pound. I had to pick a pound a day, oakum . . . old rope, unravel all this old rope, make it, you know, into a ball, like see. They used to clean torpedoes with it and all manners of jobs, see? However, I managed eventually to be able to do this pound a day, you see.

"And I had a bit of time off in my cell . . . You had a pot in there. You had a table for a bed, you know, see, and you had a pillow. I think if it was cold they'd give you a blanket, but I just laid there, you know, just night time, see? And we used to do half an hour's exercise, walk up and down the fo'c'sle for half an hour. 'Course the ship's corporal watching all the time, see, like you see in the prison."

When asked how he passed the time in the cell, Pullen replied, "Just read the Bible, that's all. Nothing else. You wouldn't have nothing else . . . And pick your pound of oakum, see. When you'd picked that, you had nothing else to do . . . Just loiter about, see, in the cell."[8]

Edward Pullen reported that he had more or less normal meals while he was confined to cells: "a couple of potatoes and a bit of meat." But other veterans of cells remembered harsher rations and slightly more varied reading fare than the Bible alone. "My diet consisted of ship's biscuit and water," said one Second World War sailor who did his time in the aircraft carrier *Indomitable:* "These ship's biscuits—for the information of those who never broke a tooth on them—were harder than any Blackpool landlady's heart, so the only possible way to eat these was to dunk them in water, otherwise you were in danger of a major dental refit. The choice of reading was either the *Manual of Seamanship* or the Bible. Having been a freethinker for several years . . . I decided to give this [latter] tome the benefit of the doubt and read it from cover to cover, which did nothing to convince me, but only reinforced my views."[9] And then there was the isolation, a marine sentry the only human being with whom the offender had any contact. Cells? "Well, that's a very, very severe punishment."[10]

But there was a still harsher punishment: detention barracks ashore, where the captain could send a rating for up to three months on his own authority, with no questions asked—or where a sailor could be dispatched for a much longer period after a formal trial by a naval court martial. Detention's reputation was fearsome—"Men doing detention in Portsmouth had a very rough time, having [myself] talked to some when they came out," reported one rating secondhand; "as near to hell as one can reach this side of the grave," said another.[11] Unfortunately, the autobiographical narratives which are the foundation of *Sober Men and True* furnish only one brief glimpse into this experience: "In detention, coal ship routine. A 50-yard long shed, one end some tons of rubble, man given a wheelbarrow and shovel, fill and double to other end, empty and return, to complete movement of all rubble to opposite end, then back again to the original end and repeat, with no time limit given. This exercise gave me a feeling of complete frustration. No time was given for a breather, but the staff in charge always seemed to know the limit of endurance. A defender [*sic*] was never allowed to walk when under detention. Although very hard, I never considered any of the treatment I experienced to be cruel to a fit man."[12]

Boys, aged seventeen and younger, remained subject to the navy's tradition of corporal punishment, which had long since been abolished for adult ratings. That it survived for boy sailors was less an aberration unique to naval life than a reflection of the larger society's belief in harsh, painful, and humiliating punishments as the appropriate way to correct young people's rule-breaking behavior. The ratings' narratives of childhood attest that many of them had regularly experienced beatings and whippings at home and in school. As practiced by the navy, corporal punishment provided a legitimated outlet for homoerotic sadism in punishers and audience.[13]

Corporal punishment took one of two forms. Boys were subject to the same "Index of Offences" in *The King's Regulations and Admiralty Instructions* as were adult ratings, but for boys the type of corporal punishment permitted was determined by whether the offense was printed in roman (less serious) or *italic* (more serious) type. Canings were meted out for the lesser offenses. Perhaps a boy hid in a ship's boat to avoid a muster, as Edward Pullen once did. The captain would sentence the culprit to six or twelve blows (or *cuts*) with a cane, three-and-a-half feet in length, thick as a man's thumb, and wrapped at either end with waxed twine to keep it from splitting when in use.[14] A boy, wearing a pair of thin duck trousers—although there is at least one report of a boy being caned naked—was held down, customarily over the ship's vaulting horse used in gymnastics, buttocks upward, and given his six or twelve strokes with the cane, blows laid on slowly and with all the force that the master-at-arms could muster. Often all the ship's boys—but never the adult ratings— were assembled to witness canings. At other times they were administered in a closed space with only a portion of the ship's officers, the surgeon, the master-at-arms, and the ship's corporals as participant-witnesses.

More public, more humiliating, and more painful were the whippings administered with bundled birch branches and saplings—cautionary theater known as *birching*. Here was an ultimate sanction reserved for the most serious offenses: desertion, theft, striking a petty officer, or a homosexual encounter with an older sailor. The punishment was typically either twelve or twenty-four *cuts* with the birches. These instruments of correction were usually hung up in the steam of the ship's galley to make them supple enough to have knots tied in them, though there are also reports of birches being soaked in vinegar or saltwater before being used. As with caning, the culprit was bent over a vaulting horse or over the ship's bits, but for a birching his buttocks were exposed and the entire ship's complement was assembled to be entertained, warned, or sickened by the event.

Chief Yeoman of Signals Thomas Wallace, who had himself experienced naval caning as a boy, described the punishment of "Paddy" Flynn, caught having sex with a pig and sentenced to dismissal from the navy: "The birching's got to be done at noon today! There's two birches hanging up in the galley in the steam. A birch is like a—sometimes you see 'em in the park with the sweeping, you know with a kind of a twigs all bound together. Well, a birch is that on the small scale. And it's hung up in the steam, in the galley, where the steam's going up in it all the time, making it brittle. It's there for about twenty-four hours and then it's taken down; and if you get twelve cuts they use one birch. But they wouldn't use a birch for more than twelve cuts; if there's any more than twelve they use another one. And it's on the bare bottom. Not on the back—on the bottom. And you're strapped over the bits and that's administered in . . .! . . .! like that. And you can see pieces of flesh flying up there. I think this fellow was in the sick bay . . . for about a fortnight before they could discharge him."[15]

The psychological effect of corporal punishment on sailors of the nineteenth-century British and American navies is contested historical ground. Those calling for the abolition of flogging asserted that the practice destroyed good men, humiliating them, breaking their spirits, and making them desertion-prone—that is, if the physical effects of a flogging did not maim or kill the punished men.[16] Those who hold a more positive view of corporal punishment argue, on the basis of anecdotal sailor evidence, that men preferred corporal punishment to alternatives such as long periods in confinement. These revisionists reinforce their position with statistical evidence which, they argue, infers that corporally punished men continued to be good, effective sailors—that, in fact, sailors accepted corporal punishment as a necessary and salutary part of life at sea.[17]

Some twentieth-century sailors told of receiving canings themselves as boy ratings, testimony that may help shed light back into the nineteenth century. "The first stroke whistled through the air and seemed to cut one in half; hence the term *twelve cuts with the cane*. This punishment was only used on boys under the age of eighteen, but required the will of a man to resist the suffering."[18] When asked what the worst part of the experience was, one rating replied: "Humiliation. Having to face, or being thrashed, in front of all my messmates, my shipmates and so forth. Your pride is hurt very, very much—more than the physical side in my case."[19]

And the aftermath? Were there lingering psychological wounds? How did the caned boy face his messmates and older sailors? According to one old sailor who had himself never been caned, the victim "got a bit amenable. He didn't want any more of that." Asked if the victim put up a front, the sailor replied, "Oh yes, he come round and say, 'Well, that's all right. I can put up with that. It never hurt me.' But all the time perhaps it did, look, you see." How did other sailors behave around the punished boy? "Never used to bother too much. Used to say, 'Well, now you knows better than to go on, don't you?'—or something like that. Never used to—used to accept it as part of the things that, you know, had to happen."[20]

The only acceptable response to caning or birching, if one was to remain a sailor, was to endure the punishment and reveal no outward sign of suffering. Arthur Crosby, a twenty-five-year veteran of the navy who ended his career as a chief petty officer, reported that over the span of those twenty-five years, he "experienced most forms of punishment, including detention, all of which I considered deserved. Men who were stroppy [a lower-deck corruption of *obstreperous*] were also prepared to take any punishment meted out . . . The general attitude of men was that 'they could take what the navy was prepared to serve out.'"[21]

In the specific instance of caning, according to Chief Petty Officer James Cox, there was an unwritten rule: "The tradition [was] you never opened your mouth. Well, I mean, if anybody was to cry or scream or anything like that . . . you were a coward. That didn't happen." When Cox was asked about his own experience of caning, twelve cuts for attempting to strike a petty officer—did it breed resentment? lower his morale? destroy his self-respect?—he replied, "I didn't think it out the way . . . Oh no, I expected it. Oh no, I wasn't severely punished. I was let off light."[22] These personal recollections appear to support the revisionists who question the long-term psychological damage inflicted by corporal punishment in the navy. The old sailors see such punishment as an appropriate response to inappropriate behavior, and the ability to en-

dure and survive it without breaking down as a vindication of one's masculinity.

Former ratings spoke with diverse and seemingly contradictory voices
when they told of their experiences of naval discipline. Some said:
"Harsh, savage, 'ours not to reason why.'" "Extremely severe." Sometimes "cruel and sadistic and out of all proportion to the 'crime.'" "Too
rigid and in many instances unfair."[23] But to others it was: "strict but
generally fair." "If one did one's job and behaved, no trouble at all."
"Very fair. If any well-trained naval rating was punished for stepping out
of line, such as his dress, his work, responsibility, absence ashore, etc.,
then he certainly deserved it." "Discipline was harsh but just. If you behaved like a mule, they had a good stock of jockey that would ride you. I
knew all this before and joined."[24]

Ratings' perceptions of naval discipline were shaped by many factors:
their own personalities; the captains and commanders under whom they
served and who set the tone for discipline in a ship; the leadership skills
(or lack of them) possessed by the ship's subordinate officers; and the
type of vessel in which they served most of their time (rigidly disciplined
battleships and cruisers or smaller, more informal destroyers and submarines). But among the seemingly contradictory memories an impartial
observer can discover an underlying common ground shared by most
sailors when they thought and spoke about discipline.

Even when their recollections of personal encounters with the navy's
disciplinary system included sanctions that seemed unfair and even un-
just, almost all ratings explicitly recognized that discipline—even severe
and strict discipline, so long as it is neither excessive to the point of sadism nor capricious in its application—is essential to the effective performance of the naval mission; it maximizes the safety of all who go to
sea in a ship; and it ensures that each sailor bears his fair share of the
ship's work. One stoker, himself from a humble (but respectable) working-class background, though not from the bottom (or rough) rung of
the Edwardian social order, added this class dimension: "The type of
people you had joining then mostly came from the lower-educated part
of the population, and if you gave people like that a free hand, you put
them all together, you would have an horrible situation. You'd never
have the health and comfort to sleep or the usual things that's necessary
. . . You're in a port. There's leave for everybody. Men come off at night.

If there wasn't discipline, you'd get a drunken man keeping everybody awake. We're probably going on watch a little while afterwards. There's one. You can have a man going on leave. He come back lousy. Used to get 'em coming back lousy. If that was allowed to go on without the discipline, you'd have everybody being infected [with lice]."[25] The conditions of life at sea sanctioned the kind of discipline the navy sought to inculcate in its sailors. "The navy had its own brand of discipline," observed one thirty-year veteran whose service included both world wars, "based on the fact that men were for days, weeks on end in what you could describe [as] a steel box: calm, storms, tropical heat. No ice water. No cool air system. This called for a special brand of discipline, a different type of man."[26]

For many—almost certainly for the best and most effective sailors—the order and discipline of a ship of war satisfy a fundamental emotional need. When asked if he thought naval discipline was a good thing, one rating replied in these words, echoed by many other sailors: "Yes," he said, "I think so. I took a pride in it really. I mean I get great pleasure from springing to attention and saluting an officer. I would enjoy doing it."[27] A former stoker looked at the same idea from a different angle. Men who were not fundamentally amenable to discipline, he explained, did not remain in the navy. They either fell into serious trouble and were discharged or found some other means to break away from naval service. He himself "was amenable to discipline, knowing that it was—you couldn't live without it."[28]

An even more basic insight into the dynamics of naval discipline was offered by one astute sailor who said, "They liked high spirits. [In the context it is not clear whether "they" are the ship's officers or the collective naval administration.] They don't want people walking about with a Bible in their hand in the navy, you know. They like to see people with spirit. They cultivate it, you see. They like to see high spirits. They like to see people alive, you see. That's the sort of people they want."[29] And how should we define "high spirits"? Robert John Jeffery remembered that during his first duty assignment at Devonport as a boy writer—this would be toward the end of 1906 and early 1907—he "was [frequently] getting into trouble. I was a gymnast in those days—jumping through windows and breaking them and holding onto gas pipes, catching [hold of those] alight, and causing that sort of boyish trouble. I was taken up before the commodore twice and when he looked at me the second time he made various noises and said, '*You'll* finish up on the gallows. No question about that!' So he said, 'I think the best thing you can do is to go somewhere else.'"[30] Whereupon Boy Writer Jeffery was shipped off to Portsmouth. No gallows for him—Robert Jeffery lived to be an old man, recording in the mid-1970s his life and successful career as a ship's writer.

In the rating's eyes the essence of good discipline rested, not in breaking men's spirits and reducing them to automatons, but in a creative tension between the navy's need to maintain order and the highest degree of seagoing and combat efficiency and the spirited, assertive individual's need to fight back against all this imposed control. The sailors' attitude is classically summed up by one man who, in the glossary to his memoirs, defined good conduct badges as being awarded for so many years of "undetected crime."[31]

Lest any reader think his statement an exaggeration, consider this story from the Second World War diary of William F. Read, then attached to the new cruiser *Belfast*. On July 29, 1939, Captain George Arthur Scott presented a rating with a long service and good conduct medal, "but as the ship was not yet in commission, the pomp and ceremony commonly performed on such an auspicious occasion had to be waived. This did not seem to affect the lucky recipient, Leading Stoker Rimington. I use the term *lucky* in the fullest sense of the term, as it is generally accepted that one has to be very lucky to keep his misdemeanors hidden for fifteen long years." Then Read added tellingly, "Furthermore, I knew Rimington very well." What makes Read's testimony especially telling is that he was the man officially charged with detecting those misdemeanors. William F. Read was *Belfast*'s master-at-arms.[32]

Ultimately the navy functioned well as an organization because its sailors accepted, internalized, and acted on its standard of discipline, while at the same time maintaining their own sense of identity through essentially harmless but morale-boosting "undetected crime." As thoughtful ratings came to realize, the purpose of the navy's externally imposed discipline was to teach and reinforce self-discipline, which the ratings themselves identified as one of the greatest personal assets gained from their lives in the navy. "I still think how good the discipline has done . . . me," Richard Rose said. "You do a job perfectly when you've been disciplined to do it."[33]

⚓

Ask the former ratings about naval discipline and the talk soon turned to officers. They—the Royal Navy's lieutenants, commanders, captains, and admirals—came from a world separated from that of their lower-deck subordinates by a social chasm that is difficult to comprehend fully in the more democratic world of a century later. Sailors were children whose families earned (or scratched out) a living by manual labor. Although naval officers of the early twentieth century were, to some extent, appointed from the old aristocracy of the British Isles, increasingly they originated from the ranks of the financially secure and the affluent middle classes, whose numbers and whose wealth had been fueled by nineteenth-century industrialization and a sun-never-sets empire. Put another way, naval officers were drawn from the 13 percent of the population that controlled 92 percent of the nation's capital.[34] Distinct in birth, education, and the route by which they had entered the Royal Navy, officers were as remote from the ratings as it was possible to be in the restricted world of a ship. They lived in their own, usually far-removed, quarters, dined with as much Edwardian grace and manners as they could transport to sea, and—that sure sign of gentility—had their physical needs catered to by servants. Most important, they knew they were entitled to be officers because a deep and unbridged social gulf set them apart from the men of the lower deck—a social gulf that ran parallel to that which separated Master from My Good Man on land. From their side of the social chasm officers ran the ship through its senior ratings: the leading hands, the petty officers (POs), and the chief petty officers (CPOs).

This description is, of course, a gross over-simplification of the shipboard reality. Maintaining social isolation (which is different from the necessary authority of command) was a challenge in a ship as small as First World War–era destroyer or submarine. Engineer officers were generally more democratic and accessible than officers in the executive branch, the latter being those officers who could (or who could aspire to) command a ship. Urged on by lower-deck agitators for change, some progressively minded senior admiralty officials attempted to develop means by which able ratings could gain admission to the officer ranks.[35] These efforts were stoutly and more or less successfully resisted by the navy's officer corps, with the outcome that, during most of the years this book covers, such attempts at fundamental change succeeded in promoting from the lower deck only a tiny cadre of second-class officers, men condescended to by the traditional officer class and disliked and distrusted (if perhaps secretly envied) by their former peers on the lower deck. A more democratically recruited officer corps would have to await the pressures of finding men to command the much enlarged Royal Navy of the Second World War and the evolution of an increasingly open society in Britain in the post-1945 years.

No aspect of naval life prompted such a mixed bag of recollections from the former ratings as their reactions to officers. At one extreme stood Leading Seaman Arthur Ford, who had no doubts about the essential rightness of a navy founded on the principles of deference: "The proper officers, you know, they were the higher-up, well-educated people and come from jolly good families, wealthy families, too . . . You had some respect for those people . . . They're born and bred . . . Anybody who's better educated than me and has been brought up in a different strata of society, I can look up to them, because possibly I could learn from them . . . I can't visualize a ship being run by somebody from the lower deck. No, I can't . . . No, it's a different class of people altogether." "You think the navy is best run by, shall we say, the upper class?" Ford's questioner interjected. "Yes, definitely," he replied. "Everybody's got their place."[36]

At the other extreme was the analytical chemist-turned-naval seaman Charles Stamp, whose First World War service on the west coast of Africa in the second-class cruiser *Astræa* brought him into contact with a set of officers, mostly Royal Naval Reserve men, for whom he could have no respect: "I am very sorry to say we have a rotten lot . . . They have not taken one little bit of interest in the men or their welfare and can be truthfully described as a selfish, pleasure-seeking, whisky-loving . . . [bunch of] jumped up 'gentlemen'—men who have not had power to command 300 men before and now like to 'swank.' They are the only 'gentlemen' and they treat the lower-deck men as 'scum.' One in particular when he first came aboard . . . used absolutely disgusting filthy language—worse than any I have heard on the lower deck (and Jack can swear, although he means nothing by it) . . . According to Admiralty rules etc. we are not allowed to work in heat of sun etc., but that did not affect the officers . . . We often had to in heat of day and often for their pleasure going ashore for leisure or a sail."[37]

Charles Stamp's take on officers at their worst is especially informed and damning, because he was himself a member of the financially secure middle class from which so many officers came to the navy. Stamp had volunteered for wartime service on the lower deck out of patriotism. His father owned a chain of London grocery stores; a younger brother, Laurence Dudley Stamp, attained eminence as a geographer; his older brother, Josiah Charles Stamp, an economist and taxation expert who was a government financial advisor during the same years that Charles was sweating in the African sun, later became chairman of the London, Midland and Scottish Railway, and entered the peerage in 1938 as Baron Stamp of Shortlands.

How can one reconcile perceptions as sharply conflicting as those of Ford and Stamp? One promising approach is to identify the qualities which men of the lower deck repeatedly attributed to good and bad officers. Despite their differences of opinion, all hands agreed that the tone was set from the top. "It always lays with the captain or commander whether the ship's company have a bad or good commission," wrote Seaman William Williams from South African waters in 1901, "for if the ship has either, the ship's company are the sufferers, as everyone in authority under them have to be more severe, so that [the] lower the rank, the greater the pressure is put on, and in some ships I believe it is little better than slavery for the lower-deck hands."[38]

At the top of the list of undesirable officers was the captain who was tyrannical, petulant, and irrationally angry. Edward Pullen remembered serving under just such a man, Charles Martin de Bartolomé, in *Drake*, between 1907 and 1909. Pullen told several stories about de Bartolomé, all of them presenting a consistent picture of a captain who made life miserable for the men of *Drake:* "Our mess was 43 Mess and we was the cleanest mess in the ship. And when Captain de Bartolomé joined the ship as a captain he came down on our mess. We had a silver cup presented by the other captain [Arthur Hayes-Sadler]. And the men used to have three-water instead of four-water rum, you see? And he had a look there . . . And then he said, 'This is the cleanest mess in the ship?' 'Oh, yes Sir.' So he says to the caterer—that's the leading seaman—'Turn your table over.' And you know where we'd been scrubbing at the top, the dirty water would get underneath, see? And some men had pieces of meat stuck on a fork under there, ready for another meal when they came down, see? And with that Captain de Bartolomé caught hold of the silver cup, flung it straight out of the port, and we had seven days' scrubbing that mess."[39]

Closely related to the petulant and tyrannical officer was the officer who was consistent in his behavior: unfailingly hard-driving and insensitive to the needs and feelings of the ratings under his command. One of the threads running through Able Seaman Percy Rooke's First World War diary is his commentary on the behavior of Heathcoat S. Grant, captain of the battleship *Canopus*. When *Canopus* coals at Abrolhos Rocks off the coast of Brazil on Sunday, December 27, 1914, Rooke releases his pent-up frustration in the privacy of his journal: "Finished at 11 P.M. This has been our hardest coaling, as we were working in the sun and the temperature was ninety degrees in the shade. Quite a lot of men collapsed during the day, and our captain expressed his gratitude by telling us that the coal *must damn well* come in faster. If not, he would walk around himself and we would know what that meant. Yes, we all knew what it meant: He would get his suit dirty and could not drink so much *whisky*." More than a month later as *Canopus* is approaching the entrance to the Mediterranean, Rooke complains: "Captain had all hands on the quarterdeck today and said when we get to Gibraltar he would expect the coal to come in faster than it had done on previous occasions." Nine hundred and fifty tons of coal are taken on board at Gibraltar, and *Canopus* steams on to Malta and another round of coaling—this time 700 tons. It is now February 8, 1915, and the men of *Canopus*'s lower deck have had no shore leave since war was declared the previous August. Coaling completed, Captain Grant gives one watch leave from 4 P.M. to 8 A.M. the following morning. The men, already voicing "a lot of discontent," are further roiled to discover that other ships in port have 60 or 72 hours' leave to *Canopus*'s niggardly 16 hours. "Can see trouble ahead," Rooke tells himself. "If we cannot get by fair means, we will get it by foul." Sure enough, despite the inevitability of stiff punishments, 69 men from the first watch ashore deliberately overstay their leave and have to be rounded up and brought back on board *Canopus*. When the second watch gets its 16 hours ashore, 59 men fail to return on time, and Captain Grant responds by canceling all further leaves, leading Rooke to confide to his diary: "Our captain is a good fighting man but would be appreciated a lot more if he thought a little more of his ship's company. He could have prevented all this by giving leave the same as other ships. 7:30 P.M.: [Captain Grant] thought better of things, served out rum."[40]

Less detested, perhaps, but still a major source of lower-deck irritation were the officers who liked to keep ratings busy at seemingly pointless work on the old theory that constant occupation prevented idle men from getting into mischief. The ratings, seeing themselves as responsible human beings, resented being treated as if they were not. When Chief Stoker James Dunn was serving in the battle cruiser *Renown* (August 1929–December 1931), he came under an engineer lieutenant commander, Reichel W. V. Reeves, who was a keen devotee of this school of leadership: "His idea was to keep men at work and you didn't get any trouble as long as they had plenty of work . . . and he believed if it was only men doing useless work, such as he'd have bulkhead doors that were painted, he'd have them cleaned off and *polished, burnished* so they were all shining, *and he had this done to keep men at work* . . . Just make-work. I would go to him and I'd say, suggest to him that the football team was playing ashore this afternoon: 'You think we could make a half a day of it?' '*Certainly not. Certainly not.* Give 'em something to do.' And, 'If you've got time you can spare like that, give 'em something to do. They'll find—keep them out of mischief.' The next officer I had was Lieutenant Commander [Robert S. E.] Hannay, who came from Edinburgh, and he, when I mentioned this to him, he said: 'Dunn, life is too short for that sort of thing.' He believed in work, but he didn't believe in that useless type of work."[41]

One could muster a degree of sympathy and understanding for an officer like Lieutenant Commander Reeves, James Dunn's nemesis, when he was as hard on himself as he was on others. Dunn remembered times when Reeves was so ill that he was confined to his bed on the surgeon's orders: "He's had me in his cabin and he's been going through routine work then. He would say, 'Bring all the papers along, Dunn, and we'll go over this and we'll go over that.' That with him laying in his bunk!"[42] But there was only resentment and hostility for officers who indulged themselves while expecting the ratings to accept conditions they themselves did not. Ratings' diaries and memoirs are rich in such stories. "Christmas day (at sea)," wrote Percy Rooke on December 25, 1914, in *Canopus*. "Signal from admiral wishing us a very happy [Christmas], which proved a very miserable one. Our officers had a very good one: best of food, drinking and singing all day while the men were on corned beef and hard biscuits and manning the great guns at night. Personally, I felt very sad that day as I recalled the happy one I had on the previous [Christmas]."[43]

One world war later a leading signalman attached to the monitor *Roberts* at Port Suez recorded: "When the yeoman of signals was out of the ship or otherwise not available it was the job of the duty leading signalman to take any messages which were received to the captain, and one day when it was even hotter than usual I happened to be on duty. It wasn't even necessary to move on the messdeck to make a person sweat. Just sitting still it rolled off, and when I took a message into the captain he was sitting in the middle of a square formed by four electric fans! My communistic tendencies were growing rapidly."[44]

Men of the lower deck especially condemned officers who consumed alcohol to excess while on duty. This criticism has already appeared in Percy Rooke's litany of complaints about his captain in *Canopus*, H. S. Grant. Able Seaman Ronald Orritt made the criticism even more explicit: "An officer who had taken too much gin during the midday meal time could issue orders of a ridiculous nature, and often of a dangerous nature, but they *had* to be obeyed and put into execution at the risk of being charged with mutinous conduct; and I may add that the officer was never taken to task." William A. Green, another able seaman, recorded with contempt in his diary just such an incident in *Canopus* on New Year's Eve, as 1914 ended and 1915 began under supposedly wartime conditions: "At 12 midnight the officers are getting very rowdy and behaving in a disgraceful drunken manner. About 12:15 A.M. 'Action' is sounded off for some reason or another unknown, after which things grew quieter. This, however, is not the first time we have gone to action stations under the commands of drunken officers."[45]

This censorious attitude on the part of the ratings demands an explanation because of the apparently blatant contradiction it displays: how could the men of the lower deck, many of whom were experienced and enthusiastic drinkers, be so critical of officers who drank? After all, they themselves had their daily issue of alcohol in the form of grog or, for petty officers, neat rum. Because none of the sailors on whose memories *Sober Men and True* is founded appears to have explained this contradiction, the historian is compelled to speculate. Almost certainly there was an element of jealousy here. The rating's daily issue of alcohol was strictly controlled; the officer in his mess appeared to be under no such constraint—he could drink as much as he wished. Whether the latter perception was true or not—no responsible captain or commander would want tipsy officers on duty—is beside the point. The ratings believed that the officers often drank to excess. But there was a more fundamental issue here: in the deference-saturated naval and civil societies of pre-World War II Britain, ratings expected officers to observe a higher standard of behavior than their own, because officers held privileged and responsible positions. An officer compromised in ability and behavior by alcohol was an affront to such lower-deck expectations.

The concept of deference leads to the final characteristic of the bad officer. That defect in command was, in the ratings' eyes, a perversion of an element essential to the well-ordered running of a ship of war: the psychological separation that must exist between officer and rating. Able Seaman Walter N. Basford explained well the expected behavior: "They were *officers* and *they brooked no argument or anything.* You were told to jump or double and you jumped and doubled. And if he spoke to you, you would stand to attention. There was never any camaraderie like between us or anything like that. He was there, and *you did what you were told.* There was never any slip-up or anything like that . . . They were there as *officers* and they let you know it [by] the tone of their voice: '*Stand to attention.*' And you stood to attention . . . There was never any slip-up and say, 'Oh, all right, you do this and I'll do that.' '*Double!*' You know, it was always abrupt. They were officers and you were not, and that was that."[46]

Ronald Orritt provided the commentary that helps to elucidate Basford's text: "There was, throughout my period of service [1924–1934], a distinct barrier between officers and the lower deck. This of course we (the lower deck) appreciated. Service in a man-o-war warrants *control* and control can only be maintained by a display of leadership. Our officers were our superiors and our leaders; therefore they couldn't maintain their positions if they were to fraternize. Very often in small ships officers became very lonely. We were aware of this and sympathetic to all officers who played their part humanely, but"—and here was where the perversion of that necessary distance between officer and rating came into play and poisoned the relationship—"there was also that distinct display of class distinction and arrogance by some of the officers who displayed themselves as Mummie's little boy who must always have his own way, and this was more or less condoned by the undisputed authority they held."[47]

If tyrannical, petulant discipline, hard-driving insensitivity to human needs, love of pointless busywork for subordinates, self-indulgence, and excessive parade of class distinction and arrogance were characteristics of the bad officer, what made a man a good officer as seen from the lower deck? This question is more difficult to answer than what made a man a bad officer, for sailors, like other diary-writers, typically used the privacy of their journals to vent anger and frustration rather than to record praise. A detested officer is likely to be better documented than an admired one.

Shining brightest in the lower deck's cluster of positive officer qualities was a genuine interest in the welfare and the personal problems of the men under the officer's command. "Now don't forget, you blokes, if ever you're in any trouble at home, the missus gone off with the milkman or anything like that, you come and see me," said the Honorable (later Sir) Guy H. E. Russell, then a young officer in the battleship *Royal Sovereign*, in a meeting with the men of his division. The sailor who told the story still remembered the moment a half-century later and honored the man: "As I say, he was a great guy."[48] For well-regarded officers these were not just idle words. Richard Rose recalled the engineer lieutenant from one of his First World War assignments as a prime example of this genuine concern as manifested in real, effective action: "The chappie [from] up in Yorkshire . . . his wife was suddenly endowed with three or four soldiers billeted on them up in Yorkshire, and of course she wrote and told him, and I think they hadn't been long married and of course he was very jealous that she'd got three or four soldiers staying in the same house and it upset him terribly. And he came to me one day and he was talking about this like and he said, 'How can I get home?'

"I said, 'Well, you can't get home.' This is out in the Mediterranean. I said, 'It's obvious you can't get home.' So I said, 'Why don't you see the engineer?' So he saw the engineer and explained it all to him and the engineer wrote away. Of course it took a long, long while to get the letters, to get to and from, because you know out there they were always sinking the ships with the mails on board or vice versa—coming to you, see—you could never guarantee you would ever get a letter, but they got this one through and the officer commanding them decided under those circumstances he'd find [other] billets for these four chaps, and I think it all ended happily."[49]

The detailed First World War diaries of yeoman of signals and Isle of Wight native John E. Attrill are of particular interest here because Attrill made a special point of recording stories of officers liked and respected by the men under their command. Early in the war Attrill, whose former vessel, the battleship *Audacious*, had been sunk by a mine on October 27, 1914, was detailed to a new assignment, the armed yacht *Lorna*, in which were two six-pounder guns, a ship's company made up of her old civilian crew, some Royal Naval Reserve men, and two Royal Navy pensioners, and a mission to patrol off the northwest coast of Scotland in search of submarines, mines, and contraband-carrying steamers. Attrill has his hands full teaching signaling to this mixed bag of naval humanity, but he finally shapes them up. Afterward Yeoman of Signals Attrill proudly notes in his diary that he was "thanked by the captain [Edwin H. Edwards, RN (retired)] for doing my best in teaching signals to the crew."

Later, when Attrill badly scalds his right foot and left knee and is laid up for ten days, Captain Edwards personally changes the dressings on Attrill's foot because *Lorna* carries no medical officer. In May 1915 Edwards leaves *Lorna* for a bigger command and Attrill laments: "I think everyone was sorry. In fact, I was more than sorry that we were losing him, as he had been very kind to us and it would be a job to get a better [captain], and I think he was sorry himself, as he always said how proud he was of the behavior of the ship's company . . . Our late captain left at one o'clock, shaking hands with everyone and wishing us luck, and I think he began to break down a bit at the finish."[50]

Back in the battleship navy and at the other end of the war, Attrill has good words for Edward B. Kiddle, his captain in *Marlborough*. When Kiddle is hospitalized because of an injured leg in July 1918, an event that leaves Commander Harry W. C. Hughes in charge, Attrill writes, "It was hoped that he would soon return." Kiddle does return to duty a month later, but in October he is promoted to rear admiral and leaves *Marlborough* for the last time. "He had been a jolly good captain and did everything possible for his ship's company," records Attrill. "He spoke to us all before leaving, saying he had told the new captain [Charles D. Johnson] that this was a fine ship's company, the best ship in the squadron, and the best squadron in the Grand Fleet. He thanked us all for [our] assistance to him . . . We gave him three cheers and later, when he left [the ship], all hands turned up and manned the ship's side and cheered him until out of sight."[51]

Personal qualities that earned an officer the ratings' esteem were not necessarily those that gained him the high regard of historians. Admiral Sir Cecil Burney, second in command of the Grand Fleet under Sir John Jellicoe, has not fared well in the historical audit of the First World War's command performance at sea. Arthur Marder has memorably dismissed Burney as "a man of powerful physique, though in chronically poor health . . . reputed to be a fine seaman . . . a hard taskmaster of the old school—orthodox, unimaginative, utterly lacking in initiative—who appeared to one officer as 'a piece of solid wood.'"[52] The growing corps of Marder revisionists have not disagreed with this evaluation. When Jellicoe was made first sea lord late in 1916, he took Burney with him to Whitehall. Historians have applauded Burney's removal from command at sea and seen his replacement by Admiral Sir Charles Madden as an unqualified improvement in the fighting capability of the Grand Fleet. The ratings' view up from the lower deck differed, however, from the historians' view down from Olympus. Here is how Attrill saw matters: "At 10 A.M. [on November 28, 1916] all hands were assembled 'aft' on board [*Marlborough*], as Admiral Burney wished to bid us farewell. It was very touching, and amongst other things he said he had to leave to take up another appointment and he was very sorry indeed to have to go, as he would willingly serve on in the *Marlborough* until the end of the war. He thanked all hands for the way they had assisted him in carrying out his duties, especially during the Jutland fight, and he hoped that we should prove victorious and safe in anything else that we were called upon to do. He evidently began to feel it very keenly at parting from us after so long. At 11 A.M. he boarded the [destroyer] *Parthian*, and as she left everybody cheered him lustily and, when last seen of him, he was still waving his hand in farewell. Everyone was sorry to see him go."[53]

Burney is the mirror image of the diarist Percy Rooke's previously quoted portrait of Captain Heathcoat S. Grant: "Our captain is a good fighting man but would be appreciated a lot more if he thought a little more of his ship's company." The contrast is a sharp reminder that those qualities that make a man an excellent commander in active warfare and battle—courage, determination, combativeness, risk-taking initiative, imagination, ability to ignore combat losses in pursuit of victory, to name a few—are not necessarily the qualities that make an officer a strong leader during the stresses and tedious routines of daily naval life. It is the exceptional officer who combines both.

Closely allied to a genuine concern for those under his command was an officer's willingness to communicate with the lower deck, to let his subordinates know what was happening. It was a quality keenly valued by the ratings. Fifty years after the fact, Ordinary Seaman Patrick Mullins remembered this from the battle cruiser *Repulse*'s role in the May 1941 pursuit of the German battleship *Bismarck:* "How much did we know, over the next momentous three days, of what was going on around us in the North Atlantic? Quite a bit, I think, because Captain [William G.] Tennant had a very good practice, once we were at sea, of speaking to the ship's company over the Tannoy system or getting one of his senior officers to do so, and telling us as much as he knew operationally. Of course he had a captive audience locked up inside this great steel box and there was no risk of leaks; but it was a wise appreciation on his part of the fact that information is an excellent aid to good morale. The spirit of the ship's company was, in fact, remarkably high, especially in such an elderly and in many ways unsatisfactory ship. The flow of information, eagerly devoured, gave an edge to everyone's keenness and, although the surface attitude was one of 'I hope we avoid that f———,' it was clear that [if and] when the moment came, they would fight the ship well."[54]

An officer could be tough and still be respected, no matter how strict he chose to be, so long as he was fair. Toward the end of December 1918 Ordinary Telegraphist J. A. (Jack) Goodwin of the battle cruiser *Lion* returned to Rosyth from leave nine hours and forty-five minutes late. He had missed the last drifter out to the Battle Cruiser Force and spent the night in the superannuated cruiser *Crescent* before finally reaching *Lion* at ten the following morning. Goodwin reported to *Lion*'s police office, where the master-at-arms welcomed him home with: "Commander's report, Monday, 10 A.M."

When "Defaulters" sounded on Monday morning Goodwin appeared before Commander Harold G. C. Franklin armed with some plausible (if fraudulent) excuses about why he was late in returning to Rosyth, "but the commander, being too old of a bird at the game himself, said there was ways and means of getting back to the ship in time, and I was old enough to know better." "Captain's report," said Commander Franklin. "Right turn. Double march," sang out the ship's corporal escorting Goodwin. At 11:30 "Captain's defaulters" sounded and Goodwin was marched up before Captain Arthur John Davies. Once more Goodwin tried his sad tale with no luck. The captain, "being a bit of a sport himself, said 'Usual scale' to the ship's corporal, who read 'Four days pay [forfeited]—Four days leave stopped. Right turn! Double march!'"[55]

To be respected, an officer not only had to be fair no matter how strict; he also needed to work as hard and be as demanding of himself as he was of his subordinates, never taking advantage of his status to avoid unpleasant duty. Recall James Dunn's dislike of, but grudging admiration for, Lieutenant Commander Reichel Reeves, who kept right on working even when he was too sick to leave his bunk. The respected officer also had to know when to let the men under his command get away with something that did no real harm. "They used to have a kit inspection," remembered Arthur Ford. "One of the dodges [tricks] there was—because, if you were anything short . . . it would be taken a note of and you'd have to go to the purser's place—the paymaster's stores—and get another one. But the favorite dodge was there: 'Only one flannel?' 'Yes, Sir, one on, one in the wash.' I were up to all the dodges . . . And ten to one, you know, the officer going round, he'd laugh, you know. They just take it, you know, laugh, you know. Any high spirits or those sort of things, they were—you know—they join in, you know. Never frowned upon anything of that description, you know. They used to get a kick out of it, I think, sometimes."[56] Here was one reason ratings so disliked officers who had themselves risen from the lower deck: such men knew all the dodges. Under them there was no opportunity of maintaining that critical margin of self-esteem in the face of a harsh and all-pervasive discipline by getting away with a few things now and again.[57]

Much could be forgiven and great respect awarded to the officer who was a brave, calm, and inspiring leader in danger. When the battleship *Albion* accidentally grounded on May 23, 1915, during the Dardanelles campaign—and, in fact, grounded directly under the Turkish batteries, which took full advantage of her crippled situation—Signalman Walter Dawson, who left a detailed diary narrative of *Albion*'s successful escape from all-too-imminent danger, positively bursts with enthusiasm for the role taken by the battleship's acting captain, Hector L. Watts-Jones: "Throughout this inferno [of Turkish shelling] Captain Watts-Jones, to whom great credit is due, maintained a perfect calm and displayed splendid coolness and courage, and, though not many men said so, he was, without [doubt], the hero of the day to everyone on board . . . Then [as *Albion*, afloat at last, moved slowly out of range of the enemy guns] someone on our forecastle sang out: 'Three cheers for our captain!' Needless to say, no second asking was necessary, and despite the fact that the captain said 'Cease fire,' the cheers rang out loud and strong for him who deserved them if anyone else did. More than one strong man who, but a few hours before, had been hurling death and destruction at the Turks with only one feeling—of wiping the enemy out—felt a lump rise in his throat as this part of the program was being carried through."[58]

After noting the qualities which ratings mentioned when they described those men whom they considered to be good officers—real and effective concern for sailors' welfare; communication to the degree possible about what's going on; fairness in dispensing discipline; knowing when to look the other way; courageous leadership—one circles back to the puzzling question asked earlier: What sense can one make of the discordant, contradictory voices with which men of the lower deck answered questions about the officers under whom they had served? Was it a navy in which "seventy percent of the officers I served under [1929–1936] acted and behaved similar to what they were referred to, 'naval pigs,' by the lower deck; the other thirty percent were called and acted like 'gentlemen,' but they were outnumbered and couldn't alter the rot"?[59] Or is this assessment more accurate: "Officers during my service

[1924–1949] were pretty genuine people and, as such, commanded automatically a good relationship"?[60]

On closer study patterns in the ratings' seemingly contradictory responses can help to explain the sailors' widely divergent reactions to officers. Ratings' assessments of officers as a class differed according to the years in which the ratings served or the portion of their service about which they were thinking when they responded to cues concerning officers. So many former ratings reported the following impression that its validity cannot be doubted: officer relations with the lower deck improved continually and consistently throughout the 1900–1945 period, reaching their best state during the Second World War, with the officer corps as a whole taking a growing interest in the welfare and the personal problems of the men under their command and with a steady lessening of officer distance and hauteur.[61]

Moreover, a rating's opinion about officers was heavily influenced by whether he served mostly in big ships—battleships, cruisers, or aircraft carriers—where relations were distant and formal, or in smaller vessels such as destroyers, submarines, depot ships, and the like. "I spent a lot of time in the Mediterranean in small craft," recalled Philip Robinson, a former engine room artificer first class. "If we were round the Greek islands on a Sunday, the first lieutenant might pass the word round that he was sailing that afternoon. Would anyone care to join? We would take tea and sugar and land. We would all skylark together, brew a pot of tea, etc. But once back on board we paid the first lieutenant the respect due to his position."[62] According to Chief Petty Officer Albert Heron, who spent most of his naval career in small ships, the senior officers of such commands had little interest in inflicting punishments for petty offenses. The first lieutenant was more inclined to call into his cabin a sailor who had gotten out of line and give him the word—"Don't let me have to speak to you again, my man, *or else!*"—than to have him stand facing the paintwork for hours.[63]

Although small ships were preferred over large vessels for their more informal officer-rating relationships, whatever the size of the ship, the ratings observed that relations were better at sea than in port and more comradely in wartime than during peace. Finally, ratings who worked closely with officers, whether as signalers, ship's writers, or stewards—or who were capable athletes and filled vacant slots on officers' sports teams—tended to have good opinions about officers because they came to know them as human beings through intimate day-in, day-out contact. "At first I personally felt that officers were *all born* at Windsor Castle, dined at Eton or Harrow, and had 'Blah!' for tea," said Leading Electrical Mechanic Kenneth Oke, who often filled in on officer teams in football and hockey during his 1926–1950 active-duty service. "Later I discovered they had mums and dads (even children) just like me."[64]

⚓

Perhaps because they had so thoroughly internalized the values of ranked Edwardian society, most of the sailors whose diaries, letters, memoirs, and interviews have shaped *Sober Men and True* were proud of their status as seamen or leading hands or petty officers or chief petty officers and seemed to feel little desire to become commissioned officers themselves. Many expressed contempt, hostility, and disdain for men of the lower deck who became officers. "Like it's the nouveau riche who are more snobbish, it's the man raised from the lower deck that is more officious. They know all the dodges and answers," snorted one former stoker first class.[65] To the country boy Arthur Ford a man promoted from the lower deck simply could not be a real officer because he did not come from the proper social class. To support his point Ford told the story of a west countryman who had been promoted to warrant officer from the lower deck: "Of course they try to put on the airs and graces when they get off the lower deck, you know." This particular warrant officer was directing a party of ratings who were being transferred from one ship to another. The men's bags and hammocks were all in a pile. The warrant officer did not want the sailors searching through the pile for their individual bags and hammocks. Every sailor was to pick up one of each and sort out ownership later. To effect his purpose the warrant officer ordered the men: "Take your bags and hammocks indiscriminately and place them over 'ere."[66]

Maybe this attitude was all just sour grapes, the ratings' way of dealing with the reality that they were forever barred from ascent to officer status. There is no way to know. But there were *some* lower-deck men who wanted to be officers and who made no secret of their desires. These tended to be men with more years of formal education than their non-complaining shipmates, men who saw themselves as equal in natu-

ral abilities with their commissioned officers, but who, because of economic or other circumstances, had been denied the opportunity to continue the educations that might have permitted them to gain officer
rank. Such men were Left in their politics (the majority of lower-deck
men, if they thought about politics at all, tended to be Conservative),
and their unhappy voices were most often heard in the years just before
the Second World War. However, as such would-be officers were the
first to point out, they were a small minority in the mass of lower-deck
men satisfied with the status quo.

One of the most eloquent of these men was the Manchester-area petty
officer telegraphist Charles R. Thomas. He belonged to the minority of
naval ratings who had attended and completed secondary school. A good
student, Thomas applied for a scholarship to pursue a bachelor of sci-
ence degree at Manchester Municipal College of Technology, but he
was not selected, a circumstance that appears to have left him embit-
tered. For a while Thomas worked as a laboratory assistant in industry,
but it was a hobby—wireless telegraphy—that was his real passion. After
a stint with a Royal Naval Volunteer Reserve wireless unit in Manchester, Thomas transferred to the Royal Navy on a seven-year enlistment in
1934. There is no way around it: Charles Thomas was a loner. As a boy
and young man, he spent much of his spare time walking and climbing
in Derbyshire and the Lake District. In the navy he tended to isolate
himself. Most ratings held comradeship to be one of the great strengths
of naval life, but not Thomas. "In the navy," he said, "one's life is
'hominibus plenum amicis vacuum' [plenty of men, friends none]. I am
very much alone."

As do most loners, Thomas spent a lot of solitary time thinking. In
letter after letter to his family in the late 1930s and early 1940s he
poured out his feelings of resentment that he was a rating while others,
less able than he (at least as he saw it), were his officers. He complained,
"I am . . . more equipped to hold a commission than the majority of the
cadets I have seen. Of course the criterion of the son's ability in the navy
is the father's ability to either manufacture jam or make boots and shoes
out of compressed paper . . .

"Essentially the services . . . consist of two very divergent classes. The
officers come either from the old aristocracy or from the capitalistic
middle classes and the men in the ranks from the working class. The

standard of education is very low in the working class . . . The man with a secondary school education is in an uncomfortable position. He is often equal in education to the average officer and superior in common sense but has only the same prospects in the promotion racket (a true word) as an average rating. Naturally, the officer class does not impress me as much [as] it does the average rating because I can see through the veneer and realize that it is only in such an exalted position (and believe me it is) because of a grievous fault in the social system . . .

"There is a lot of 'eyewash' in the newspapers about the navy being short of officers. If they can't find any out of a hundred thousand ratings, well, they ain't looking hard enough.

"There is too much of one class controlling everything in this country and the sooner everything is thrown open to everybody the better . . . People outside the services do not realize that the services are controlled by a class of people who elect their own successors and are independent of Parliament . . . How much longer are they going to recruit officers from the chosen class? How much longer are they going to put money and social position before efficiency? . . . It is appalling that in such times as these, when we need every man in authority to be of the finest type, that we have an obsolete and utterly useless system which is a dead weight on our fighting efficiency . . . [But] it is natural that [the class of people who control the navy] will not favor any scheme which, though it would mean an immeasurable increase in efficiency, would mean their losing control of a long-held prize . . .

"I writhe under the unfairness of the present system."

When Thomas's ship, the cruiser *Leander*, was at Las Palmas in the Canary Islands in October 1936, the old battleship *Schleswig-Holstein* arrived on a training cruise with German naval cadets. Thomas talked with one of them ("he spoke perfect English") and learned that, under the Nazi system, the cadet had been sent to a labor training camp after he finished school. From the camp he had been selected, on the basis of ability, to be educated to become a naval officer. Not surprisingly, Charles Thomas approved of the National Socialist approach: "This seems to be a good idea, education and not social standing being the qualifying condition . . . I should like, when I finish my seven years, to get a movement going amongst the younger people to force the throwing open of the services and the abolition of the society side of it all. The first thing is an efficient fighting machine for defense, and for this you need all the technical brains which come from the classes which are not allowed under the present system to enter [the officer ranks]. It is, of course, a huge swindle."

Thomas wanted a system of admission to officer training based on national competitive examinations which would measure, in addition to intellectual abilities, physical fitness and character, and that would provide a psychological profile of the applicants. Admission to the examination was to be open to all men between the ages of sixteen and twenty-five, including those already in the navy as ratings. While under training, both single and married men were to be paid a sufficient allowance so that lack of money would be no bar to access by the able, whatever their financial circumstances.

Thomas knew that to accomplish his plan he would need allies inside and outside the navy: "It will . . . be necessary to enlist the sympathetic aid of progressive serving officers and of the educated thinking civilians." Nor was Thomas under any illusions that he spoke for anything more than a minority of the men on the lower deck: "I have broached the subject of a new system of recruiting officers with numerous men in the navy and army and, not so strange to relate, the only people who support my ideas are the ex–secondary school boys. The southerners, especially those from the country districts [a description that perfectly fits the deference advocate Arthur Ford, one might note], are still in the old feudal days, proving themselves staunch supporters of the old country families. It would be useless to expect support from men in the services if any determined effort were made to compel the 'inner circle' to alter the whole military system."

Almost certainly the Second World War and its voracious demand for officers would eventually have brought Thomas the status and the opportunities he coveted. Whether he would have joined or led a campaign for a more open and democratic method of officer recruitment, whether he would have applauded the deep changes that the war of 1939–1945 accelerated in British society, must be forever unknown. Charles R. Thomas died on April 9, 1942, when the aircraft carrier *Hermes* was sunk by Japanese dive-bombers in the Indian Ocean. He may have been an agitator-prophet of the post-1945 Britain that came to be, but in the Royal Navy of the late 1930s Thomas was still a lonely minority voice.[67]

3

The Finest and Most Sincere Crowd of Men

Teamwork is as essential as discipline to the smooth operating of a warship. In *Keeping Together in Time: Dance and Drill in Human History*, William H. McNeill argues eloquently that coordinated military maneuvers, such as close-order drill, bond soldiers emotionally and make them effective members of a military organization far more than do rational arguments or material rewards.[1] Although McNeill focuses primarily on armies, his argument holds just as true for naval ships, where raising anchor by hand, filling a coal bunker, or firing a big gun demands as high a degree of bonding, teamwork, and split-second choreography as the most elaborate field maneuvers.

If this is so, it is not surprising that many twentieth-century ratings said the best aspect of their naval service was the comradeship. "The lower-deck ratings were the finest and most sincere crowd of men I have ever met in my life, and I am proud to have served with them," said one former sailor. "I would join up again if I were fifty years younger." Nor was his an isolated opinion; it was part of a swelling chorus in which ex-sailor after ex-sailor joined his voice. In the navy, said Mechanician First Class Raymond Dutton, who served in the 1930s and 1940s, "I enjoyed comradeship to a degree I believe unavailable in any other walk of life."[2] Coming at the same idea from a different angle, First World War signalman Edgar R. Baker recorded a telling incident in his diary. At the conclusion of his training at the signal school at the Crystal Palace in July 1916, Baker and other newly fledged ordinary signalmen were offered a few words of advice by their commanding officer, Lieutenant Mather, who was himself a former man of the lower deck. What stuck in Baker's mind was Mather's admonition: "A man at sea was better to stand well in his mates' eyes than in the eyes of his officers." When Baker re-read his old diary in 1960 he inserted this note: "Later on I found this to be correct." Then he added: "The chaplain also gave us advice, but his was not so valuable."[3]

The notion of comradeship is essential to understanding the men of the lower deck. It was a bond which penetrated every aspect of a rating's life. But because it was a part of shipboard life that was taken for granted by virtually all sailors, the essence of comradeship was rarely described or analyzed by these men of the sea. When asked to speak about comradeship, Leading Stoker Richard Rose chose to talk in terms of a specific incident from his service in the battleship *Irresistible*, in the latter part of 1913, and of a shipmate from Portsmouth: "Believe me, [*Irresistible* was] just like an old lady. She'd come up in the air there and shake her skirts and down again underneath the waves.

"And this chappie—Green his name was—believe me, he suffered absolute vile seasickness . . . Lifeless he was. The moment that we went to sea he lost all power over his legs and arms. And invariably he used to go down the stokehold—and here comes the comradeship again there—you'd stick him in the [coal] bunker and, well, other people . . . but that's the comradeship, see? This chap, he felt so ill they got him down in the stokehold to do his watch [and then] stuck him in the bunker out of the way till the watch ended. Someone else do his job for him."

Wouldn't Green have been in serious trouble if it had been discovered that he was absent from duty? asked Rose's questioner. "Oh yes, yes," Rose replied. But "I don't think anyone ever spilled the beans. We had a good chief [petty officer] in charge of the stokehold. That's where the humanity of the navy came to its being."[4]

Petty Officer Edward Pullen told a story of comradeship from his wartime service, 1916–1917, in the destroyer *Ready:* "We had what they called Rudolph gear, I think—expanding voice pipes, you know, that stretched all along the decks . . . The captain [Lieutenant Commander Alfred G. Peace] called [the able seaman stationed to look out for torpedoes] up [on the voice pipe] in the night. Couldn't make him hear. He sent for me, said, 'Go and find out if that man's asleep.' I went along and he was asleep. His name was Moore. We used to call him 'Pony' Moore. He was asleep all right. So I broke this Rudolph gear, see? And I said to the captain, I said, 'That Rudolph gear was broke. That's why he couldn't hear you.' [The captain] took me and this able seaman on board the *Sandhurst*, our parent ship. He said, 'If I thought you were sheltering that man,' he said, 'I'd have you shot, both of you.' Because, he said, he had lost a destroyer in the Dardanelles just like that. I saved that man's life. And he had no punishment for it. But they was doubtful about what I was saying, see?"[5]

As revealing as these two stories are, they are also misleading. Comradeship was more than simply sheltering one's messmates from the consequences of their own weaknesses and follies. Plumber First Class William (Jock) Batters caught best the essence of comradeship in his memoir, "Harry Tate's Navy." He wrote with his Second World War experiences in mind: "The sailor fought for more than just his life, for that was cheap enough, to be sure. When a sailor 'belonged' to a ship his main loyalty was to the ship and his mates. If they endured enough together, his family came second. How other can you explain the actions of men who, when their ship was going down, were seen to go below, although the order for 'Abandon ship' had been given? . . . Whatever this kink was—and it was the antithesis of self-preservation—it really existed. There must still be many who can remember the feeling."[6]

Comradeship is key to understanding the thoughts, ethics, and actions of sailors. It may be a mysterious and elusive quality in lower-deck life, but it *is* possible for the historian to explore the shipboard world which nurtured this spirit. By identifying elements of naval life that fostered comradeship, as well as others which tested its strength, one can come closer to understanding the growth of this powerful bond.

⚓

An external mark of comradeship was the naval uniform. This reminds those of us who live in a different century that the past is, indeed, a strange country. True, regulations required it, but ratings took real pride in wearing the naval uniform whether they were on or off duty. "I loved [the uniform] myself, and I don't want to boast and brag, but I had the prize for the best-kept kit for two years running when I was in the training ships," recalled Leading Signalman Reginald Ashley. "So it was a popular uniform?" "Yeah, it was to me," Ashley responded. "I loved it." "'Course," added Leading Seaman Arthur Ford. "You'll always get one or two a bit slommacky, but generally speaking they took a pride in their dress. And they took a pride in being in the Royal Navy, they did."[7]

When Reginald Ashley, after speaking of his pride in the naval uniform, added with a laugh, "I reckon I was one of the best-dressed blokes in the navy," he was not talking about wearing the ready-made uniform issued by the navy through the ship's store. "Oh yeah, you get a pusser [uniform], well," said Able Seaman Walter Basford—and he, too, laughed—"you'd get a bag hanging out here and all that kind of thing. And you could get a lump out the back."[8] The uniform that showed one's pride as a member of the Royal Navy was custom tailored and it had been *tiddlyvated*—a sailor word unlikely to be found in any standard dictionary, but one derived from *tiddly* in the sense of "dressed up" or "smart looking."

Although sailors could and did have uniforms made by shoreside tailors, particularly in foreign ports, where the work was a good bargain, the common method of acquiring the desired uniform was to go to the ship's store, purchase the required amount of regulation uniform cloth, and take that to a shipmate who owned a sewing machine and had set himself up in business as a tailor in his off-duty hours. Walter Basford explained the process. First you buy the blue serge, "then you take it down to this bloke, the tailor—well, he called himself a tailor—well, he'd made a few hundred suits and he was all right with it, too! He would measure you right round, and you'd get a jolly good-fitting suit for six bob then." The uniform jumper and trousers were simple to make. Once the shipboard tailor got the knack of it, he could run up two suits in an evening. And the results? "They were different altogether [from the navy-issued uniforms]," reported Chief Yeoman of Signals Thomas Wallace. "The trousers were wider and, well, I mean it's— when they got [uniforms] from the pusser's they were just made anyhow. You know, they just dropped on you. Where, if you had 'em made, they fitted in tight. It was much, much different." It was important for the suit to fit snug and well, explained James Kelleher, "to show out our youthful figures." And not to shipmates, to be sure. The custom-made uniforms were meant to be worn ashore on leave, in large part for a potential audience of women. Those one or two slommacky-looking fellows aside, sailors—especially sailors on shore—were instinctive dandies. "I tell you," said Edward Pullen, "I think sailors in them days, they looked wonderful fellows in their uniform, because the great majority wore high-heeled shoes, like the Spanish shoe, you know, and the baggy trouser. And they always fitted so well, you know. Of course you had no braces or anything like that, see? Always fitted tight round your waist."⁹

Much as a sailor might love the navy and its disciplined regimen, asserting his individuality was an essential part of life on the lower deck. Here was where smart dressing—*tiddlyvating*—came into the picture. Sailors could order perversions of the naval uniform—white silk scarves or cap tallies from ships with more virile-sounding names than the one on which a rating was actually serving—by mail from James Ward, 90 Markhouse Road, Walthamstow. These uniforms might look great while home on leave and far away from the master-at-arms, but they would never be allowed in barracks or on shipboard. "Well," explained Thomas Wallace, "if you were on HMS *Black Prince* or HMS *Emerald*, oh, you couldn't wear that cap ribbon. You used to write to [James] Ward and get a *Vengeance, Revenge, Powerful, Terrible*—they were the favorite cap ribbons. They used to send for them cap ribbons . . . The only time you wear it [was] when you were on leave . . . because girls come along—'Oh, look at the ship he's on—*Vengeance!—Terrible!—Powerful!*'—flirt."¹⁰

More common alternatives to mail-order tiddly were the small alterations a sailor could make to the regulation uniform to proclaim his individuality. Standard-issue cap bows could be unstitched and retied in more spectacular ways. Some angles at which the naval cap could be tilted were not exactly by the book. With the aid of shipboard tailors, trouser legs were widened, jumpers cut a bit longer, and flannels made snugger fitting. Collars could be scrubbed and scrubbed until the coveted light-blue color was achieved, then ironed to make them shine. The denim edge of the grey-striped workshirt might be feather-stitched. Anchors, other nautical symbols, and mottoes could be embroidered on flannels and cholera belts—unseen and ignored by the authorities, but known to the wearer and seen, of course, by those who encountered the sailor partly undressed.

Naval authority in the persons of the ship's duty officer and the naval police fought a containing action against these perversions of the uniform and their perpetrators. For the sailors it was one more game that kept life interesting and bearable. The field of battle was shipboard inspection, which took place before a sailor went ashore on leave. In the front line of the skirmish were the shock troops, the master-at-arms and his regulating petty officers. One master-at-arms recalled a typical encounter as a shorebound leave party formed up: "As soon as they were fallen in I would take a casual check round to see everything, as I thought, was more or less correct . . . I would look for the silk [and] lanyard properly worn and everything, the collar, and that every man was in the rig [that is, uniform] of the day that was piped . . . see the collars are properly cleaned, things like that; that he's had a shave before going ashore; if he's a non-shaving fellow, that his beard was more or less cut and trimmed and things like that which the officer-of-the-day would pick up [when he inspected the shore party] . . . I might find that [a man's] jumper is a bit on the long side and it's not a service dress. Probably got—he's bought one ashore, you see—what we call *tiddly*, you see—and he was trying to get ashore with that on. Well, *if* I noticed things like that, he wouldn't be seen by the officer-of-the-day. I would say, 'Woit! Whoosh! Out! You've got a shore suit on there which you know the officer-of-the-day won't pass.'"[11]

Here, looked at from the other side of the skirmish line, is how one rating saw the battle of wits and uniform: "Going ashore . . . well, what we used to do, you see, because your flannel part that shows in front—you know, there's a certain section of your neck shows flannel, doesn't it? Well, perhaps that's the only part that gets grimy, you know. And then, when you want to go ashore, you see, you got to have another [clean] flannel ready, see. So what they used to have, what they call a *dickey*, a little flannel, you know, that covered that part. And you tied it round your chest, you see. Well, that was easily rubbed out, like rubbing out a pocket handkerchief. You put one of those clean ones on the front, you see, and then when you're inspected when you're going ashore, you see, at night—because they always inspect you, the officer walks along—it looks nice and clean. Didn't matter about the other [unseen] bit, you see." Would the officer ever check to see if a sailor was wearing the whole flannel? "Not much. No, not much."[12]

Although the officer-of-the-day, the master-at-arms, and the RPOs had the weight of authority on their side, and though the skirmish was fought over and over, thousands upon thousands of times, it was an encounter in which no victory could be final so long as sailors went ashore in uniform knowing that they would find there an audience of women.

⚓

Comradeship heavily influenced the type of ship in which ratings preferred to serve. The conventional image of the Royal Navy during the First World War and the interwar years is that of a force of big ships—battleships, cruisers, and later aircraft carriers, units manned by approximately one thousand officers and ratings. But most sailors said that, if given a choice, they would much rather serve in small ships: destroyers, submarines, or river gunboats in China, vessels with complements of fewer than one hundred men. Many voiced this preference even though the small ships were, by universal admission, far less habitable and offered much less by way of off-duty entertainment than did the big ships.

"Destroyers must be terrible in rough weather," thought Ordinary Telegraphist Charles Thomas after a day's training at sea in January 1935. "How the messdecks are kept clean in good weather is a miracle, as about twenty men live in a space as big as the ordinary house-sized kitchen."[13] Thomas Wallace, who personally preferred small ships to big ones, explained the sleeping problem: "There was room for some hammocks to go up, but not all . . . A hammock is a very comfortable thing to sleep in when you've got it slung up, but you didn't have the space to sling 'em up in a destroyer. I think out of about, say, fourteen [men] there was about room to hang up six hammocks. The remainder [of the hammocks] was [spread out] on the lockers, on the table, and on the deck!"[14]

Then there was the utter lack of privacy in a small vessel, the inability to get away from one's shipmates. "Well, that was the trouble," recalled Reginald Ashley, another sailor who preferred to serve in small ships. "I mean, for writing letters, you had to write letters with one end of the mess table and perhaps somebody else was reading or playing cards [at] the other end, you know."[15]

Edward Pullen, who definitely did *not* like duty in small ships, thought the hernia which sent him back to the big ships was almost a blessing in disguise. He vividly remembered the conditions in the destroyer *Ready* during his October 1916–May 1917 service: "There was no life at all aboard a destroyer. If I was to tell you the truth, you can't stand up. When I was in that *Ready* you couldn't stand up, you couldn't sit down and you couldn't walk about . . . And we always had a rope round us, you

know, see, because . . . it was quite easy falling overboard in a destroyer
. . . And the water used to come down just like a waterfall all the time.
And you could never cook nothing. I used to boil a dozen eggs before we
left Scapa . . . And as soon as we put to sea perhaps I'd break an egg and
eat it, look see? That's the only way. You lived an awful life. It's almost
awkward to be able to tell anyone the life you can live there, see? You
couldn't make a cup of tea, because the seas was continually washing
over. I've seen our captain [Lieutenant Commander Alfred G. Peace] up
there with his oilskins on day and night, clearing out [that is, vomiting]
all the time. A terrible life, really. I know the only way I could find any
comfort, we had a collision mat in the fo'c'sle part. I used to go down on
my hands and knees and hang onto that collision mat there, stop there
for hours, hands and knees."[16]

For all the physical difficulties, small ships offered bigger compen-
sations: a relaxation of the spit-and-polish busywork and the snap-to-
attention discipline epitomized in the master-at-arms and the regulating
petty officers of the battleships and cruisers—functionaries happily lacking in small ships. "You kept the ship clean," said Thomas Wallace, "but
otherwise everything was easygoing." Chief Petty Officer James Cox
elaborated: "You see, men of my type, men who could stick the sea, always volunteered for destroyers if they could get them, you see. I always
tried to get in a destroyer if I could. I never liked the big-ship life. You
see, there was more discipline in a big ship. You had to obey the King's
Rules and Regulations [*The King's Regulations and Admiralty Instructions*].
You had naval police to enforce those regulations, see that they was carried out, whereas in a destroyer you've got no naval police. The only
man you've got aboard there to carry out discipline duty is the coxswain.
Well, he's also a seaman. He's also the purser. He issues all the rations.
And he also takes the ship in and out of harbor and looks after all the
navigation charts and things like that. He's a pretty busy man. But he's
in charge of all the discipline. But, on the other hand, he hasn't got
many people . . .

"But, on the other hand, the discipline was free. The discipline was
easy. The work was harder. Your work was harder because every man
had his job to do. And if he didn't do it, nobody else did, you see?"[17]

Even more important in the small ship was a strong spirit of community: closer, more personal relations between officers and men than ex-

isted in large ships, as well as the amelioration of status rivalries between, say, stokers and seamen. "Actually," said Reginald Ashley as he reminisced about his service in small vessels, the hardships of close-quartered living "made people more pally with each other. I mean even the officers, you know, was very good to you . . . [In] the submarine service, I mean, the officers and men were very close together. Well, in my own experience, I mean, I was with the same captain all the time. He wouldn't have anyone else."[18]

⚓

Comradeship began in a ship's messes. When one thinks or speaks of messes and messing in today's navies the mental image is one of *general messing:* food prepared by professionally trained cooks and served cafeteria-style to any and all of the ship's company authorized to eat in a particular mess. A different system, called *canteen messing,* prevailed in most ships of the Royal Navy until well into the middle of the twentieth century. It was a system with which, a few small modifications aside, any naval sailor of the eighteenth or nineteenth century would have been right at home. Men of the lower deck were assigned to messes of anywhere from ten to twenty-five men—but typically fifteen to twenty individuals—who were expected to eat together, day in and day out, for the duration of the commission. Changes of mess and messmates were possible, but the expectation was that the membership of a mess would remain stable. Messes were segregated by branch: telegraphists ate with telegraphists, and stokers ate with stokers. There was further segregation by rank: petty officers had their own messes, chief petty officers theirs. Curtains provided symbolic separation from men of lower rank.

No First World War–era battleship survives intact in which historian and tourist alike can experience a sense of the three-dimensional reality of canteen messing. But visitors to the mid-nineteenth-century's HMS *Warrior* at Portsmouth harbor can see carefully restored eating arrangements that changed little in the years which separated *Warrior* of 1860 and *Iron Duke* of 1912. Between each of the broadside guns on *Warrior*'s main deck is a wooden mess table, supported by metal cleats set in the ship's side at its outboard end and suspended from a metal crowsfoot at the inboard extremity. Each table is capable of accommodating eighteen hungry sailors, who sit on wooden benches and eat from metal plates and basins. The table can be unrove, the benches collapsed, and both stowed out of the way. At the outboard end of the table and built into the bulkhead is a combination rack and cabinet with shelves and slots to hold plates and basins and with drawers which may be used to store tea or flour. At night hammocks are slung in the space above the tables. Higher still, between the beams which support the upper deck (as well as along the bulkhead), are secured the implements necessary to work *Warrior*'s big guns.

So, too, was the arrangement in 1900 or 1918 or (in many ships) in 1930. Each mess still ate at its designated long wooden table suspended from the deckhead on metal crowsfeet and often with the ship's guns as mealtime companions. The tables could still be unrove from their metal supports and stowed fore-and-aft along the ship's side or hoisted up out of the way when the messdecks needed to be cleaned. Messmates still sat for their meals on long wooden benches, which, like the tables, could be unshipped and stowed. "Now that mess when it was normally full—it was always full—you all had a job to sit down there," recalled Joiner First Class George Michael Clarkson. At the bulkhead end of the table were a drawer for the mess's knives and forks and racks for the crockery plates from which the men ate and the basins from which they drank. "[We were] generally reduced to about three drinking out of the same basin," remembered Arthur Ford, "because they got broken. Somebody else was short and they went around at night and pinched some of yours. You know, that's what used to go on. And you'd finish up, you see, three drinking out of one basin." Here, too, were stowed the mess's common utensils: one big black pot for making a potmess from a shin of beef; several large tins for making stews; nets for boiling peas, beans, and potatoes; the tea urn and the rum fanny. A two-drawer wooden cupboard held tea and flour. At the opposite end of the table was the bread barge, a cone-shaped wooden tub, its top covered in white canvas, where leftover bread was stored for between-meal snacks. The bread barge also served as the traditional seat of the youngest member of the mess.[19]

Sailors often compared eating as a mess with dining as a family at home, and the analogy was an apt one. The leading hand assigned to the mess, the *killick* in sailorspeak, was an authoritarian father-figure. "It didn't matter whether you liked him or whether you didn't," recalled Walter Basford. When asked if the leading hand was ever the shy type and got pushed around by lower-ranking sailors, Basford answered, "Oh no. No, they were all assertive. Oh yeah. They were on the ball the whole time. Yeah, yeah." Basford paused, then continued, "No, no, no. He was on the ball the whole time. He was there. [The leading hand] was responsible [to the commander] for your mess."[20] He was also almost always the caterer of the mess.

The word *caterer* demands explaining, and that explanation leads directly into the Royal Navy's system for supplying food to the lower deck. The navy issued certain basic staples—bread, fresh or preserved meat, fresh vegetables, sugar, tea, chocolate, and condensed milk—to each mess. (Appendix 3 gives the full details of the daily ration.) Beyond these basics, the mess was allowed four pence per man per day toward the purchase of food items—beans, peas, cabbage, turnips, onions, bacon, and tins of fruit—to enrich the basic supplies according to the mess's taste. The mess would decide as a group, occasionally with the leading hand playing a dominating role in the decision, which food items they would purchase either from the paymaster's stores (extra quantities of basics) or from the ship's canteen (supplementary foods). If at the end of the month, when the paymaster's office delivered the mess bill for purchased food items, the total bill came to less than four pence times the number of days in a month times the number of men in the mess, the savings would be credited in equal amounts to each man in the mess. In reality—at least if the former sailors' memories can be trusted—this rarely happened. More commonly, a mess would eat too well and the mess bill would be greater than the sum of the monthly food allowance. In that case, money would be deducted from each rating's pay to cover his share of the deficit. A good caterer avoided this problem by being attentive to detail and careful at bookkeeping, so that the month's mess bill came out equal to or less than the collective allowances for food purchases. Ratings who wanted a little something extra were free to visit the ship's canteen and sign a chit for any food items they desired, with the cost to be charged against their monthly pay.

Together with the caterer, the cooks-of-the-day were the key figures of the canteen messing system. They were not, as the name might suggest, trained food-preparation professionals, but simply one or two members of the mess picked in rotation by the leading hand. A cook-of-the-day's job was to collect the day's ration ingredients, prepare any dishes that required cooking, take those dishes to the galley, where they were actually cooked by the ship's cooks and cook's mates, set the mess table, brew tea or cocoa, collect the mess's grog ration, retrieve the cooked food from the galley, and clean up after the meal had been eaten. George Michael Clarkson vividly remembered what it was like to be cook-of-the-day: "That meant that the night before you were being cook the next day . . . you drew potatoes, peas, anything that was wanted for the next dinnertime. You'd peel the potatoes. You'd put the peas in [to] soak.

"And then you started the next morning. 'Hands to cocoa and wash.' You had to nip to the galley to get the cocoa. Then [at] breakfast time you had to put up [for your mess] the stuff that was for breakfast. There was no—the [ship's] cooks didn't do any cooking. None at all. The cooks only boiled hot water and they put your stuff in the oven that you brought up and they took it out when you called for it. That was all they done. They never prepared anything at all. But the cook-of-the-mess done that. So in the morning you took the breakfast up. It might be kippers or anything like that—that was, if you were [in] home [waters]—and then you went up and wet the tea. You collected the kippers—whatever it was—and you brought it back into the mess. By this time you'd laid out the knives and forks and everything all ready. And then they came down to breakfast.

"As soon as breakfast was over you had to wash up. And you imagine washing up twenty-five lots of greasy plates. You always had a job to get hot water somehow or other. You got to go to the galley to get that. And then you had to wash up and get the dinner up to the galley. Now you didn't get any—you had about a quarter of an hour to do that in after the others fell in . . .

"The meat you used to draw from the meat screen—usually a marine or a naval seaman who was called *the butcher*. And he cut up the meat. You didn't know what sort of meat you were going to get. And so you'd rush up—you're always in a hurry. You got the meat and the butcher'd say, 'Number Seven Mess, here you are.' And he'd take a drop kick with it. And you picked it up and you decided—you had to decide and you had to learn quickly—what to do with it, whether it would be a straight rush or whether it would be a stew or whatever you would do with it.

"A straight rush, of course, you'd put it in a dish, put the spuds around it and a few onions, and that went up the galley. You never worried about puddings—you never had time . . . If it was a pie, you had to know how to make a pie. You had some weird and wonderful concoctions there from those of us who'd just joined. And if it was a case of making a pie, it meant that you had to cut the meat up, put that up to the galley. And then you had to sneak away from your job, because you had to fall in about a quarter of an hour after the others and start work. Well then, you went to your boss—if you were a seaman, your captain of your top . . . and say, 'All right to nip down to the mess and make a bit of clacker [a pastry or piece of dough spread over with currants and jam and cooked]?' 'Yes.' So you'd rush away down the mess, because if you were caught on the messdeck, you were in the wrong, you see. And then you rolled out this stuff, made your dough, rushed up the galley and pleaded with the cook to let you have this. You had a bit of wood with the number of the mess on [it] tied under the handle of it there. Back again, roll this out, put a lid on it—the *clacker*, as we called it—and back to the galley. Now then you were back to work again.

"Dinner time was twelve o'clock. A quarter to twelve the bugle would go then or a pipe: 'Cooks to the galley.' And you went to the galley then. You're all lined up in a queue. 'Number Seven Mess.' Chuck it out. 'Number Twenty-one.' The two cooks carried that away. And they had to cut that up and serve those twenty-five hungry so-and-so's. And then by the time they'd finished serving that lot out—because you didn't dare give one too much, they had to be equal proportions—and then you had yours, what was left. And then you kept on saying: 'Come on lads, get up top.' 'Open the door.' 'Go away for a smoke.' So that you could wash up. You had to wash up and get that stuff away."[21]

At this point—the clean-up—Arthur Ford picks up the cook-of-the-day's story: "Oh yes, you have to do all the washing up. And very often they sling half the utensils down the chute, you know, [with] the washing up water. There's a chute on the side of the ship, you know, what you tip the stuff down out in the sea. You'd hear knives, forks, and spoons go rattling down. There must be a hell of a lot of those at the bottom of the sea."

Arthur Ford laughed: "Oh yes, yes. 'There they go! There they go!' they used to say." The loss of the utensils was commemorated in a short verse:

Tinkle, tinkle, little spoons;
Knife and fork will follow soon.

Funny? Sure, but the mess still had to put up the money to purchase re-
placements the next time an admiral's inspection loomed: "When they
came round all these things [were] supposed to be laid out on the table,
you see. Well, there should be enough there for everybody . . . They
were all collected and put round in circles, you know, made up all facing
one another and then the spoons and then the forks, you know. But, of
course, [if] you've only got about half a dozen, you couldn't put [up]
much of a show." Arthur Ford laughed again. "Then that means to say
you got to go and buy a lot of knives, forks, and spoons, you see."

The job of cook-of-the-day was not something the navy taught ratings during their basic training—or later. Sailors were expected to learn
on the job. If the mess was big enough, two men were assigned as cooks
each day. A new man with no cooking skills would usually be paired with
an experienced sailor until he had learned the job.[22] Some ratings took to
the task with a natural affinity. "A good many navy men learned to cook,
same as I do meself. I can cook anything," said James Cox. "I do now for
the wife." Within the limits of the navy-supplied food and the mess's
willingness to pay for extras, the dishes prepared and how they were
fixed were the prerogative of the cooks-of-the-day. "So you never knew
what you was going to get," Cox explained. "Sometimes you'd get some
good cooks and you had damned well-cooked food. Another day you'd
have a shin of beef on top of the potatoes and have a rough cut."[23]
No amount of practice made some men good cooks, especially if they
just wanted to get by with the minimum effort their messmates would
tolerate.

The cooks-of-the-day, whether skillful or lazy, were responsible for
four meals. Although some men remembered Sunday breakfasts that
featured bacon and eggs or eggs and sausages or kippers, most of the
time breakfast was an eat-and-run affair washed down with tea. "Well,
I'd say a couple of mornings a week you might have kippers or bloaters
or a bit of fish of some sort," remembered Chief Petty Officer Albert
Heron. "But it always seemed to be that there was no time in the morning to sit down and have a decent breakfast. You was always rushing
around. And there was so much for the cooks to prepare. Of course you

had jam and marmalade always on the table, so you could have a couple of slices of bread and butter and jam or marmalade and take it from there." The sailor who wanted to start the day with something more substantial could always nip along to the canteen, purchase an egg and a rasher of bacon, take them to the galley, and have the ship's cooks fry them up. Or, less ambitiously, he might simply buy a penny's worth of cheese to quiet his growling stomach.[24]

Dinner, the midday meal, required much more attention from the cooks-of-the-day. It was the centerpiece of the mess's common dining experience—not to mention the meal at which the day's keenly anticipated rum ration was served. Men who fancied themselves excellent shipboard chefs could remember their favorite offerings to their messmates: "Take a straight bake. That would be a lump of meat that you drew from the butcher off the block. And you'd bring it down to the mess, have a look at it, wash it, say, 'Right, well that's all right for roasting.' Then you peel your potatoes and carve them into halves so that they fit nice into this great big dish capable of holding enough to supply twenty-four. Then you'd peel a few onions, mix those up to make a bit of a savory taste with it, and that would go—oh, if you had some spare margarine . . . baste it with a bit of margarine—and take it up to the galley."

"Oh yes, you could have had toad-in-the-hole. Toad-in-the-hole would be sausages which, of course, you bought from the canteen. And you laid them in the dish, twenty-four or forty-eight sausages; or perhaps twenty-four in one dish, twenty-four in another. You made your awning—you used to call the top crust that went on these dishes the *awning*—make an awning over the top, which was, of course, a covering of flour and what-have-you and pastry. And some of the sails were cut off—the bits of dough that was left over—make ivy leaves and, in the center, put a rose. You know, so many layers of duff [dough], and then turn 'em over, cut it, and you got a nice rose there, see? . . . And with that you'd have perhaps boiled potatoes. You may have baked potatoes—just as you wished—and, again, cabbage perhaps and carrots. Something like that."

"Now you also had a potmess . . . You put it in a great big pot and cut up all the meat, put it in the pot; make dumplings, put those in; put onions, put potatoes in; carrots—any veg you could get hold of. Put all that lot in and take that up the galley . . . and that would be a potmess. And with that you'd probably have cabbage, which was cooked in a string bag."

"Then you'd say, 'Well, I tell you what, we'll have a few currants today.' Get a bit of flour. Your [mess] table would be all scrubbed ready and your rolling pin there. Roll out a bit of duff and a few currants and raisins, mix them up, roll up your duff and put that into a dish, grease your dish and take that up to the galley . . . and that would be your afters or sweets."[25]

The rest of the day's meals were hasty pick-up affairs. "Well, there's not much to be said about tea," remarked Bert Heron, the rating who provided the most information on shipboard cuisine. "Once again, you might find that someone would buy some cake or something like that [from the canteen], but normally tea was either bread and jam or bread and marmalade or bread and paste and a cup of tea. And in fine weather take it out on the upper deck. And that was that."[26]

Supper was marginally more elaborate and required some effort on the part of the cooks-of-the-day, but it was nothing like dinner. Leftovers from dinner, if any, could be reworked as supper. Eggs and sausages were another possibility, or cheese and pickles. Then there was canned rabbit and canned salmon. "Salmon. You got a salmon issue in those days," remarked James Cox. "I mean, salmon's extravagant these days. But salmon was a regular issue in the navy in those [days]. You could get as much salmon as you wanted, really, because there was always plenty of fish, tins of fish, available . . . It came in your ration. And they used to accumulate in the mess shelves, because people didn't always want them. And we'd have that for our supper."[27] The fish was usually made into fishcakes, which, along with herrings in tomato sauce (*red lead*), were remembered as standard fare by many of the former ratings.

Eating appealing and nutritious food in adequate quantities was a critical component of morale as well as physical and mental health for sailors—then as it is today. "Good food, like, you know, and you were happy then," said Walter Basford. Thinking back to his experiences as cook-of-the-day, Arthur Ford added the dimension of quantity to Basford's emphasis on quality: "Anything went down so long as it was food. They'd eat anything as long as they were filled up." Equally important, eating together as a surrogate family—"they just run [the mess] same as you would at home" (James Cox)—bonded the members of the mess and was the smallest building block from which the bigger society of the ship was constructed.[28]

⚓

To this point, the narrative has told of typical fare served on board ship, but the quality of meals could vary spectacularly. Indeed, the food served depended on whether the ship was in port or how long it had been at sea, its size, whether there was refrigeration on board, and (occasionally) whether the officers gave a damn about how the ratings were eating. Ordinary Seaman Wilfrid Smith wrote to his mother from the monitor *Erebus* at Durban in February 1942 to explain just how well sailors could eat when their ship made the right port: "One very good thing about a visit to port is the very good selection and variety of 'eats' that one can enjoy aboard for a few days afterwards. For instance, during the last few days we have had runner beans, very fine cabbage, tomatoes, watermelons, lettuces, potatoes, good butter, brown bread, etc. (Apparently white bread is unobtainable here, although I personally consider this an advantage.) And, procurable from our caterer aboard, oranges, apples, peaches (1d each), and some really splendid black grapes at 7d a pound. Actually, I suppose the only time I cannot say I am well fed is after a week or so at sea, when, usually owing to the heat, the potatoes have gone bad and the bread has either all been eaten or what remains is probably moldy, and there are no fresh vegetables or meat—when, in fact, we live by the tin-opener and ship's biscuits. Then it is indeed a treat to see land again and all that it means in the way of fresh supplies and who knows what unexpected treat in the fruit line and a run ashore."[29]

Then, too, a sailor's ship was afloat in an ocean full of fish. When opportunity offered, fishing was a great way to bring variety to the mess's meat-dominated menu and—best of all—with no addition to the monthly mess bill. "All day today," Signalman Walter Dawson recorded in his diary in the battleship *Albion* on December 3, 1914, at Simonstown, "our ship's side has been practically lined with men fishing. Hand lines only are used, but a tremendous amount of really splendid fish was caught, the bulk of it being fine large mackerel."[30] But when the ship was small, the passage between ports long, and opportunities to find one's own food unavailable, life at the mess table turned grim. Richard Rose remembered days and weeks of poor-quality food during his First World

War service: "A destroyer could only take one day's bread to sea and one day's meat. Potatoes and anything like that was a bit different. So, consequently, the first day at sea you got meat and potatoes and bread, see, but after that you were—you weren't on your own, because they supplied biscuits, ship's biscuits—and ship's biscuits are not all that palatable at any time—and bully-beef [boiled salt beef].

"Well, when they run a bit short of bully beef . . . they open what they call salt pork. And there's nothing more hideous on earth than a piece of salt pork in your mouth. A person there that I know always threw it straight over the side. I think a lot of other people did. Some of it was barrelled, oh, as far back as Nelson's days, issued by the victualing yard, Portsmouth, and it tasted vile. It was green sometimes. What you were supposed to do was soak it for a bit, twenty-four hours, and then put it up the galley and hope for the best.

"You used to sometimes get split peas from the store—from the paymaster's store or from the coxswain's store—and those split peas, that was about the only palatable part of a meal was the split peas, but invariably the salt pork was humped straight over the side."

Whether or not the legendary salt pork had really been aging *en cask* since the Napoleonic Wars, the experience of drawing rations such as these was one that twentieth-century men of the lower deck shared with their counterparts of the eighteenth and nineteenth centuries—if for far shorter periods. "You always had a fair supply of ship's biscuits," recalled Albert Heron, "but I'm sorry to say that most of the ship's biscuits I ever saw had weevils in them. But there, you got used to it. You took no notice of them and you just ate the biscuits—weevils as well."[31]

The culinary hardships of salt pork and ship's biscuit were an expected, if not welcome, part of naval life, to be tolerated with as much good humor as possible. More destructive to morale was bad or inadequate food, the responsibility for which could be traced to the navy or to the ship's officers. The navy was a huge, remote, and amorphous organization. The ship's officers were concrete and right there, targets for ill will whenever food problems surfaced. Of course no experienced sailor was going to blame the ship's officers when a remedy was beyond their control, as when the demands of active-duty cruising made conditions grim in the second-class cruiser *Glasgow* in South Atlantic waters during the initial weeks of the First World War. Maltese canteen staff had left the ship on the declaration of war. Supplies were running low and there was little hope of replenishment before the ship reached Montevideo. "I have not wrote about what food we have been having, as I don't [like] complaining," Able Seaman William Hawkes confided to his diary on September 4, 1914, "but all I can say is I am very grateful there is a bakery in the ship or otherwise we would be properly starve[d], but the captain [John Luce] has the same food as us, so we have no cause to grumble, and he tries his best to get all the fresh food he can."[32]

Contrast this with the experience of Ordinary Telegraphist William Blamey in the armed boarding steamer *Hazel* in the eastern Mediterranean early in 1916: "The food we get is disgraceful—scandalous. Surely the navy allows us enough. They always have on other ships I've been on. Here we have 'dishwater' to drink, accompanied by 'bully beef and biscuits' every meal. It nearly kills us. We shall soon be thin enough to do the vanishing trick through the eye of a needle. Enough of that now in here [his diary]! But just a word more. The officers [mostly Royal Naval Reserve, Blamey notes elsewhere] naturally feed well, while we!— well, really, is there such a thing as food? We've no bread, no beef, and more than often no potatoes. Two days we did have beef. It nearly drove us all from the mess. It was Greek beef and must have been some old dogs about 800 years old. There was one advantage about it though. We never had the trouble of carrying it about. It always walked itself . . . I believe if I don't get off this ship . . . soon, I shall do something willfully so as to get punishment and so get discharged to another ship that way."[33]

Telegraphist Blamey need not have the last, bad word about officers and lower-deck food. From the Second World War diary of Master-at-Arms William F. Read in the cruiser *Belfast* comes evidence that a good senior officer understood well the importance of wholesome food in adequate quantities to the morale of a ship's company. "That same night," August 22, 1939, Read recorded, "the commander [James Gregson Roper] saw a representative body in his office and told them he had heard rumors that the food was insufficient, a state of affairs which he deeply regretted, although the catering was outside his province. He said that he had gone into the matter and that he was satisfied there were grounds for complaint and that he had taken steps to have matters made more satisfactory. His action was very much appreciated, because it proved that he had the interests of the ship's company at heart. In my capacity though as master-at-arms I had already seen enough to realize his anxiety for the comfort and wellbeing of everybody."[34] Fortunately for the men of the lower deck, commanders like James Gregson Roper appear to have been the norm rather than the exception among the Royal Navy's officers.

⚓

A mess was more than just a place to eat—whether one ate well or badly. It was the physical space on which the off-duty hours of the lower deck centered. If the sea were smooth enough, a sailor might be writing a letter at one end of the mess table. Another could be stowed away reading a book from the ship's library. Perhaps one messmate had taken down his ditty box and was looking at a photograph of his girlfriend while another was busy with a bit of tiddly work, embroidering an anchor on his pillowcase. This sailor might be busy doing macramé—mantle covers and antimacassars for the family at home—that sailor making rag rugs. An older man could be at work tying an elaborate knot, a work of mysterious and high skill sure to impress the relative newcomer to life at sea. A small group of men might be having an amicable and protracted argument, a not uncommon occurrence according to Edgar Baker. "Somehow the conversation turned on fate and for hours, from 10 P.M. till 2 A.M., we argued it backward and forward," recorded Baker in his First World War diary. "Arguments were one of the pet amusements in the RN. Sometimes they would be about ships. Then they were interesting. Sometimes about any silly subject. I have seen the mess almost in blows over the question 'Is marmalade jam?'" Some messmates had wandered off to the upper deck: perhaps to smoke, perhaps to gather around a banjo player and sing. Others would have gone quietly to a remote and secure hideaway to indulge in a forbidden—but still (and perhaps because forbidden) popular—game of chance.[35]

Present, too, were rough physical games, seemingly pointless to the non-seafarer, the main purpose of which appeared to be the release of tension through aggression. Edward Pullen described a game which could be played by four or five men. One sailor was *It*. He stood, arms crossed, with his back to the others. A messmate smashed into him, "hit him pretty hard, look see?" The man who was *It* was required to guess who had hit him. If he guessed wrong, he remained *It*, absorbing the body blows of his mates, until he correctly identified his attacker, whereupon the attacker became *It*. The game continued until the players grew tired and quit. "Stupid rubbish, really," said Ted. "A bit of a pastime, I suppose."[36]

But that was exactly the point. Except for those men who had evening and night watches, the sailor's workday traditionally ended with quarters at 4 P.M., followed by tea and sometimes by a general drill such as an abandon-ship exercise. Thereafter, barring some emergency, a man's time was his own. In port he could (and probably would) go ashore to entertain himself. But at sea there was no place to go but the messdeck or the upper deck. Monotony was a daily companion. "Well, we put to sea just a week ago today and we have been there ever since!" Wilfrid Smith wrote to his mother in December 1941 from *Erebus*. "I must confess a sight of land once more will be most welcome, as seven solid days of sea and sky are apt to become a little boring, to put it mildly." Smith's contemporary, the civvy-street journalist and hostilities-only writer Ray Wilkins, at sea in the cruiser *Gloucester*, was even more eloquent about monotony: "We work, talk, read or write, and the sea moves by and the days pass . . . The sea seldom changes in my view. I do not belong to the sect whose sentiments are touched by the sights of oceans. I regret to say I am wooden and unromantic about the sea. It is just so much water to me. If I feel like a bout of nostalgia, I go up on deck at night and stare up at the stars and moon and mope. Most times though I stay below and, if I am not working, read or write or sleep. Occasionally I go up on deck after tea, while it is still light, and walk up and down with [another writer]. You would probably think it funny if you could be on the upper decks of our ship at about this time of day. You would see pairs or threes or fours walking backwards and forwards over a narrow strip of deck at a furious rate. It looks comically pointless, as I discovered when I stood aside the other day and looked on at the rite."[37] To cope, a sailor fell back on his inner resources or joined messmates in search of collective ways to fight the tedium of emptiness and idleness.

Some sailors in the mess were purposefully—and profitably—busy in their off-duty hours. These were men who, either individually or, more typically, teamed with mates in *firms*, were earning extra money by doing skilled, necessary, or unpleasant jobs for their shipmates. Shipboard tailors produced the made-to-measure uniforms that ratings preferred to the standard issue. The *snob* repaired boots and shoes. Barbers kept hair and beards in a tidy state that forestalled the negative attention of one's divisional officer or the master-at-arms. Perhaps the most popular firms were the ones that went in for *dhobeying*—doing laundry. On shipboard each sailor was responsible for the washing and pressing of his own clothes. The facilities were primitive and the task difficult. "We only had a tub, you know," recalled Arthur Ford. "And if you went to the galley for some hot water, they looked at you like poison, you know, I mean to say. Although they're supposed to supply hot water, it wasn't always so easy to get it, you know." James Cox elaborated: "Washing and maintaining clothes? Wash your clothes whenever you like—in your own time of course. And there was official times for hanging it. Used to have clothes lines rigged when you came into harbor, perhaps two nights a week or something like that. It had to be [up] after sunset and down before sunrise in the morning, which didn't give much chance for drying anything. So most clothes used to be washed on deck in the evening. You know, just sit in a bucket. And you'd wash your clothes. And you'd wash 'em out. And then you'd get down the stokehold and over top of the boilers. You know, one of the stokers or petty officer in charge of that boiler room would rig lines up. And you used to ask his permission and perhaps give him a couple of bob—come to that in some cases because pay wasn't a lot. And he'd let you dry your clothes.

"Same with getting hot water. In some ships you could get hot water . . . from the galley. In other ships you put a few coppers in the box for the cook. Or you might be friendly with a stoker petty officer down in the [stokehold]. You'd be able to take a bucket of water down in the stokehold, put a steam pipe into it, turn on the steam, and hot your hot water like that, you see? But hot water . . . it was never allowed for. You used to find your hot water where you could to wash your clothes. So you can bet your life, if you got a bucket of hot water, you'd put shirt, pants and flannel and everything through that one bucket and then wash it out with a good lot of clean, fresh water, see? But the hot water was very scarce."[38]

There were some small improvements in shipboard laundry facilities after Ford's and Cox's time in the Royal Navy, but right through the Second World War the basic challenge of doing one's laundry remained essentially what it had been in the Edwardian battlefleet. Early in 1942 Wilfrid Smith explained the difficulties to his mother back home: "We have been wearing tropical rig for some time now [the monitor *Erebus*, in which Smith served, was rounding Africa, headed for the Indian Ocean], i.e., white shorts, shirt, and white cap, black shoes or boots, and black socks or stockings. But I must say I shall always prefer the blue suit, although weather conditions of course are the governing factor in these affairs. The trouble with this tropical rig is that one is never finished washing. One wears the white shorts while working about the ship and, needless to say, at the end of the day, when one has done perhaps a bit of painting or scrubbing or sweeping, etc., said infernal shorts are anything but white, and so once more one repairs to the bathroom, which incidentally is totally inadequate in size, and once more one attempts to produce a clean pair of shorts with the aid of a bucket (if able to borrow somebody's) or a bowl (if they are not already all in use), a bit of Persil and soap and a lot of elbow-grease. And then perhaps there will be some socks, a shift, towel, shirt and one or two other odds and ends which also require restoration to something like whiteness. I can assure you our bathroom in the dog watches presents at times a scene that has to be seen to be believed! However, I suppose there are worse things at sea!"[39]

With do-it-yourself laundry conditions such as these it is easy to understand the popularity—and the profitability—of the dhobeying firm: fellow-sailors who did others' laundry for a price. Able Seaman Robert L. Fagg, who briefly participated in a two-man dhobeying firm in the destroyer *Lark* in 1916, charged these tariffs for his services: collars, one pence each; singlets, one pence; flannel shirts, two pence; drawers, two pence; pair of socks, two pence; towels, two pence; overalls, six pence; hammocks, six pence. Bert Heron remembered at least two dhobeying firms from his Far Eastern service in the light cruiser *Carlisle* in 1919–1920: "In each case there were two people involved. One would do all the dhobeying and the other would do all the collecting, come round the mess: 'Chuck out your dirties. Chuck 'em out.' You know, take a big bag round, laundry bag—and then in the evening he'd take it up and then they'd combine and start scrubbing. And then they'd rinse it all out— plenty of water—rinse it all out and then roll it up. And they would get permission then from the engineer officer to go down to one of the boiler rooms—one of the two or three boiler rooms—to hang it all up. But of course it had to be hung up properly—not in the way of any machinery—and it had to be taken down at a certain time. So, in that case there was four chaps involved. Two separate dhobeying firms, two [men] in each."

In a well-run ship the business of setting up a dhobeying or other firm was not a free-enterprise affair; it was more a matter of state-regulated capitalism. A sailor who wanted to start a firm—say, cutting hair—put in a request to his divisional officer. The divisional officer then turned to the master-at-arms. "About how many barbers do we already have, Master?" "Well, Sir, at the moment one good barber, Joe Soap. He's carrying on the work quite well. I don't see any reason why we shall need another one." Request denied. Whether a bribe or a promise of a kickback to the master-at-arms secured the desired permission, none of the former ratings revealed. Of course there was no question of a payment to one's divisional officer; that was unthinkable. But some sailors did recall payments to cooks and engine-room petty officers who made life easier for dhobeying firms. Indeed, the system offered an excellent opportunity to purchase the jaunty's benign blessing. Because there is no shortage of authentic stories of corrupt masters-at-arms ashore, it is hard to believe that the shipboard master-at-arms did not, at least sometimes, get his cut of the money being made by these profitable firms.

Using up most of one's off-duty hours in pursuit of the firm's business, often working when one's messmates were fast asleep in their hammocks, typically appealed to older, married sailors who wanted to make extra money to send home to their families, but held little interest for the unmarried sailor with no family to support. Robert Fagg, a single man who was primarily motivated by the desire to earn more money for his runs ashore, soon disbanded his dhobeying firm when he discovered how difficult and time-consuming the laundry work really was. But for the security-minded rating in a good-sized ship on a long commission, the opportunity was golden—if it could be seized. Albert Heron recalled two shipmates who made sufficient money—even after payments to co-operative cooks and engine-room staff—from a one-commission dhobeying firm to have saved about £150 to £200 apiece by the time the ship paid off at the end of the cruise. It was enough for them both to purchase the Portsmouth homes in which their families lived.[40]

⚓

While some messmates were improving their finances, a smaller number were busy improving their minds. Here one moves away from the mess as basic social unit toward the entire ship as a little society-at-sea. James Cox participated in organizing one such self-improvement effort: "When I came home with the submarines, which is a tedious journey home from Hong Kong all the way across in the [depot ship] *Titania*, going at about six or eight knots all the time and ten thousand or twenty thousand, well, fifteen thousand miles—well, coming across the Indian Ocean, say, you'd be about four or five days. Well, we got up lectures, you see. Went round the officers asking them if they was interested in anything special or any men or doctors or anyone like that, anybody was interested in anything special, would they give a lecture? And we'd put them down for a lecture on a certain night on [the] fore messdeck or [the] after messdeck or the foretop messdeck and so on.

"Say you'd institute a lecture on football, a lecture on rugby, a lecture on venereal disease—get a doctor to do that, see? Now you went to the skipper, the skipper—I remember once listening to a lecture on the Reform Bill, a lecture on the importance of the Suez Canal, and all things like that which used to pass away an evening very, very nicely, because you learnt the—also, say, a lecture on the way the government runs the country or the customs in Parliament, things that you don't usually learn, don't usually know. We used to think up these things and ask different people if they knew anything about it, would they give us a lecture on it, and so on."

It would be easy to overemphasize activities such as these and imagine a navy full of upwardly mobile men intent on self-improvement. Cox admitted that he was exceptional rather than typical. When he left the navy James Cox expected to join his brothers in managing the family business (which he eventually did), and he consciously tried to prepare himself for that role. As for his shipboard peers, "The average petty officer in the petty officers' mess was—liked to play cards, gamble, or make mats or something like that for his wife. Or some would read and so on. Most people were rather selfish as regards their spare time." Some sailors bent on self-improvement had to deal, not just with passive negativity, but with the active hostility of their fellow ratings. Just try attending a course to raise your level of educational attainment, reported Stoker First Class Henry Boin, "and your mates all turn around and if— you sort of, you had to have a very thick skin, otherwise you was thought you was doing a bit of, you know, [trying to be better than them] to be quite honest. Because, as I say, the men those days was very, very crude—very, very crude."[41]

Shipwide concert parties were more likely to generate general enthusiasm than was a culturally enriching lecture or a class aimed at enhancing one's education. The concert party was typically a self-organized and thoroughly rehearsed variety show made up of individual and group songs, instrumental performances, skits, and magic—whatever talent the ship might be able to produce. Concert parties took time to prepare. One every two or three months was the best a ship's complement could expect, but dancing—that might happen any night. To amuse yourself, "you'd do a lot of dancing," Cox recalled. "Any part of the deck where there was a space, between a pair of turrets or something like that. Somebody would get on deck with—they'd get the piano up on deck. And that's where [the] majority of sailors learned to dance. But they danced in their bare feet all the time. You'd do your waltz, your Valettas, your different dances . . . foxtrots, quicksteps, quadrilles and all those old-fashioned dances we used to do on board ship, yeah. Nearly every night was dancing."[42]

Lectures, concert parties, and dancing were events that built bonds of comradeship among the entire ship's complement, officers as well as men, because everyone participated. Rank and status were temporarily downplayed. Indeed, it was not unheard of to see a midshipman or a lieutenant with a seaman or a stoker as his dancing partner. Nonetheless, the fundamental bond that made an individual ship an effective unit in a larger navy was formed not on a makeshift dance floor or lecture hall, but in the mess. It was here that loyalty grew, a point dramatized in a story told by Richard Rose.

A mess in which Rose was leading hand instituted a swear box. The idea was that if one messmate caught another swearing, the offender had to put a specified sum of money in the swear box. When the ship reached port Rose would open the swear box and distribute the money equally among the members of the mess. "It's amazing the sum of money that can collect," said Rose, chuckling heartily. "Used to say it just shows you what villains we are." Now in this mess there were two Welsh lads, twins, who came from a farm near Llanelly. Both were committed chapel-goers. Neither ever swore. But each day the twins put money in the swear box so that they might contribute their fair share to the collective shore-leave fund.[43]

Arthur Ford pointed to the manner in which food was served in the mess as another mark of the way the mess built loyalty, trust, and cohesion. He contrasted naval messing with mealtime arrangements in the army, where everyone lined up and one corporal put so many potatoes on each plate and the next corporal in the mess line added a certain amount of cabbage. In a naval mess the serving pan was passed around the table. "You cut off a piece of meat which you think is your fair share and take so much cabbage and a couple of potatoes . . . And you were sort of trusted to, if you understand. We liked it better that way, because we liked to feel we got that community spirit, you know, that you sort of thought of somebody else, you see . . . We liked the more being-at-home style, you know."[44]

Although mentioned less often by former ratings than its role as agent of socialization and builder of community, the mess also functioned as a place of lower-deck self-governance. It offered an alternative, and often more acceptable, means of behavior control than a ship's officer-dominated disciplinary system, even if the latter was the ultimate sanction which made the former possible. Here is a story James Cox told to make his point: "Now in the old days, now especially in the POs' messes and the chief POs' mess, there's a lot of routine and tradition kept up . . . They had all white covers on your seats and things like that. But there was also certain rules laid down in the mess. You see, you wasn't allowed to come into the mess in a overall suit, for instance. If you was working in an overall suit, you had to take your overall suit off and have a wash and that and come into the messes. Although perhaps you was only in your shirtsleeves or jersey, something like that, but you had no dirty clothes on, you'd never sit on the white cloths [in dirty clothes] or anything like that.

"There was a president of the mess, you see. A senior chief was in the mess, and he'd run the mess—according to the rules of the ship of course. And anything untoward he would report or suppress. For instance, I know a case now in my mess out in China. We had a chief PO in our mess, a chief stoker, who had borrowed some money off one of our bumboat men, Old Ugly as I used to call him . . . Well [Old Ugly] come to me one day and he said that Chief PO So-and-So had borrowed so much money from him and he could never get it back. So immediately I went up to that chief PO and I said, 'Look,' I said, 'we have a certain tradition to keep up. And we have to show a certain amount of integrity,' I said, 'to these people.' And I said, 'You've got to pay that debt. If you don't pay it, I shall report you to the president of the mess.' Well, he didn't pay. Well, I reported it to the president of the mess. And of course we had a mess meeting. Mess meeting. 'Come in.' That PO was charged and [we] wanted to know why he hadn't paid it, you see. Right. But he was censured by the president of the mess and given so long to pay it. And if it wasn't paid to him, to the president personally, then he would report it to the captain, you see? So we kept trouble away from the captain . . . We judged our own people in our own mess and kept up a certain amount of integrity in the mess, you see?"[45]

⚓

If all this talk of comradeship and messdeck life seems rather remote from the real world and authentic people, if these messmates are beginning to look and sound too much like paragons of Edwardian middle-class values, a gallery of typical shipmates, as remembered and described by the old sailors, should correct any skewed perspective: "Jock Page was a rascally Glaswegian who had two green eyes tattooed on his bottom. When at sea his hammock was pitched next to mine and when he clambered in these green eyes leered at me as he rolled into his blankets."[46]

"There were several [of my shipmates] who you could never ever imagine taking up civilian life again, as some of the 'strokes' they pulled sound incredible. One bloke was a past master at unsealing a one-pound tin of tobacco, taking out the contents, filling up the tin again with dried tea leaves which he collected for just this purpose, and then putting on a top layer of tobacco and resealing the tin, which he would flog ashore to many of the ready buyers. Of course you could only do this once, in one pub, otherwise the expectation of life could be very short."[47]

"H. was one of the finest and yet one of the worse men I have ever met. I admired him very much, and his faults were greatly outweighted by his virtues. He had absolutely no morals, drank like a fish, would steal anything from stores or dockyard (never from a pal); a confirmed gambler who lived with another man's wife and literally found a wife in every port. On the other hand he would do anything to help a shipmate and was kindness itself to any youngster who got into any trouble. When he gambled he played fair; when he borrowed money—and he would borrow from anyone—it was always returned at the end of the month and he would ask the loan of it for another month if necessary. A splendid seaman, he would do the most dangerous job with a laugh. I have seen him go up the mast on a rough day to help a boy who was nervous."[48]

"Baldwin was a tearaway AB in an adjoining mess, apparently trying to live down, in the eyes of his shipmates, the story that he was the son of a commander. He used to boast in detail about his sexual exploits ashore and hold up stained items of clothing in support of his tales. He was forever showing off his strength and not so much picking quarrels as seizing every chance to bear down on people. He once caught hold of me on some pretext and forced me to the deck. I merely remained inert until he let me up again."[49]

"A telegraphist was boasting how many times he had crossed the line [the equator] and was naturally getting on people's nerves. He mentioned Father Neptune and an old rating said dryly, 'I suppose he's the man who joined the navy after you.'"[50]

"One rating [in *Lucia*, the submarine depot ship at Kilindini Harbor] never seemed to move, apart from paydays and mysterious trips ashore with some large parcels. I met him one day where he rested in his hammock, a fishing line attached to his big toe, the line leading out of an open port, whilst he read the latest semi-porno magazine. What his precise function was aboard no one seemed to know, but he used to catch a lot of fish and sell these to hotels ashore, with very little effort and the added bonus of being paid by the Admiralty for reading and angling."[51]

"We have a bore on this messdeck with a novel technique. He ought to have been a parson, because he speaks to you as if he were addressing an audience and reading from a previously prepared sermon. He approaches and speaks the key word. Suppose it is 'market gardening.' This means: 'I am about to commence a conversation on market gardening. You must listen and not interrupt.'"[52]

"Another rating [in *Lucia*] was a huge Glaswegian with a beard like a whin bush. He would go ashore, talk of endless conquests and incredible

feats of prolonged sexual activity, and one night returned, heavily re-
freshed, with six huge pineapples. He bellowed in a huge voice, 'All
richt, yer miserable set of shits, Sassenach-faced bastards, I'm a fucking
commando,' and threw these heavy fruits at all and sundry and, in fact,
one of them demolished a locker door. He was later on taken away by
several large ratings who 'accidentally' dropped him a few times on his
way to the cells."[53]

⚓

Even for young men who had grown up in large families hovering near
the edge of poverty, the unrelenting intimacy of life in the navy could be
a shock. A sailor slung his hammock wherever he could find a free bil-
let—and it might or might not be near where he ate. "At night there are
hammocks everywhere," Charles Thomas reported home from the
cruiser *Leander* in the mid-1930s. "Some men sleep in the gun turrets,
their hammocks tied to any projecting mechanism of the guns. I sleep
over the main electric motor which works the capstans and consequently
when the anchor is lowered the roar is deafening." Sailors found sleeping in a hammock a comfortable experience. "The more it swayed," said
one, "the more relaxing I found it." But the business of sleeping mir-
rored the crowded conditions found everywhere on the messdecks.
"Now then," said James Cox, "the conditions on the messdeck of a
night. Remember you're sleeping like that in hammocks. You see"—he
gestured, placing his hands end-to-end, the fingers running between
each other—"the head of one between the foot of the other. You're allowed eighteen inches between each hook. Let me tell you, you're sleeping very, very close. And you can't help it, because there isn't the room."
Whether a man was eating on a mess bench or sleeping in his hammock,
conditions were always the same: "You were shoulder-to-shoulder all
the time. Yeah."[54]

Nowhere was the lack of privacy more obvious than in the heads, or
toilets. "They were the same as prison lavatories," reported George Michael Clarkson, who after he left the navy entered the prison service as
an officer in charge of maintenance parties and workshops and there led
a life as full of interest (and danger) as his naval years: "They were the
same as prison lavatories, where you can see a fellow's feet and you can
see his head . . . And you're sitting in rows there. And then there's a

queue as well, standing facing you, waiting to have their go. And the only time you moved is every now and then when the water was let go and you used to rush round. And it was just one lavatory with so many seats."

"There's these metal partitions like partitioned off," explained Arthur Ford, adding his perspective: "Well, down below . . . a big trough, you see . . . Every so often what they call the captain of the head—that's what they called him, he was the one who looked after that head, you see—he'd pull a lever, you see. And in would come a flood of water, you know. And if you happened to be sitting on there, you know, you got nearly washed overboard."

Arthur Ford laughed, then continued: "When he thought there was too many getting in there having a mike, you know, he just pulled the old lever. They soon scampered. It didn't half come down there I can tell you! Would nearly wash you out of the place."[55]

George Michael Clarkson saw conditions such as these, similar as they were to the arrangements he later encountered in the prison service, as part of the navy's fabric of control: they were intended to maintain a certain moral degradation through humiliation. Others took a more benign and less conspiratorial view. Conditions similar to these—or worse—had been part of shipboard life since human beings first went to sea countless years before. If the navy was slow to begin to meet twentieth-century standards of privacy, it could as easily be attributed to the heavy hand of tradition—always a controlling shipmate in the Royal Navy—as to more manipulative motives. Even Clarkson admitted, "Well, you can get used to everything. Nobody liked it, but it was the best you could get then." "You learned to accept what was coming to you, and you abided by that," recalled Walter Basford. "You knew you had to put up with it and you thought to yourself, 'Well, I've got twelve years to do'—which we did have those days, 'cause we couldn't sign for anything less. We signed for twelve years and that was your lot and you accepted those things then. Well, I was always pretty well on the ball, most things, and I thought to meself, 'Well, that's it.' And you know, that was it."[56]

Perhaps *getting used to it* is a less accurate description than *accepting the inevitable*, because several sailors testified that they never really got used to the lack of privacy and personal space. The desire to be alone was

always there, no matter how cheerfully one accepted shipboard conditions. "You know," commented Arthur Ford, "you sort of get that feeling that you want to get on your own sometimes—you know, occasionally. You see, you always got a crowd round you. You see . . . you get that
feeling, you know, that you'd sort of be nice to be on your own, you
know." For the typical rating the lack of privacy was an enduring problem that could never be solved in an active-duty warship, even when the
navy made explicit efforts to improve lower-deck conditions. "In the
Royal Sovereign class of ship . . . they had a recreation space," remembered George Michael Clarkson. "But that was overcrowded. And in
these small cruisers they had recreation spaces, but then you couldn't go
up there. They'd probably have a piano or something there. Some amateur bandsman would be up there bashing away on that. Just like when I
was in the [light cruiser] *Dauntless* [March 1930–July 1932] we had a
crowd of cooks who formed a band. And they were right on top of us in
this recreation space, day and night, blowing saxophones and bashing
away on drums. You couldn't get away from the noise. There's no such a
thing as peace until *pipe down* at night."[57]

Did crowded conditions and lack of privacy on the messdeck create an
atmosphere ripe for arguments, quarrels, fights, and violence? Not according to Richard Rose: "Funnily enough, I've never seen a quarrel—
never seen a fight, can we put it that way?—on our messdeck in all the
ships I've had. Yeah, I've heard quarrels, but mainly over stupid things,
you know . . . You would think that tension would be built up by being
so closely closeted together, but, no, I found that sailors, on the whole,
were jolly good people to get on with. They were human. They were always ready to help someone else."[58]

The notion that "sailors were jolly good people to get on with" was
affirmed and reaffirmed by former ratings. But Rose's statement regarding a lack of messdeck fights seems just too good to be true. Negative
suspicions are fueled by other men's memories. William Batters's recollection of messdeck life is not quite so Rose-tinted: "Generally, when
the ship had been at sea a few days, we got on each other's tits. After a
week you could expect a few fights"—especially around the time of the
daily issue of rum.[59]

"Yes, oh yeah. There was always a bit of friction now and again—bit
of a row going on," recalled Walter Basford. "A bloke'd get overwrought

and fed up and things like that, and just somebody'd talk about something and he'd pick him up about it . . . That's right. I have seen fights down there [on the messdeck], like, you know. Nobody interferes in the fight—just let 'em go on. Unless a leading hand is there. Then the leading hand—his job is to maintain, you know, everything on the messdeck, and he'd have to stop it then. Otherwise, if he didn't, he'd be on the carpet. That was his job, to see that everything went along all right on the messdeck."[60]

The recollections of John Davidson provide a leading hand's perspective on just such a situation: "It was not altogether easy to live in a mess alongside fifteen men from all walks of life and, as leading seaman, to be responsible for discipline . . . On [one] occasion at sea a couple of ratings were shouting at each other and scuffling. I was tired, coming off watch, and before they could react I grabbed them both by the collar and banged their heads together. This took them by surprise, and I was amused to see that I was eyed somewhat warily thereafter."[61]

The potential for violence—serious violence—was always present. Most of the time it was held in check by the navy's strict discipline and by the ratings' self-discipline. "If it hadn't been for the naval discipline, it would have been hell on board ship," said Edward Pullen. Once in a while a bit of that hell erupted. Edward Pullen (then an ordinary seaman) served in the battleship *Caesar*, the flagship of Lord Charles Beresford, in 1904–1905. Although he belonged to the seaman branch, Pullen still had to do six weeks of stokehold training. One day Ted came up to dinner from the stokehold and sat down at the mess table opposite a seaman named Sturgess. "He was about five-foot-ten," the half-a-foot-shorter Pullen remembered, "and he had a five-bob piece tattooed on his chest."

"That's doing you good down the stokehold, Ted," said Sturgess in no friendly tone of voice. Ted Pullen was not the type of man to let such a remark pass unchallenged: "Do some of you people good to get down there." Then "[Sturgess] put his foot under the table and shot me right up against the securing chamber of the gun. We didn't have knives and forks in them days. But we happened to have a black-handled knife belonging to the bandsmen's mess—next mess—in our mess. And it was pointed like a bayonet. And I jumped up with that knife and I stuck that into his chest about, I should think, two inches at least. He jumped over the table and grabbed that, rushed to the sickbay." Within minutes the master-at-arms appeared and announced: "Quarterdeck, Pullen." There the officer-of-the watch declared: "Commander's report, Pullen." The commander passed him on to the captain. Pullen was almost certainly punished, but he did not tell—perhaps because he did not remember—that part of the story.[62]

Whether it was an eighteenth-century naval ship or a twentieth-century one, the potential for the crowded, no-privacy conditions of a messdeck to generate tensions that could escalate into violence was constantly present. Navies had in place a disciplinary system to discourage such violence and to throttle it when it did explode. But that system was hardly foolproof. There were too many men and too many remote corners of a ship to make constant surveillance possible. As Ted Pullen well knew, in the navy a man was his own first line of defense.

⚓

One source of potential messdeck tension was strictly banned: talking politics. "Never. Not allowed," said one former petty officer, who speaks here for many.[63] Or was it?

When ratings were asked to recall which of the two major parties the lower deck supported, only about half of those who responded named a party. Of these, two-fifths said a majority of the lower deck favored Labour or the Liberals and three-fifths replied that the lower deck was Conservative in its political sentiments. These perceptions were, to a degree, influenced by the years in which a man was in the navy. Sailors who served in the 1930s and 1940s were more likely to see their messmates as Left-oriented than as Conservative. First World War ratings, by contrast, perceived the lower deck as Conservative turf.

A thirty-year veteran who attained the rank of chief petty officer saw the lower deck's support of the Conservatives "as a natural thing." He did not explain himself, but one of his contemporaries did elaborate: Labour's policies were hostile to the best interests of the fleet, and the party had a record of reducing pay and emoluments for the lower deck. Moreover, Labour's support for the Bolsheviks in the years of the Russian Revolution and after alienated other men of the lower deck who had observed conditions in Communist Russia firsthand or who had seen the plight of refugees from the Revolution in places such as Istanbul. But not all sailors viewed the Conservatives as natural friends of the lower deck and its interests. Able Seaman Ronald Orritt, who served between 1924 and 1934, was certain that the lower deck was Labour country with no love for the Conservatives: "Lady Astor [Nancy Witcher Astor, Viscountess Astor, Conservative Member of Parliament from Plymouth and the first woman to serve in that body] was bitterly hated by servicemen and their families. I recall that it was she who was supposed to have stopped the one shilling per day hard-laying money for men in destroyers and submarines and all small craft, coupled with other mean recommendations against servicemen."[64]

Whether their answer to the hypothetical question "How would the lower deck have voted?" was "Labour" or "Conservative," all the former sailors affirmed that party politics were rarely, if ever, discussed on the lower deck. Some attributed this to the young age at which future sailors entered the navy: "When one joins as a boy, what does one know of politics? We put that down to civvy antics." Others saw sailors as people who, by and large, just were not interested in party politics: "Other things seemed of far greater importance . . . Up to the age of thirty most of us would, if asked, have voted as directed." If a Sunday newspaper appeared in a mess, it was the sports pages that drew the most attention. To still other ratings this lack of interest in politics was viewed as the virtue of being apolitical: the navy was there to defend Britain, no matter which party was in power. Or was it simply a visceral conservatism? a fundamental acceptance of things the way they were? "Many had the complex of the inevitability of a divided nation of master and man, officer and rating, rich and poor," recalled Chief Ordnance Artificer Leslie Nancarrow. It was not a long step from there to apathy: "We didn't know or care who the prime minister was half the time, the impression being: If nothing very much has altered [in the navy] since Nelson's days, what could politics matter or politicians do to alter our lives?" explained Able Seaman Alan Pitt.[65]

If the lower deck had a natural disinclination toward the politics of party, this leaning received powerful reinforcement from tradition and authority. "During my twenty-five years service, as a leading signalman [and] senior petty officer," said Roland Purvis, "I forbade on the messdeck any discussions on politics, women, and religion"—three potentially controversial subjects likely to disrupt the harmony and comradeship of the mess. Many other veterans of the lower deck reported similar prohibitions in the messes—although most recalled only politics and religion as taboo, with ample, free, and enthusiastic discussion of women and sex. "Mainly loyalty to the country was practiced, particularly if this point of view was expressed by a PO, who usually was annoyed with any opposition," said William A. D. Bailey. He should have known, for he himself had been an acting leading hand, presiding over a mess, before he left the navy in 1919. The petty officers and leading hands did not have to enforce these prohibitions on their own. They had powerful reinforcement from higher authority. "On more than one occasion," recalled Leslie Nancarrow, "we were told by the captain [that] the party in power was our bosses and we had little right to challenge authority in any way."[66]

An exception to the general consensus on party politics and the lower deck comes from Able Seaman Arthur Adams, who asserted: "Yes, [politics was discussed on the lower deck] very frequently. Because it was a red-hot topic, talks had to be camouflaged. In every ship I was in I found the discussions very impressive. We used the media of writing home to parents and friends and of acquainting them of certain facts relative to our conditions and getting into touch with MPs and local councils. We made arrangements regarding having certain papers sent to us stuck away in food parcels . . . Most of us were progressives, believing in a cooperative and labor society. Yes, politics were talked about more than one knew." But Adams is far from an impartial witness—and may not be a reliable one. Although a capable sailor, Adams was deeply alienated by the conditions he found in the navy. He developed a far-from-enviable disciplinary record: four entries of *Run*—that is, desertion—and a total of sixty-seven days spent in cells on seven separate occasions. After his fourth desertion, in August 1919, the navy just let Adams disappear— good riddance!—a departure he was later able to have changed to an SNLR (services-no-longer-required) discharge through someone's political influence. Arthur Adams's memory of politics being hotly discussed is probably accurate, but this memory is of debates among the small circle of disaffected activists for radical change of which he was a member—not of the reality among the apathetic majority.[67]

One note of caution: the preceding review of politics on the lower deck derives entirely from memories recorded after the fact, not contemporary documents. Although there is little basis on which to challenge the widely held perception that the lower deck of the first half of the twentieth century was *generally* apolitical, there were thoughtful individuals who swam against the current—recall Charles Thomas and his denunciation of the elite monopoly of the officer ranks—and there were times of crisis that rattled even the satisfied complacency of a petty officers' mess. Two diary entries, one from each of the wars, provide rare contemporary references to lower-deck political talk. The first was recorded by Ordinary Seaman Charles Stamp, who stood a night watch in the second-class cruiser *Astræa* in African waters in August 1916: "Long jaw with PO Roscoe about navy life, people, etc., etc., in general. He is strong objector to Labour Party owing to their lack of foresight, etc." The second is found in the diary of Leading Telegraphist Archibald Richards, on board the aircraft carrier *Formidable* in March 1942: "Quite an argument developed in the mess today and out of about eight chaps only one was for imperialism. The others were enthusiastic for the Russian regime."[68]

The best assessment from the evidence concerning politics and the lower deck appears to be this: the majority of sailors were not concerned with party politics, an attitude which received powerful reinforcement from the navy. A few men did think and (less often) express opinions about political issues. Those ideas could be expressed freely, without penalty or repercussion, so long as any perceived threat to authority did not seem too immediate. Arthur Adams crossed to the wrong side of that line.

⚓

Was there at least one additional (and natural) human trait working against the spirit of comradeship in the Royal Navy of 1900–1945? Did an informal, and possibly tension-producing, hierarchy exist among the men of the lower deck? Of concern here are not such official gradations as boy, ordinary seaman, AB, leading hand, petty officer, and chief petty officer, but whether there was, among men who were seemingly equal in their official shipboard standing, an informal hierarchy of status derived from the kinds of work they did—the roles they filled in the ship.

As with all such unofficial hierarchies, prestige was in the eye of the beholder. When asked if there had been much difference in status among the branches of the lower deck, a former petty officer with twenty-eight years of active-duty service responded: "Not really—only what the lower deck made themselves." Although it was not quite that simple—there were navy-created factors that fed the perception of a status hierarchy—Harry Sowdon's remark is one of those key insights that flies straight to the heart of the matter. Because perceived status was so subjective a quality, there was little consensus among the informants. When asked if status differences existed, one old sailor responded, "None at all." Another reported that they were pervasive.[69]

But here is where the big ships—small ships dichotomy comes into play once again. Differing perceptions about the existence of a status hierarchy were driven by whether a sailor was thinking about, say, a destroyer or a battleship when he spoke. In small ships the conditions of service all militated against the creation of status hierarchies.[70] Everyone was thrown into a small space; all had to get along as equals to survive. Informality was the keynote of interpersonal relations. Even the handful of officers were far less distant—if still officers.

It was in the big ships—the battleships, the cruisers, and the aircraft carriers—where there was the critical mass of people required to incubate real social distinctions, that lower-deck hierarchies of status flourished. Because they were perceived, subjective hierarchies, not every sailor would have agreed on the relative status of the branches. But—ignoring these individual variations for the moment—wherever a status hierarchy did exist, it ran (top to bottom) from the ship's writers and sick-berth attendants, down through the communications branches (wireless operators and signalmen), the officers' stewards and the supply branch, through the torpedomen and the gunners, to the seamen and finally bottomed out in the engine room with the stokers.[71]

The higher-perceived status of the sick-berth attendants, the ship's writers, the telegraphists, and the signalmen was the product of two factors. For one, there was the perception that the Royal Navy picked the most intelligent of its recruits to be trained for these jobs. "It wasn't exactly expressed, but . . . the wireless man would think to himself, 'Well, I got more brains than what a bloody seaman has.'" Or so said James Cox, himself a member of the seaman branch. For another, men in these high-status branches worked on a daily basis side by side with the commissioned officers, were required to be better dressed on duty than other ratings, and basked in the glow of this exaltation-by-association. One sailor recalled: "We of the Communication Branch . . . thought ourselves the 'lords of creation.'"[72]

Not surprisingly, status rivalry was most intense at the bottom of the hierarchy—between the seamen and the stokers. Only the existence of stokers prevented the seamen from being the lowest rung on the lower-deck's perceived status hierarchy. No wonder the seamen worked so hard to assert their importance! Then, too, stokers suffered from a negative image: big, strong, illiterate, dumb guys, all brawn and no brain, recruited to do the ship's heavy lifting in torrid, coal-soiled engine spaces. As with most stereotypes, this one was a little true and mostly false, but it stuck to stokers with the adhesive excellence of Tar Baby. Even stokers themselves saw an element of truth in their image. Stoker Henry Boin laughed when he said, "Well, you see, life was very, very different in those days [around the First World War period], you see. And the man that joined the navy—or the man that joined for a stoker at any rate . . . he was very, very illiterate. All he was there for was his strength mainly, because they were great big fellows."[73]

Members of the seaman branch flaunted their role as *sailors* in the most fundamental meaning of that word—the men who sailed the ship and fired its guns, the men of the executive branch. The glamour of the seaman branch even tempted the joiner George Michael Clarkson, who as a tradesman had objectively a better job at better pay, to apply to transfer to the seaman branch. "You always would like to, we'll say, be in the fighting . . . And when I was out in the Red Sea [1915–1919] . . . I remember there was a young leading seaman on there. And he was only— he must have been about twenty, where in the ordinary course of events you had to have about nine years service in before you were a leading seaman. And I thought, 'Coo, if only I could get in the seaman branch, I'd be interested.' Actually, I loved the seaman side of it. And I put in to turn over to the seaman branch, ready to drop in wages and everything. But I wasn't allowed to, because in the navy you're not allowed to change over to a rating beneath the one that you already hold, you see? And I would have liked it. As I say, I was always in a racing boat's crew. If there was anything like sailing or anything [and] they wanted volunteers, I'd always be in it."[74]

It stuck in the stokers' craw that the navy's command system perpetuated the hegemony of the seaman branch over the engineering branch. As Chief Stoker James Dunn explained, a stoker petty officer or a chief stoker might be in a boat on ship's business, but the coxswain of the boat, even though he was only rated a leading seaman, was the man in charge: "He gave the orders"—not the senior (and perhaps more experienced) stoker petty officer or chief stoker.[75]

Ship's cooks occupied the most ambiguous position in the hierarchy of perceived status. One sailor, William Bailey, thought that the cooks were treated with favoritism. In his opinion, the cooks' perceived status ranked them with the officers' servants and the supply branch and just below the wireless and signals ratings. But James Cox, asked for his view of the man at the absolute bottom of the status ladder, replied: "Well, I think the cook, poor old *Slushy*, as we used to call him. I mean, the most maligned men in the ship, man who done his best, worked the hardest, and I think he's mostly despised, I think. Well, if you call it *despised*. I mean, we used to [say], 'Oh, he's only a slushy.'"[76]

Reginald Willis, a former chief petty officer cook, recorded what it felt like to be poor old Slushy. A strong sense of self-worth was required, especially when it was a case of cook versus member of the seaman branch: "When [a seaman] came for his dinner, if it was a roast dinner, some of 'em—just one now and again—tried to teach us one now and again.

'You haven't browned these bloody potatoes.'

"Well, when a man spoke to me like that, even when I was a cook's mate, I took no notice of him. I just turned me back on him. I'd go away to the other side and do something. I'd come back. He says:

'Chef.'

'Well.'

'Potatoes are not browned very well are they?'

'Well, they're browned enough to suit me,' I said. 'I'm cooking it. If you're not satisfied, you know what to do. The only thing,' I said, 'I could do is to put it in the oven and do what I can with it.' I said, 'At least,' I said, 'they're cooked. If you want to make a fuss, take it on the quarterdeck [and complain to an officer].'

"No, they wouldn't do that . . . They used to think they were cocky and they knew all about it. Yeah, I'd sooner deal with anybody in the navy than an able seaman. They were a bloody nuisance—excuse my language, won't you? That's my opinion of them, and I lived twenty-two years with them . . . The cooking branch was something that they thought they could come along and browbeat. Yet, they'd come along and browbeat you at times for certain things which they knew nothing at all about. A seaman knew everything. 'I know this.' 'I know that.' 'I know the other.'

"Now, a funny thing. You take the stoker side, men that do join at eighteen and over. Different class of chap altogether. You couldn't wish for better. Now why should a seaman be that different? I don't know. I've never found out. But we used to get [the seamen]:

'I want so-and-so-and-so.'

'Well, you can't have it.'

'Right. I'll go and see the commander.'

"I've said to 'em, 'Son, you can go and see who you blasted well like. I don't care' . . .

"You had to stand up to 'em or otherwise they'd trample on you. Oh yes. I never did like a seaman, although there's good and bad. Now give me any other branch . . . According to the seaman [the cook] was a non-entity."[77]

Status perceptions, it bears repeating, were highly subjective. This is certainly clear from the letters of the upwardly aspiring loner Charles Thomas. Although he was himself a member of the communication branch, Thomas had little respect for his supposedly high-status peers: "The major part of the navy W/T personnel are long-service men who join the navy straight from elementary schools at the ages of fifteen or sixteen in many cases. Naturally, their level of conversation is not very high. I find it difficult to listen to some and with others never try." In Thomas's world-turned-upside-down it was men supposedly at the bottom of the status ladder who stood tall: "In other branches, such as seaman and engine room (stoker), there is, on the average, a finer type of man, especially in the latter, where men are recruited between the ages of eighteen and twenty-five."[78]

⚓

Comradeship could be a fragile bond subject to intense stresses that were an unavoidable part of naval life. Had it not been fragile, there would have been no need for the unwritten tradition of No politics, No

Religion at the messtable; Edgar Baker's companions would not have come close to violence in an argument about whether marmalade was jam; nor would Edward Pullen have stabbed his messmate Sturgess in the chest with a knife. Naval disciplinary records abound with sailor-to-sailor incidents that are the antithesis of comradely behavior. But here is the real danger in writing history: permitting such incidents and the records in which they are preserved to block out the bigger truth—that comradeship among sailors was a powerful and essential bond. Whatever the irritations of daily living, the bond held far more often than it broke. Without it, the Royal Navy of 1900–1945 could not have been an effective fighting force—nor could any other navy.[79]

4

I Never Thought I'd See Daylight Again

Men of the lower deck needed all the discipline, teamwork, and comradeship on which the navy depended when they came up against the anxieties and perils that were an essential part of the sea life they had chosen. It is impossible to understand the behaviors that have inspired the sailor's roguish image without first comprehending the stresses and dangers to which the naval fighting man was exposed. No stress was more intense, no danger more real than facing an enemy in battle at sea. To this truth the sailors themselves are the most appropriate, the most credible, and the most eloquent witnesses.

Early on the morning of Tuesday, December 8, 1914, First Writer Henry S. Welch, clerk to Captain John D. Allen of the armored cruiser *Kent*, washed up with no particular sense of urgency and sat down in his mess to enjoy breakfast in a leisurely fashion. *Kent* was anchored at Port Stanley in the Falkland Islands as part of a squadron—battle cruisers *Inflexible* and *Invincible*, armored cruisers *Carnavron* and *Cornwall*, second-class cruisers *Bristol* and *Glasgow*, and armed merchant cruiser *Macedonia*—searching for the German squadron of Vice-Admiral Maximilian Graf von Spee, composed of the armored cruisers *Scharnhorst* and *Gneisenau* and the light cruisers *Leipzig*, *Nürnberg*, and *Dresden*, which had annihilated the British armored cruisers *Good Hope* and *Monmouth* in the battle of Coronel off the Chilean coast on the first day of November. The British force had put into Port Stanley the day before to coal and expected to sail in search of the Germans, who were thought to be in Chilean waters, on the afternoon of Welch's leisurely breakfast. Then, as Welch recorded in his diary, at 8 A.M., "we had a signal from the C. in C.: *Kent* to weigh anchor. I thought we were just to go out on guard at [the] entrance to [the] harbor till others finished coaling, but a few minutes later another signal came through: 'Two enemy cruisers in sight.' 'Gee whiz,' thought I, 'something doing.' Squadron now cast off the colliers and commenced raising steam for full speed. *Kent* proceeded to the mouth of the harbor at 8.20 A.M. and cleared for battle. Ship's company looking highly pleased. All woodwork, ladders, timber, etc., being thrown overboard. I went and stowed the wireless logs and signals down in the tiller flat and then, with my notepad, pencil and watch, got up on the upper bridge with the captain and started taking down notes. I could see the enemy then steaming along parallel to the land towards the entrance of the harbor where we were stationed. We kept the flagship informed of their movements. One was a four-funneled cruiser, the other had three funnels.

"Things were now getting exciting, and I think all the men were jolly delighted at the chance of a scrap. The thoughts came crowding in—home, wife, child and all that a man has dear to him. The possibilities of the day occurred to me, but there was no time to think of the danger. All that seemed to trouble me was that the other ships in harbor were so long getting under way. The business on hand gave one very little time for thoughts. I had to write all that was taking place. I fear that my hand was a trifle unsteady with the excitement, but I got plenty of detail down."

About 9:15 A.M. two salvoes from the old battleship *Canopus*, aground on the mudflats of Port Stanley as a fixed harbor defense, caused the German cruisers (later identified as *Gneisenau* and *Nürnberg*) to veer away for a few minutes. Some minutes later the Germans sighted the tripod masts of *Invincible* and *Inflexible* and realized for the first time that the British had at Port Stanley ships devastatingly more powerful than anything in the German squadron. *Gneisenau* and *Nürnberg* turned away to the southeast to rejoin and warn the rest of Spee's squadron. By 10 A.M. the British ships were coming out of Port Stanley and steaming in pursuit of the slower-moving and less powerful Germans, whose only (and slender) hope was to flee in a southeasterly direction. From Welch's vantage point on *Kent*'s upper bridge "things were now growing very interesting. Ship all cleared for battle. All men not guns' crews and special-duty men were standing easy, so they all got up on the forecastle to see how things were going . . .

"At 5 minutes to 1 the *Invincible* fired the first shot with one of her 12-

inch guns . . . All our men on the forecastle gave one huge cheer when they saw the flash of the gun. Everyone seemed full of secret joy at the prospect of a fight. It is hard to describe my feelings at this time. Thoughts of danger found no room, owing to the exciting interest of it all. No one, I think, seemed to give danger a thought. Every man and boy looked like a lot of schoolboys going away for an outing . . .

"At 1.28 p.m. the *Scharnhorst* and *Gneisenau* altered course to port and our two battle cruisers did the same, which brought the two heavy ships on each side on parallel courses running away at right angles from us on the port hand . . .

"The *Invincible* and *Inflexible*, now matched against the *Scharnhorst* and *Gneisenau* respectively, took all the attention we could spare for the time being. They got away with each other at a great speed and were blazing away at each other at a range of about 13,000 yards. The shells of the enemy were dropping short for some time, but some of the 12-inch shells from our two ships were getting there all right. From my station on the upper bridge I had a splendid view of the fight. I saw one shell (fired by the *Inflexible*) strike the side of the *Gneisenau* amidships and burst. It must have been real hell near that part. The splash and the flame seemed to reach quite two-thirds to the height of the mast. What effect it did have I don't know, but I thank heaven I was not on the *Gneisenau*. The shells seemed to be falling thick and fast all around the two enemy cruisers. Some of theirs, too, seemed to get round our two. And so they went on and all the while getting farther away. My last view of them as they got in the haze of the horizon seemed to impress me that one of the German ships was on fire. This was officially reported to our captain a few minutes later both by the signal boatswain and from the foretop fire control . . .

"At 4.26 the *Glasgow* [which had been engaging *Leipzig*] turned completely round to starboard and ceased firing and took up a position on [the] starboard quarter of *Cornwall*. *Leipzig* now started letting go at the *Kent*, as *Kent* was still sending a continuous fire across her. Things commenced to get warm, and the shells from the *Leipzig* were whistling and screeching all round us. It was very cheerful up on the upper bridge, for the shells were coming straight at us from ahead and dropping all round our bows, some passing between the bridge and the fore control. Captain, navigator [Lieutenant Commander James R. Harvey], signal boatswain and I stuck it up there till 4.35 P.M. Then the captain turned to the navigator and said, 'I think it's getting too warm up here, Harvey. We will get down in the conning tower.' So down we went under the bridge in the tower. We were all drenched by the water thrown up by the exploding of shells close to the ship below water. One shell burst on the water's edge about ten feet in front of our bows. Ye gods! it was lovely— only a trifle further and there would have been a few gaps among us. Just now the *Cornwall* opened fire on the *Leipzig*, so we gave our attention to the ship on the left on whom we had gained somewhat [*Nürnberg*]. I noticed one great thing about the speed of the *Kent*. She seemed to be going very strong. I have since found out that we were doing 25 knots and at times 26. The *Kent* had never yet done more than 23½. Our engine room staff worked like heroes down below and all were full of enthusiasm.

"At 4.45 P.M. we were just over 11,000 yards behind the *Nürnberg*, so we opened fire on her. At 5.5 P.M. the *Nürnberg* replied with four of her after guns and the real 'business' for the *Kent* started. The *Glasgow* and *Cornwall* were both after the other two cruisers [*Leipzig* and *Dresden*].

"Our speed served us well, for at 5.45 we had lowered the range to 6,000 yards and gave it to her hot. She was compelled to stop her running away, so she turned to port (so did we) and prepared to have it out with us. The *Nürnberg* and ourselves were now heading away to the left, at right angles, from the other ships, and so we lost sight of the *Glasgow* and *Cornwall* and two enemy in the haze.

"Now we were at it in deadly earnest. The crash and din was simply terrific—first our broadside going off and shaking our bodies to pieces, deafening, choking, and nearly blinding us; then the shells from the enemy hitting us and bursting, throwing death-dealing pieces of shell and splinters of steel in all directions and nearly poisoning us with the fumes. Shells were screeching all round us, and as they whizzed by the bridge and the deck I could feel the rush of air. Some were going through the funnels. One hit the corner of the fore turret casing, glanced off and tore through the deck into the sickbay, crumpling and tearing steel plating as though it was paper. One went through the chart house just over my head. Another burst just outside the conning tower and sent a perfect hail of pieces of shell in round us. I have since found that three pieces struck the armor and chipped it six inches on either side of my head

[and] on a level with it. I remember feeling something strike very near me and then stooping down and picking up the fragments of shell at my feet, but didn't dream that they had nearly been the means of putting my will into execution . . . About two minutes later there were two fearful explosions very close to us in the fore part of the ship. One, just under the conning tower in the petty officers' WCs caused absolute wreckage of the show. I went down after the action was over and never did I see such a mass of mangled and crumpled ironwork and piping. Pieces of sheet steel were torn and twisted as if they were sheets of paper. The other explosion was on the waterline at the ERA's [engine room artificers'] bathroom. Here a hole was blown out of the side of the ship as large as the door of a house and everything inside absolutely made into mincemeat. This explosion entirely swamped us up there in the conning tower. This was at 5.50 P.M. My clothes were saturated before, but now I had the additional luxury of standing ankle-deep in water as well as being soaked through to the skin. It was frightful cold, too. Possibly the need of food and a good hot drink made me feel the cold more. Luckily I had managed a couple of whiskeys and soda during the day, which no doubt alleviated matters a little.

"Our shell fire was now telling with awful effect on the enemy. *Nürnberg's* foremast was shot clean away at 5.58 P.M. and four minutes later she caught on fire between the foremost funnel and the forebridge. Our lyddite must have caused awful damage and devastation and death aboard her. I have since heard (from the statement of one of the *Nürnberg's* crew we saved) that *one* shell of ours killed 50 of her men outright . . .

"The enemy was still game, but I could see that we were getting the upper hand. Several of her guns were smashed clean up and one of her 5.9-inch guns on the forecastle was blown overboard and the other was falling about the deck. She seemed to be badly holed below the waterline and got a heavy list over to starboard. Her upper works were a picture—funnels all splintered and torn and jagged pieces sticking out. Nine of our guns were firing in salvos at her, and practically every shell found its mark and exploded, throwing pieces of steel splinters in all directions. It must have been a terrible slaughter aboard of her. We were only 2,800 yards apart now and both firing away full bore, although she could do little now as her guns were nearly all knocked out. She seemed to get the fire under control a little but, poor devils, our shells were bursting all over her and they had little chance of properly putting the fire out. At 6.15 P.M. our topgallant mast was shot away, which carried away our wireless aerials. A shell burst in our wireless room and made an Irish stew of all the instruments—a lovely sight it was: coils of wire and bits of things all over the deck in confusion just as if about 500 alarm clocks had exploded there.

"The *Nürnberg* seemed to be trying to get into a position to get us at a disadvantage or to try and torpedo us, but our captain wasn't having any. Every move on the board was ours, and we had the enemy on toast every time. At 6.30 P.M. she ceased firing but she kept her flag flying. We ceased firing at 6.36 to see what the game was. I think all her guns must have been done for, for she fired one shot which didn't reach half way across to us. At 6.42 P.M. the fire on board her burst out very fiercely and became a roaring furnace. I could see there was no possible hope of her getting out of it. Her flag was still flying and she was steaming about. I think she was trying to get a torpedo at us, but nothin' doing. We hoisted the signal 'Do you surrender?' at 6.52 P.M. and gave her another broadside, ceasing fire at 6.57. Half a minute later she hauled down her flag in surrender. She was now heeling over to starboard and gradually sinking. The men on her were jumping off into the water, clinging to all sorts of buoyant articles. It must have been simply horrible. The water was icy cold and the exposure following the battle soon made it a point where the fittest only could survive. The *Nürnberg* was now an awful sight—mast gone, ablaze, guns all disabled and falling from side to side with each lurch of the ship, the upper-works battered about, and the ship sinking. I fear I shall never efface the awful sight from my memory.

"About 7.15 P.M. we saw one of the German sailors in the water very near us, so the work of 'humanity after victory' commenced. At 7.26 the *Nürnberg* gave a sudden lurch to starboard and sank smoothly down into the deeps amid a mass of wreckage and dense clouds of smoke. The sight was one of fearful awe, and yet she turned over and sank with a graceful gliding motion, as would a cup or a tumbler pressed over in a bowl of water. Those who went down in her were game to the end, for we saw a party of her men standing on the quarterdeck waving the German ensign (tied to a pole) as she sank, and so they went down into their watery grave. One can only feel that they were brave men and died as their beloved Fatherland would have them. They fought well and to a finish.

"We did all in our power in the work of rescue—steamed up to the spot where she sank—but we could only get ten of the poor beggars aboard and only seven of them lived. No doubt those who were not killed or wounded had little life left to struggle in the icy water, and many must have been sucked down with the ship. We stayed there till after dark trying to find more of them, but [with] no success. All our boats were riddled with pieces of shell or splinters, but thanks to our carpenter staff in their smart work of patching up, the boats were away in twenty minutes. After dark the captain dismissed me, as there was nothing else to record, so I went down to the aft deck where the German survivors were being restored to vitality. I worked hard on one for more than an hour and a quarter with Dr. [Edward A.] Schäfer's [prone-pressure] method [of artificial respiration], but could get no life in him. Only seven of the ten could we bring to after much hard work and hot stimulants. Although I have mentioned the name of the ship we sunk pretty often in these few pages, I must say it was not until these survivors were picked up that we actually knew it was the *Nürnberg*. In the Pacific battle off Coronel, where the *Good Hope* and *Monmouth* met with disaster, it was the *Nürnberg* which went out afterwards and fired 79 shots at the disabled and sinking *Monmouth*, our sister ship. So, truly, we have avenged the *Monmouth*. I really believe it was in the *Nürnberg*'s power to have saved many of the *Monmouth*'s crew. Instead, she simply shelled her until the last part was visible above water. Noble work of which the German nation should feel proud. Thank God I am British.

"So ended this wonderful and exciting day, full of vivid drama and horrible details. Here we were about 150 [miles] out at sea with our coal bunkers nearly empty—battered and lonely, but victorious—probably 50 or 60 miles away from any of our ships. We mourn the loss of four of our men, two others dying, and eleven seriously injured and burnt. My poor friend George Duckett, the captain's steward, who was ambulance party in the midship 6-inch gun on the starboard side, was one of the two dying of awful injuries and burns. Poor fellow, he passed away this evening, as also did Private [A. C.] Titheridge of the marines. Our casualties now are six dead [and] eleven injured. The shell which caused these deaths and injuries entered the 6-inch gun port and burst just inside. It was an awful shambles there. The place was in flames when the explosion occurred.

"The shell which exploded in the wireless room completely wrecked all the transmitting instruments but left the receiving gear intact. At midnight we were receiving long strings of frantic signals from the admiral [Sir Doveton Sturdee] in the *Invincible*—'*Kent, Kent, Kent, Kent*, Where are you? *Kent, Kent*'—and on and on all the night, but we were unable to reply. We heard him ordering ships to go and search for *Kent*. When we reached the mouth of the harbor this afternoon [December 9] we met the *Macedonia* just setting out in search of us. Didn't they just cheer us when they saw us loom up out of the mist and signal that we were the *Kent* and had sunk the *Nürnberg*. Their cheers just about made us feel a wee lump rise in the throat. It seems the admiral was full of anxiety on our account, and all thought we were gone sure enough. So did the people ashore in the Falkland Islands. The *Macedonia* sent the admiral a message: '*Kent* entering harbor. Sunk *Nürnberg*.' A few minutes later we had one from the admiral: 'Well done.'"[1]

At Port Stanley Welch and his *Kent* shipmates learned that four of the enemy ships had been sunk, with tremendous loss of German lives but with relatively light British casualties. Only *Dresden* had escaped and was steaming hard for the Pacific Ocean, where, in March 1915, *Glasgow* and *Kent* finally cornered her and she scuttled herself after a brief, honor-saving action.

First Writer Welch's narrative of the battle between *Kent* and *Nürnberg*, recorded in his diary the day after the events he described, must be one of the most vivid and detailed descriptions of a naval battle written by a rating fresh from the scene of combat. For that reason—and because Welch could tell a great story—it has been quoted at length. But Welch's is far from the only contemporary diary entry to describe the exhilaration or the terror of staring death in the face. This, from another war and another ocean, is by the diarist and ordinary signalman Harold Osborne, a Birmingham postal worker turned hostilities-only sailor. The date was Tuesday, November 25, 1941. Osborne was serving in the battleship *Queen Elizabeth*, which had sailed from Alexandria in Egypt the day before in company with the battleships *Barham* and *Valiant* and a destroyer screen: "Up at 4.30 A.M.; action stations dawn . . . I had been

craving for action, but after today I'll stay in Alex[andria] for the duration if they will let me . . . At 11.40 A.[M.] one torpedo bomber shadow-
ing us practically at sea level . . . Shadowed all day; action stations practically all day with the three enemy aircraft which never came within
range once. Then at 4.20 P.M. the most momentous thing in my life—
I shall never forget it. During this time the [destroyer] *Jackal* had in-
vestigated a contact or sub at [3:15] P.M., but after circling three times
carried on.

"Later, at 4.22 P.M., I heard three distinct taps on the side of the ship
while I sat in the mess. I immediately dashed on deck and saw two tin
fish strike the *Barham* amidships and one aft. The sub [U-331] surfaced
right ahead of us to aim her fish. The *Barham* took a heavy list to port.
The poor souls were all congregated on the upper decks, ready to jump;
then she blew up, and the smoke rose to 1000 feet in a second, yellow
and black stuff. She sank straightaway. It was terrible—worse tha[n] that.
I don't expect any will be saved. The sub being so near to any survivors
and our bows, we steered to port. The [destroyers] *Jervis*, *Nizam* and
Hotspur were detailed to bring in any survivors but could not
depthcharge the fiend because of the swimmers, if any, so the sub got
away. How she got inside the [destroyer] asdic screen God only knows,
but the *Jackal* was very near as we turned and came back over the same
course. We had been loafing all day up and down the same course. The
whole terrible happening was over in five minutes, and after the smoke
cleared not a scrap of wood or anything was left to suggest a majestic
battlewagon was in full sail, colors flying, five minutes before. I shall
never forget it. Never . . . It was a marvelous yet grim sight all the way
through. Everybody shocked to their marrows at such a terrible sight . . .
The sub certainly was lucky and a clever chap. He was only 50 yards
range away, but gee! am I thankful to God it wasn't us, and it was so near
to us, crossing our bows, too. All the ship's co[mpany] slept on top decks
this night except a few." "Still feeling the effects of such a loss," Osborne
confided to his diary when *Queen Elizabeth* and *Valiant* returned to the
relative safety of Alexandria harbor at midday on November 26. Nor
was that the end of the psychic trauma. Two days later Osborne revisits
in memory the terrible event so many had witnessed: "No one yet has
got over the shock."[2]

From the Mediterranean of 1941 one can travel back to the Mediterranean of 1915, the Dardanelles campaign, and the diary of Able Seaman Percy Rooke, who wrote of March 11: "I left [*Canopus*] 6 P.M. this night in the picket boat, with officer in charge, to enter the enemy's minefield with seven trawlers . . . It was a very dirty night. Never shall I forget that night as long as I live. We were close to the shore, and I think that they fired everything at us from a[n] 11" gun to a pistol, and the screaming of the shells were enough to drive you off your head . . . We destroyed several lines of mines. After [we had] been in the minefield for about four hours we returned to the ship at 8 A.M. the following morning, after [we had] been in the boat for fourteen hours without anything to eat or drink, cold and wet through. I was very bad after it, as it had shaken my nerves very much . . . We were lucky to get away with our lives."[3]

Each of these three sailors attempted to describe the gut-wrenching danger, the fear, and the horrors of combat. Surely each felt, graphic as his words may seem, that he had failed to convey the intensity of the experience. So far as one knows, none of the three crossed the thin line between a psychic strain almost beyond endurance and combat neurosis or psychosis. Perhaps these diarists—each writing in the immediate aftermath of the events, not weeks or years later—used his journal as a means to distance and objectify the terrible memories and remain thereby on the narrow road of sound mental health.

One sailor who recorded lasting psychic wounds from combat was a signalman in the destroyer leader *Kelly*, although he wrote his memoir some forty years later, not in the shadow of the event. "That torpedo [which struck *Kelly* on May 9, 1940, while the ship was searching for German minelayers] broke my nerve," he wrote. "Before I always slung my hammock and undressed before getting into it, but afterwards I never slung it nor undressed when the ship was at sea. I slept as best I could on the lockers, always ready to go to the flag deck at a moment's notice should anything happen. What is more I was never happy below decks once the ship had left harbor. At every bump and bang, be it only a wave breaking against the side, I went hot all over . . .

"I was always glad that my job kept me out in the open on the bridge or the flag deck. I don't know what I would have done if my action station had been in a magazine or if I had been a stoker always in the boiler room when on watch. I wasn't afraid of drowning, but I had a constant fear of being taken down inside a ship. Also I was afraid of being afraid, and I was glad I was in the navy: Even if I wanted to run, there was no place to run to."[4]

What was it like to be in a boiler room during combat? and how did a man cope with the danger and the fear that the signalman in *Kelly* would have found unbearable? That experience was captured in an interview with James Dunn, who describes his service as a stoker petty officer on board the destroyer leader *Gabriel:*

INTERVIEWER: You said . . . how during the war, the First War anyway, when you were at sea, what it was like to be down below in the engine room. It was quite frightening obviously, wasn't it?

DUNN: If they ring down *Full speed,* like they did a couple of times, and you're supposed to be just on the verge of meeting the enemy, believe me it's a frightening experience. And I had just one little young stoker that had come straight out from working in a factory in Bristol, and he was the only one down with me. There was only him and I down with these two boilers and thirteen sprayers on with this roar of air and you're waiting for to be blowed sky-high at any minute.

And I've been out mine-laying like that [on August 2, 1918] and two destroyers [*Ariel* and *Vehement*] were blown to bits just beside us, because when we went out to lay these mines just off Heligoland the Germans had laid mines beforehand and we run onto the minefield. One destroyer blew up. The other one went to stand by her and she blew up. We only saved about half of the two crews of those.

INTERVIEWER: And you knew this could happen at any time throughout the war?

DUNN: You knew that this could happen at any minute . . .

INTERVIEWER: And all the time you were at sea, in the period and throughout your time at sea, you were below the waterline and you knew, really, that if anything happened, a torpedo—

DUNN: You had oil tanks up at the side of you. You had oil underneath you. And you had 250 pound of steam all round you. So—

INTERVIEWER: Do you become philosophical about it?

DUNN: Yes. Yes. I got—in the war I used to have one thought in my mind: If I had one more leave. As long as I could have that one more leave, well, anything could happen—and it would, I thought. But if I could only go ashore once more.

INTERVIEWER: You'd be happy?

DUNN: That was my philosophy.[5]

Battle, though the most obvious danger in a rating's life in war at sea, was far from the only source of anxiety and fear. Even so, sailors had relatively little to say about the risks they encountered and the fears they had to master as they went about their daily tasks. A rating's life and work demanded a high degree of physical bravery; there were powerful expectations on the part of the sailor's peers, his officers, and the Royal Navy that he would deny any fear as he worked in that dangerous everyday world. The idea that the navy likes men with high spirits implied that sailors had a light-hearted or thick-skinned attitude toward danger. Many sailors must have shared the feelings recorded by Petty Officer Edward Pullen; few felt free to admit to them: "Let us come on to a ship called the *Drake* again. We're going under the Firth of Forth bridge. Now we're going to strike topmast . . . Commander shouts out to the petty officer, White, in charge of my group: 'Petty Officer White, get a good able seaman to go aloft with you, strike topmast.' Now we had to go up there, you know. And as that topmast was going down—all the bluejackets down below was lowering it, see—there was me and 'Knocker' White, this petty officer, just enough ground for us two feet to stand on after we'd pulled the fid out, see? And he—I always remember him saying: 'Don't let's skylark on here, Ted,' see? And as that mast went down, there we was holding our both hands like that. And I think many a time in bed of a nighttime I've shouted and the wife have asked me what's wrong. I think it was the recall of that, see?"[6]

The danger that Ted Pullen and "Knocker" White apprehended was well grounded in reality. (White's "Don't let's skylark on here, Ted," reveals much about Pullen's reputation among his shipmates.) The potential for serious accidents and injuries was ever present in a sailor's life and work. Such accidents and injuries rarely found a place in sailors' diaries or memoirs, lending special significance to the writing of the chemist-turned-ordinary seaman Charles Stamp, who recorded an incident from 1916 in the second-class cruiser *Astræa*, then operating off the west coast of Africa. Although dinner had been piped, a work party of which Stamp was a member was ordered to raise anchor from the Cameroon River, where the cruiser had been coaling and pumping water for her boilers. "We had her up, 'catted' her, and were just lowering [the anchor] on [its] bed when something went wrong with [the] capstan and it took charge. I was thrown but managed to scramble clear of the wire. It was a miracle nobody (let alone the whole crowd of us) was [not] killed. I thanked God as never before for His protecting arm. Rotten old ship ought to be sunk!" But later in the day, after a brief call at Fernando Póo, luck ran out: "We had catted [the] anchor and got it level with [the] bed when again the capstan took charge. I was thrown forward and nearly over [the] side but cleared the wire, bar the skin on my right ankle and big toe and a bruised knee. The wire jammed, and on picking myself up . . . I saw poor Newell round the capstan, the wire passing across [his] thighs—crucified—big toe hanging by [the] skin, head cut, and the weight of 3 ton 5 cwt. across his body by this one wire, yet not a murmur from him. The C.Y. [chief yeoman] took charge and, all praise to him, quickly put on luff and [the] fellows pulled as never before. They got him out and down to sickbay. Later we heard that he had broken one leg near [the] thigh with a compound fracture (bone out) lower down. Internal injuries not known . . . Newell saved Atkins by pushing him away but has paid the penalty. Two near escapes. I thanked God again and again."[7]

No routine aspect of a sailor's life was more rife with danger than that most hated and filthy of tasks: coaling ship in the days before and during the Royal Navy's gradual conversion to oil as a power source. It was work that had to be performed all too frequently when a ship was cruising routinely—and even more often under wartime conditions. To cite but one case, *Indefatigable*-class battle cruisers, completed in the years just before the First World War, carried between 3,170 and 3,340 tons of coal, but burned 192 tons of that coal each day steaming at economical speed (14 knots), 530 tons per day running at three-fifths power, and 790 tons under battle conditions, when they might attain speeds approaching (or occasionally exceeding) 27 knotts. Here, to capture the ratings' enthusiasm for this job, is a small sample of the dozens of coaling entries in the First World War diary of James J. Eames in the battle cruiser *New Zealand*, one of the *Indefatigable* class. Eames had just turned sixteen and was rated boy when the entries begin. By the date of the last entry he was a nineteen-year-old AB and a veteran of the battle of Jutland, his rapid promotions a mirror of wartime conditions:

May 27, 1915: "Coal ship—we ARE smiling?"

November 15, 1915: "Coal ship, 1,000 tons. I am so glad I joined."

February 10, 1916: "1 P.M. started to coal—Are we moaning?—No— not some."

March 27, 1916: "Arrived Rosyth. Coaled 1,200 tons. I wish I could get hold of that man who first found coal."

January 10, 1917: "Raining. Coaled 350 tons [at] night. O' why? O' why did I join?"

March 25, 1917: "Arrive Scapa. Rough sea, strong wind, rain, snow and cold. What a day! Coaled 900 tons. A rotten coal. Dust everywhere."

November 5, 1917: "7 P.M. Arrive Rosyth. Raining hard but got to coal ship just the same. Finished coaling 12 P.M. . . . Turn in about 1:30 A.M. Why couldn't they leave the coal until the morning? Was they afraid that it wouldn't be raining then? It's the navy all over!"

November 27, 1917: "Coal 250 tons. Who wouldn't be a sailor, aye?"

March 5, 1918: "Firing practice. Anything to burn coal, so we can coal again soon."

July 22, 1918: "King's visit. He ought to come when we're coaling."[8]

Preparations for this dreaded duty typically began the day before the coal was brought on board. "A shadow would come over the ship as soon as you heard you were coaling," Joiner First Class George Michael Clarkson explained. All the doors in the ship's superstructure would be sealed over in a semi-futile attempt to fend off at least some of the coal dust that would penetrate every part of the ship. Ship's boats were hoisted outboard and the crutches in which they normally rested when not in use were taken up and stowed away, and the resulting empty bolt holes filled with oakum. Iron chutes were rigged between the upper deck and the coal bunkers, passing directly through lower-deck living spaces on their way. Here another semi-futile attempt would be made to seal around the scuttles where the chutes passed through the messdeck. The sealing job must have stopped some dust, but enough would seep through anyway to cover every surface with a thick layer of black grit.

On coaling day each man and boy in the ship, right up to the commander, had an active (and dirty) role. All hands, officers and men alike, wore old clothes, often ludicrous outfits intended to add a light note to a detested task. Vaseline poked up the nostrils and spread around the eyes offered some defense against the clouds of coal dust with which they would soon be assailed. The collier came alongside—perhaps as early as 4:30 A.M.—and a party of sailors boarded her to begin shoveling coal into large sacks that held two hundredweight apiece. When an appropriate number of sacks (that number varied from one ship to another) had been filled they were assembled in a hoist and swung over to the warship, either by the collier's steam winches or by the warship's derricks, and dropped on deck. There a crew jumped to the arriving hoist, released the straps, and loaded the bags on handcarts or trolleys manned by seamen and marines, who then sped away to a designated scuttle (or coaling hatch) in the deck from which a chute led to a particular bunker. With enough experience the trolleymen learned the precise motion that would tip a sack off the truck in just the right position and with the required momentum so that the men stationed at the chute could, in turn, tip a bag's contents down the chute in one smooth and (seemingly) easy maneuver. The empty sacks were tossed to boys—or perhaps to telegraphists, who were excused from other coaling work for fear they would injure their hands—to be hurried back to the collier and filled once again.

Meanwhile, members of the marine band, also in old clothes and with their instruments increasingly clogged by the hated coal dust, were playing lively tunes. Large cans of lime juice placed around the deck—their contents soon liberally mixed with coal dust—offered the closest thing to refreshment available until dinner: big cold sandwiches of bully-beef with perhaps tea or cocoa, although one veteran sailor remembered dinners of salt pork and pea soup, with the smell of the cooking pork permeating the ship for hours before and after dinner. Bully-beef or salt pork, dinner was a brief respite only; the work started up again all too soon. Circulating through the apparent pandemonium was the commander, accompanied by a rating with artistic talent. The latter carried a large blackboard on which he had drawn a foaming pint of beer over the legend: "The sooner you get it in, the sooner you get ashore and have one of these."

By now, between the ragbag old clothes and the coal dust, officers were indistinguishable from ratings. Coaling provided the primary occasion when naval hierarchy and deference were relaxed for a day: "That was the only time that everybody could swear at each other. An officer, if somebody ran over his ankles with a truck—it was dangerous—he could say 'You bloody fool' or something like that. And you could turn round and say, 'Who the hell are you talking to?' And you could call him just the same. And there was nothing ever done about it . . . Everybody was brought down to one level there. Everybody was as good as anybody else, because you could say what you like, you could do what you like . . . You went back to normality as soon as you washed your face, as you might say. Now you're talking about the only time that [officers and ratings] ever really mixed to be equals . . . The idea was that the officer was working just as hard as you were on the same job, so you were all equals there."

When several ships were coaling together competition was fierce, with each ship attempting to get the most coal in the fastest. Competition exacerbated what was already a risky situation. As "the two-ton hoists came over [from the collier] you had to catch 'em quick and get 'em away on the trolleys . . . And if you didn't get that two-ton hoist away quickly, there was another one dropping on top of it. It was real dangerous. There was always at least half a dozen in the sickbay with broken legs or arms, injuries of some kind. It was a competition—rush all the time.

"Unfortunately nearly every coal ship I heard of some poor soul lost their life . . . The common danger was the slipping of bags off the hoist or sometimes the hoist wire breaking itself and the whole hoist, coming inboard, would sometimes settle around the men that was working in the collier hold filling the bags. And sometimes it would happen on the upper deck itself where men were waiting for the hoist to be dropped and then suddenly the wire would break and then the coal come down on top of them. That has happened on many occasions . . . I've seen a hoist wire break, and I know one man that got killed. There was no hope once one of those hoists—you've got about two ton of coal falling on you right away solid. And of course you simply had to pick him up and then repair the wire and then carry on. They didn't stop work because of the man being killed. He was taken away to the sickbay and that was all you could do about it."

Where were the stokers and what were they doing amid all this frenetic activity? At least some of them were down in the ship's bunkers waiting for the coal from those tipped-up bags to come pouring down the chutes. "Stokers used to go down there on coaling ship and they'd sit in the corner and wait for their turn to come," said James Dunn. "They wouldn't be pouring coal into all the bunkers at the same time. They do so-many at a time to keep the ship even-keeled and all this. Now a couple of stokers—and I've done it—have gone down in these bunkers and set there waiting their turn. Then the coal starts pouring down. You can hardly see. You're breathing all this dry coal dust, which you're bringing up for three or four days afterwards off your lungs. And you know that's what gave me, I always imagined, bronchitis that I've always suffered from. But there was nobody to guide you and say you shouldn't do this. You had no need to go down those bunkers till there was so much coal in it, really . . . You weren't forced to go down them [the bunkers] till it was necessary to start throwing that coal into these corners, you see, and gradually building up. But you went down there to be out of the way, see."

Coal dust, bad as it might be, was not the only danger to the stokers down in the bunkers. Leading Stoker Richard Rose tells how close he had come to being buried alive by incoming coal: "You just sit there and wait for this lot coming down . . . Of course, all the coal dust—the moment it hits the [bottom of the bunker], see, up comes the coal dust and you can't see a thing. You've got oil lamps . . . And after about five minutes the coal dust used to put the oil lamps out, so you were in utter darkness there. You just hoped—all you used to do, you used to sit right at the back there and let the bloke [the petty officer topside in charge of dumping coal down the chute] work it out himself. When he found he couldn't get no more coal down the chute, he knew you'd got enough, see? So you used to wait till the dust settled and light your oil lamp—and invariably you had matches and cigarettes on you—light the oil lamp again—they didn't give much of a light—and clear all this lot away, throw it back [in the corners of the bunker]. That used to be the hard work, throwing it all back in the corner . . . And the moment chappie up the top saw this lot moving down the chute, so he'd pour [more coal down]. Well, that's how I got caught in a bunker, like that."

The petty officer at the head of the chute was expected to know the capacity of the bunker, and he was supposed to be keeping track of how much coal had gone down the chute into the bunker. "He kept on, this chappie up the top. Proper clueless he was . . . Every time we moved some coal, so he filled [the chute] up again, see?

"Well, come to the stage when we'd filled the bunker right up and we'd got nowhere to put the coal that was coming down the chute, see? We was pushing it back by hand. We couldn't use a shovel, because there wasn't no room. We're laying right up close to the bulkhead, which we would call the ceiling, between the coal and there, and we daren't move this lot. Every time we went to move this lot, so this rooster up the top was filling it up again. So we were trapped, absolutely trapped, and there we lay about two or three hours. Couldn't breathe. The heat was terrific, we were so confined, you see . . .

"And this other chappie [the sailor in the bunker with Rose] he got in a hell of a [state]. Well, I did too, I expect, and we didn't know—we couldn't communicate with this bloke up the top, and the moment we moved anything so down come another load. And there we were for about two or three hours. It seemed eternity, it did. I don't suppose it was as long as that, but it did seem like that. We daren't smoke because of the heat. And eventually this chap up the top must have realized that he'd got us trapped. And the only way he could do it—he couldn't communicate with us—it was too far up to communicate. That was a bad fault of the system, that was, really . . . Oh, I'll never forget those few hours!

"And what [the petty officer topside] had to do was to lower a chap down by his feet, head first, into a bucket . . . He took about two or three hours, this chap. They hauled him out while they pulled this bucket out, see, because a chute's only about that wide, see? That chap that was being lowered down, he must have had some nerve, too. If the rope had broke, I don't know what would have happened to him. Anyhow, he was able—this chappie that was lowered down head first, he eventually was able to shout down: 'Are you all right down there?' We could just hear him. And we said, 'No, we're trapped.' He said, 'I thought the [fucking] idiot had done that.' Anyhow, it was through him that we got communication [and were eventually rescued].

"We could have reported [the petty officer responsible] and of course probably done him a lot of harm. But we didn't. He apologized and all

On the threshold of a naval life. George Michael Clarkson, sixteen years old but claiming to be eighteen, as a newly entered carpenter's crew at Portsmouth, early in 1915. (Geoffrey Clarkson)

The third-class cruiser *Amethyst*. Although *Amethyst* is larger than a destroyer or a tender, this photograph conveys a sense of the intimate scale and the companionship valued by sailors fortunate enough to be assigned to smaller ships. (© National Maritime Museum, London)

When a ship was at sea, being in the navy meant being on the job twenty-four hours a day, seven days a week. *Above:* Holystoning the deck. *Below:* Stoking the fires in a coal-burning battleship's engine room. (Imperial War Museum, London)

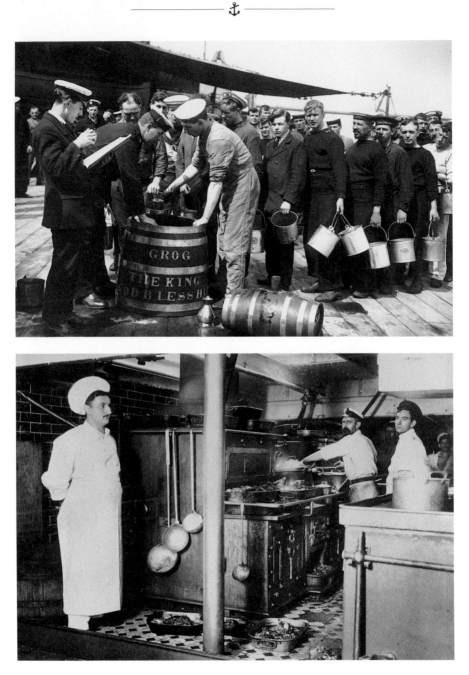

Above: Rum cooks in the battleship *King George V* line up with their fannies to receive the daily grog ration for their messes. At left, the steward checks his book to determine the number of tots each mess is entitled to receive. The barrico or breaker lies on the deck in the foreground, next to a measure. (Imperial War Museum, London) *Below:* Ship's cooks in the galley. To judge by the pans sitting on the tile deck and the stove, dinner that day was a roast of beef with potatoes. (Imperial War Museum, London)

Above: Messdeck in a light cruiser, probably *Concord.* Note the benches, the tables suspended at their ends by metal supports, and the racks at the bulkhead for storing the mess crockery and utensils. (Imperial War Museum, London) *Below:* The mess as home and recreation space. At left, sailors listen to a phonograph. A card game is in progress in the center; one absorbed player, apparently a stoker, is still wearing his soiled coveralls. To the right a man reads the tabloid *John Bull.* (Imperial War Museum, London)

Preparing for the much-hated kit inspection, in this case in *King George V*. Each rating must lay out in a specified pattern the articles of uniform and the gear which he is required to possess. (Imperial War Museum, London)

The master-at-arms precedes the captain at morning inspection in the battleship *Rodney*, July 1943. "I would look for the silk [and] lanyard properly worn . . . and that every man was in the rig of the day that was piped . . . see the collars are properly cleaned, things like that." (Imperial War Museum, London)

Captain's report, *Rodney*, July 1943. It is not recorded whether the sailor with his back to the camera is a *defaulter*, about to be punished for a disciplinary infraction, or a *request man*, perhaps a rating seeking a compassionate leave because of an emergency at home. (Imperial War Museum, London)

Muster by the ledger. Each sailor marches before the captain in the order in which his name is recorded in the ship's pay ledger (open on the table), salutes, tells the captain the ratings which he holds, the number of good conduct badges he has earned, any special pay increments to which he is entitled, again salutes, and marches off. To the captain's left (the viewer's right) the master-at-arms checks his muster book to account for any sailors absent because of special duty, leave, or illness. The petty officer writer standing to the left of the master-at-arms (viewer's right) is probably holding the ship's disciplinary record, a big book which contains a sheet for each sailor. According to the master-at-arms who described this little-mentioned ritual, "the object of mustering by the ledger is to give the captain an opportunity of seeing each man in the ship individually." (Imperial War Museum, London)

Laundry in a bucket, destroyer *Arrow*, about 1941. "You can bet your life, if you got a bucket of hot water, you'd put shirt, pants and flannel and everything through that one bucket . . . But the hot water was very scarce." (Royal Naval Museum, Portsmouth)

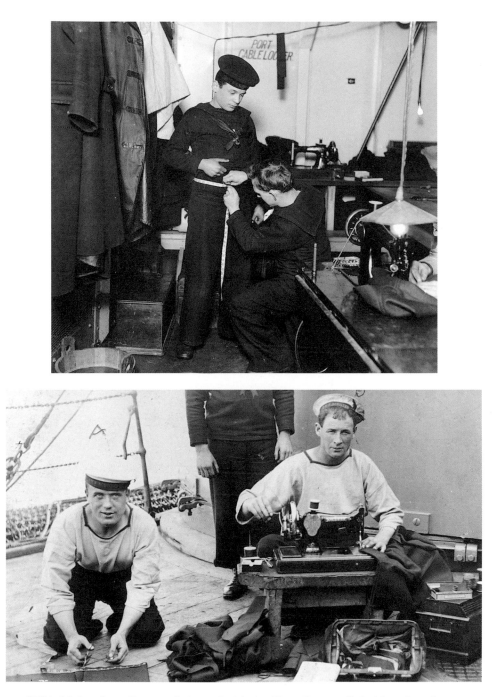

"This bloke, the tailor—well, he called himself a tailor—well, he'd made a few hundred suits and he was all right with it, too!" *Above:* Measuring for just the right fit in the battleship *Royal Oak*. Cutting out the fabric (*below left*) and sewing it up (*below right*). (Imperial War Museum, London)

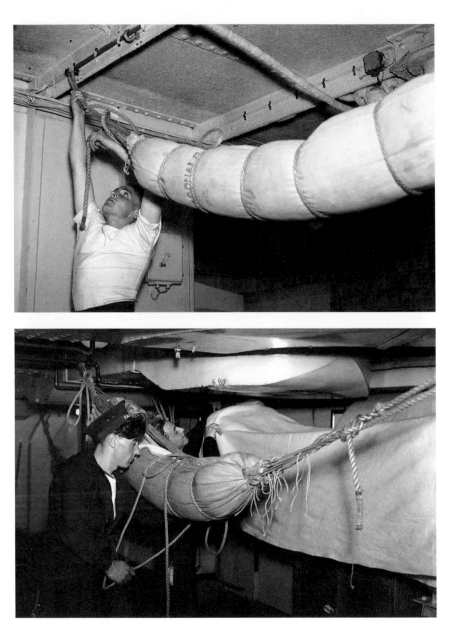

A sailor goes to bed in *Rodney*, 1940. *Above left:* The hammock is secured to a steel hook in the overhead beam. *Below left:* Releasing the hammock's lashings (*foreground*); spreading out the bedding, which has been secured inside the hammock (*background*). *Above right:* The art of getting into a hammock. *Below right:* All snug for the night and a bit of reading before "lights out." (Imperial War Museum, London)

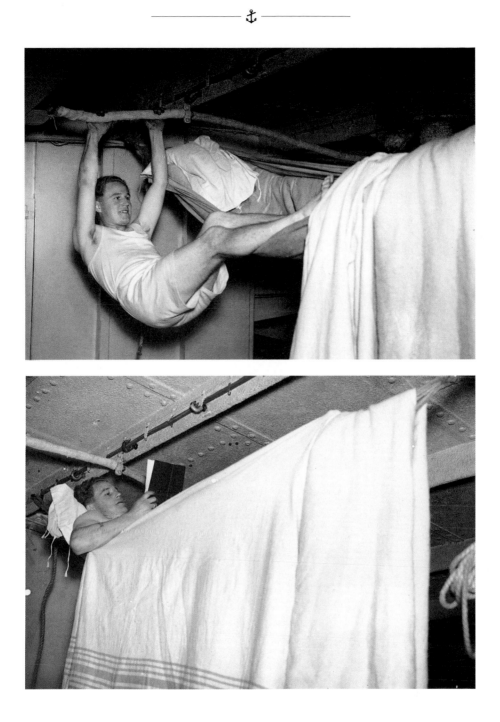

The most dreaded task in a sailor's life: coaling. *Above:* Filling sacks in a collier, either before dawn or after nightfall. (Wilfrid Pym Trotter, *The Royal Navy in Old Photographs*) *Below:* Moving filled sacks to the bunker hatches on handcarts or trolleys. (© National Maritime Museum, London)

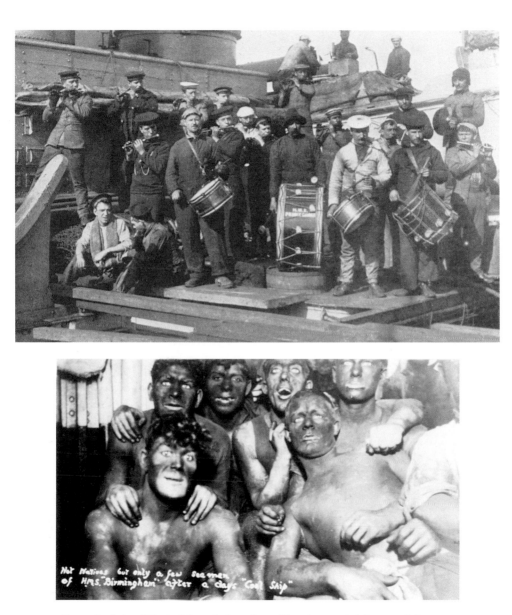

Not Natives but only a few Seamen of HMS "Birmingham" after a days "Coal Ship"

Above: And the (Marine) band played on. Keeping up spirits—and the pace of work—during coaling. (Wilfrid Pym Trotter, *The Royal Navy in Old Photographs*) *Below:* The effects of a day of coaling in the second-class cruiser *Birmingham*. (Royal Naval Museum, Portsmouth)

A stoker descends into one of his ship's bunkers through a coaling hatch on the main deck. He will trim the coal as it pours down the chute that leads from the coaling hatch to the bunker. (Wilfrid Pym Trotter, *The Royal Navy in Old Photographs*)

Catching a quick nap during a respite from the exhausting task of coaling. (Royal Naval Museum, Portsmouth)

ONE OF THE "WRENS"

Cross-dressing in the navy. The bewitching sailor on the right is costumed and made up for a concert party in the light cruiser *Calypso*. (Royal Naval Museum, Portsmouth)

Above: The second-class cruiser *Forth*'s funny party, Christmas 1916. Clowns and mummers were an important element in the Royal Navy's annual ritual of status reversal. (Imperial War Museum, London) *Below:* Jazz band in the submarine depot ship *Titania*, ready for a concert. (© National Maritime Museum, London)

Pay day in the destroyer *Kelvin*, August 1940. This happy sailor is now ready for leave ashore. (Imperial War Museum, London)

Libertymen from *King George V* head for shore. No trouble getting these sailors to smile for the camera. (Imperial War Museum, London)

A rare image of sailors engaged in a favorite activity—drinking beer—in this instance at Limassol, Cyprus. (Royal Naval Museum, Portsmouth)

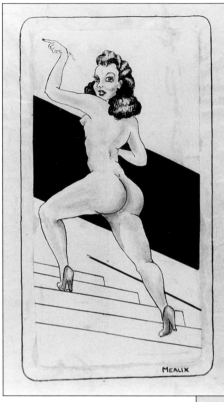

What are sailors thinking about almost all the time? Two (among many similar) illustrations from *Potmess*, the Second World War ship's magazine of the cutter *Totland*, reveal the answer. (Royal Naval Museum, Portsmouth)

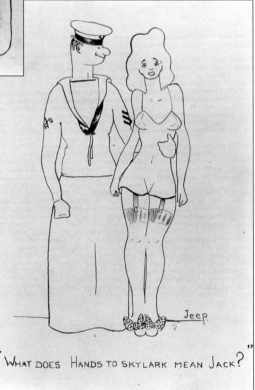

"WHAT DOES HANDS TO SKYLARK MEAN JACK?"

The only known photograph of Royal Navy sailors in a brothel—specifically, Acting Plumber Fourth Class William Batters and unidentified shipmates from the repair ship *Resource* at Le Sélect, Oran, in 1937. Bill and Sonia are at the far right of the picture. Batters preserved Le Sélect's business card, on the back of which Sonia wrote her name. (Imperial War Museum, London)

Sailor and family man. Yeoman of Signals John Edward Attrill, his wife, Mabel Elizabeth Stamp, and their daughter, Dorothy, born in August 1916. The three inverted chevrons on John Attrill's left sleeve are good conduct badges. He also wears his long service and good conduct medal. (Leslie H. Attrill)

that afterwards, and I said, 'Never in my life.' I said, 'If I've got any hair left,' I said, 'it must be white.' Oh, I never thought I'd see daylight again. We was right up close, jammed up to the ceiling. And they daren't let the bottom of the bunker go, see, because it [would] vortex, you see, immediately, see. The coal would have gone down like that [*Rose made a gesture with his hand*]—we'd have gone down there with it—so send a horrible death. So they never did do that. They knew that much."[9]

Ratings had little to say in their diaries, letters, memoirs, or interviews about the shipboard toll of illness and their reactions to it. Once again Charles Stamp, by now promoted to able seaman, is a valuable witness: "Took our mail [to the White Star liner], also Corporal Cook, invalided home, nervous breakdown . . . The climate and arduous conditions [in African waters] telling on men—each mail takes one or another home. Some dozen or so have been invalided and at present nearly 50 are either sick or on attending list. This out of [a ship's] company of 320. Last quarter had 77 days on salt provisions. It's a marvel that more are not down."

The next month—June 1917—brought another detail of sick men headed home. According to Stamp's diary, "This lot made fourteen invalided since we left Simonstown in August [1916]. Seven with heart trouble, three with TB. The staff surgeon, [John Bourdas], trying to get twelve months the limit for any man out here. Captain [Valentine E. B. Phillimore] won't agree. Staff [surgeon] also trying to get us . . . tropical pay—he thinks we deserve it. One stoker down bad with malaria, temp 106°; had to sponge him with ice water. Another (an AB) [with] dysentery . . . Have [myself] had a touch of malaria—temp up for a couple of day[s] 100° and over but took plenty of quinine and feel better now. Ship['s] company health very poor, lot of sickness."[10]

Death at sea from causes other than combat, though less common than it had been in earlier centuries, was still a shipboard companion and still a traumatic and depressing experience for the dead man's surviving shipmates. One death that occurred as the battleship *Albion* was proceeding from the Cape Verds to Gibraltar early in 1915 was recorded by Signalman Walter Dawson. His narrative parallels in words and mood many an eighteenth- or nineteenth-century diary entry about a similar shipboard event: "This morning, when the hands were turned out, the sad news was heard of the death of one of our ship's company, a boy named [Leonard G.] Ellis, who had died at 3.15 A.M. as a result of blood poisoning brought about through a scratch. At 4.30 P.M. the funeral was held. The ships [the armored cruiser *Cornwall* was in company] were stopped and the burial service read by our chaplain, the Rev. Norman De Jersey. Full funeral honors were given and the three volleys were fired by 26 able seamen who formed the firing party. On the conclusion of the service we again proceeded on our way, with a gloom overhanging everyone which lasted for a few days, especially among the deceased['s] messmates."[11]

Thin fare, these few quotations about accident, illness, and resulting death. Accidents, fatal or crippling, appear only occasionally in the sailors' contemporary records or later memoirs. Sexually transmitted diseases aside, ratings say even less about illnesses, especially the chronic or disabling conditions that were the direct result of the inherent risks of naval life and the unfamiliar viruses and bacteria the sailor encountered as he traveled the world. Diseases of mind and body were real problems—no doubt about it. Charles Stamp's diary entries offer a brief revelation of their constant presence. James Dunn's recognition that there was almost certainly a direct connection between his work as a stoker and the bronchitis he developed later in life is a telling (but rare) acknowledgment of the link between naval life and post-navy health problems. Perhaps accidents were mentioned more frequently because they were sudden and dramatic events, whereas disabling illness was often a slow process, a non-event. Or, even more likely, behaving as if the ever-present threat to health and life did not exist was a means of coping with the stress of constant danger. Add to this the perceived cultural demands of Edwardian masculinity. A *man* did not complain about how he felt— he toughed it out in silence. Whatever the reality may have been, the unwritten rule was that sailors were to be strong and uncomplaining—as witness the fact that any boy who cried out or screamed during caning or birching was labeled a coward.

⚓

Not every anxiety experienced in lower-deck life derived from combat or work-related accidents or the diseases of an unfamiliar environment. Sometimes the stress came from inside a sailor: intense doubts about his ability to carry the growing burden of responsibility as he moved up from leading hand to petty officer to chief petty officer. Many men thrived on seniority. "In my experience," said George Michael Clarkson, "the longer you'd been on the job, the easier it became. I mean, when you began to get, we'll say, the senior by years, if you like, in the mess you could tell the others to get under the table and coil the bootlaces down. You had an easier time. The people above you had more respect for you than they would for the youngsters. You knew the ropes. You knew the job, and it became easier all the time. You knew how to get out of jobs you didn't like."[12]

Petty officers and chief petty officers occupied difficult positions. The ship's commissioned officers, almost always remote psychologically from the ratings and drawn from a different social class, ran the ship through the POs and CPOs. The latter had to command men whose social origins were the same as theirs and who may have been their peers and messmates only days or weeks earlier. For petty officers (and more especially for newly made petty officers) future advancement depended, not on what the ratings thought about them, but on the officers' perceptions of how effectively they were doing their jobs. "Well," reported James Cox, himself an experienced PO and CPO, "all petty officers and chief petty officers, say, they line themselves up with the captain. If you got a good, strict captain, you got a very good, happy ship, because by having a strict captain, the petty officers' duties are made easier. And the men *know* that they've got to obey. There's no skim-shanking and going down below and having half an hour off or a fag here or a fag there and all that kind of business. But if you've got a[n] easygoing captain, the petty officers are not backed up enough. So they don't enforce the regulations too hard. They just let things go along easy. It depends absolutely on the captain, how the captain—I would rather be with a strict disciplinarian than I would with an easygoing officer any day . . . There's no doubt about it."[13]

POs and CPOs were segregated from the subordinate sailors in their own messes, their own heads, and their own bathing facilities; they were waited on in their messes by lower-ranked ratings, and allocated their own section of the upper deck in which they could walk, talk, and smoke, secure in the knowledge that no seaman or stoker or telegraphist could intrude upon their defined space. But more fundamental in defining their new role than any of these external marks of advancement over their former peers was the manner of command that newly made petty officers assumed with their promotions.

As with any other class of human beings, petty officers and chief petty officers were not all cut from the same mold. Some men of the lower deck remembered cordial, informal relations with their POs and CPOs. A few even recalled them as father-figures to the younger and less-experienced ratings. But these recollections all came from men who had themselves risen to petty officer or chief petty officer status. Or they were the memories of sailors who had served in destroyers, submarines, and other small ships in which relations between superior and subordinate were close (physically and psychologically) and informal. Or they were recorded by members of the engine-room branch, in which stokers second class and stokers first class felt a greater bond of comradeship with their stoker petty officers and chief stokers than typically existed in the seaman branch.

Those who remembered cordial relations between petty officers and men of the lower deck were definitely in the minority. Especially in the big ships, POs and CPOs maintained their elevated status over the mass of lower-deck men by a combination of distance, authoritarianism, and zero-tolerance discipline. The word most frequently used in describing petty officers was *bastard*. "On duty [petty officers were] strictly 'navy,'" recalled one sailor who himself never advanced beyond leading hand. "Even more so upon the part of 'newly mades'—very much 'beggars on horseback' until it was toned down by their more experienced fellows or the sobering effects of events." One CPO admitted that, while relations between petty officers and their subordinates were "fairly good . . . there was . . . that certain type of PO who was after 'red ink' recommends for CPO and always trying to impress higher-ups how good he was at the expense of junior ratings."[14]

Given such an atmosphere it is understandable why Acting Leading Signalman William Bailey would say that relations between subordinates and petty officers were "not very 'pally'—sometimes quite bitter if witnesses are absent." Perhaps Bailey was thinking of an incident similar to the one described by Second World War Able Seaman John E. Needham, who remembered "a very objectionable petty officer, who must have been seven stone wet through, but had—as one of the older ABs observed—'more cackle than a cow had cunt.' A nasty bit of work, this PO and . . . [he] had a very near miss with an 'accidentally' dropped pot of paint from the masthead which fell from a great height and dropped very adjacent to his feet. We all knew the culprit, but nothing could be proved, but some wag muttered, 'Good try!'" According to Needham the paint-pot drop did have a salutary effect: thereafter the offensive petty officer was "a changed man."[15]

Buried somewhere inside even the hardest, most irritable PO or CPO was a human being, and occasionally a subordinate caught a brief glimpse of that human being. The Second World War rating John Davidson experienced such a moment in the antiaircraft ship *Tynwald* sometime in 1942. "I was impressed," he wrote in his later memoir, "by the efficiency of the regulars, CPOs and POs. They knew their jobs inside out . . . One severe disciplinarian PO was at an action station with me and spoke with real feeling for the navy, and as we looked out to sea he said to me quietly and simply, 'I was an orphan. The navy has been a good father and mother to me.' He never again seemed quite such an ogre."[16]

As James Cox said, not every seaman who could pass the examination for petty officer was fit for the job. There were some "that never had— what can I say?—who never had the power of command, if you might as well say. He never had that way to lead a man." If such a man was sufficiently self-aware he never sought to advance beyond seaman or stoker or some equivalent rank during his twelve or twenty-two years in the Royal Navy. The story of one rating of the 1930s and 1940s illustrates well the importance of knowing one's limitations. He left a vivid record of a man who, until he was put on the spot, failed to realize that he could not cope with exercising authority himself. This leading signalman was promoted to yeoman of signals and the self-revelations began: "I couldn't be a big enough bastard. If I said to a man 'Do this' and he turned round and said 'Get knotted,' I wouldn't know what to do. Correction: I would know what to do, but I wouldn't be able to do it. I didn't have what the navy calls 'power of command.' I would be thinking how I would feel if the positions were reversed."

Things got worse when the newly minted yeoman's ship, the destroyer *Hero*, finished her repairs and went to sea: "Another of my failings became apparent: I have great difficulty in making decisions. My brain seems to go numb when faced with a choice between two or more apparently equal options . . . What with my inability to make decisions and the captain expecting me to yell and shout like a madman as I'd seen other yeomen doing [even when it was not helping to get the job accomplished], I'd had enough. Why the hell had I wanted to be a yeoman in the first place anyway?"

Recognizing the severe personal liabilities under which he worked when placed in a position of authority, the sailor voluntarily relinquished his yeoman of signals rating and reverted to leading signalman. Within a few years even this much responsibility became intolerable: "I had been hanging onto the leading rate, wondering how long I would be able to keep it. I had always had great difficulty in exerting authority . . . always felt so self-conscious . . . It wasn't in my nature to boss people about."

And so the leading signalman descended yet another rating, back down to signalman.[17] His may have been an extreme case, but because most people have a natural tendency to present themselves in the best possible light, to tell of successes rather than failures, one appreciates all the more this unique record of the psychological stress, not to say intense suffering, that could ensue when men were asked—or pushed themselves—to rise to positions of greater authority for which their personalities were unsuited.

⚓

From the terror of battle, through an awareness of maiming or fatal accidents as ever-present shipmates, to the anxiety of responsibility, the naval sailor was vulnerable to a spectrum of psychic stresses—some potentially so powerful as to threaten his sanity. James Dunn, trapped below in *Gabriel*'s boiler room, held on by thinking: *If only I can get ashore once more. If only I can have one more leave.* A fuller examination of how sailors coped with the multiple stresses of life at sea must now take center stage.

5

This Rum It Was Wonderful Stuff

Monotonous food. Strict and relentless discipline. Daily close-quartered living devoid of privacy. Boredom, day after uneventful day at sea. Battle. Dangerous, fear-inducing work. Unpredictable accidents. Sudden illnesses—sometimes deadly. Long absences from home and family. Burdens of responsibility. No human being could endure these indefinitely and without respite. Where did men of the lower deck turn for the relief, relaxation, and renewal needed to cope with the stresses of naval service?

Religious faith is one source of comfort to which battleship-era ratings might have turned to cope with the multiple hardships and anxieties of their lives. But to link sailors and religion is to run up against a firmly established stereotype: sailors by nature are not religious people. Many sailors themselves confirmed this idea. Religious sailors? "They would be very few and far between, you might say," responded Leading Seaman Arthur Ford. "You had one or two, but it didn't carry much weight in the navy."[1]

The obstacle to challenging such a stereotype is that it is difficult—or perhaps impossible—for one person to know whether another individual does or does not have real religious faith, whatever may be the outward pretensions or appearances. If the Roman Catholic James Kelleher is to be believed, there were as few atheists in ships under enemy fire as there are reputed to be in foxholes. Kelleher's duty assignment, the antiaircraft ship *Carlisle*, was in action off Crete in May 1941 and taking frequent evasive action to avoid German bombs. "Well, if there was a time when prayers could be said, it was now," Kelleher recalled, "and while on the ship I had words with certain personnel regarding their religion, and they had assured me that they were confirmed atheist[s] and did not believe in God. Well, I noticed during this action that these self-same people got down on the knees and invoked in their prayers the help of God. I certainly know that I did."[2]

Situations of imminent danger aside, it is true that religious sailors were a minority in the navy—though they were probably a larger minority than Arthur Ford realized or was willing to admit. "I knew and served with many a GOOD Christian" in the navy, said Chief Petty Officer Albert Heron, a man whose testimony is valuable because he himself reveals no particular religious commitment of his own in either memoir, questionnaire, or interview.[3] But discovering the religious rating's most private thoughts and feelings—reaching the fundamental roots of his behavior and values—is a difficult challenge. Two diarists from the First World War may take us as far as we can go into that inner world. Charles Stamp, the chemical analyst-turned-hostilities-only sailor, at sea and en route to South Africa, spent a Sunday afternoon in July 1916 tormented by his situation: "Unless I think of future times and my old life, this [naval] life will drive me mad." But an evening service with hymns lifted his mood a bit and made it easier to cope: "Undoubtedly 'Eternal Father Strong to Save' must be sung aboard at sea with half-gale of wind like there was [tonight]. One realizes more what the words mean. And how many who sing in brilliantly lit churches, amid friends and acquaintances, with life and perhaps trams, etc., outside [the] door to their home—how many realize what the words mean as they would realize did they but feel the roll and pitch of the boat, the whistle of the wind, and the night coming on darkly—and not another vessel in sight and miles from land?"

Arrival in Simonstown and shore leave gave Stamp an opportunity to walk about with a like-minded shipmate named Davis. "Lovely to have a talk without swearing, blasphemy, oaths, etc., and the usual naval language. Jove, how glad I shall be to get back in civvies again," he confided to his diary. With evening came an opportunity for the Methodist Stamp to attend Wesleyan Chapel: "What a lovely service! The real old hymns but full of new meaning. It is hard to believe one is all these miles from home. If one forgot the mixed congregation, it was like a little gospel service in [a] village. It did me a world of good in heaps of ways."

In his ship, the second-class cruiser *Astræa*, Stamp chose to attend the Church of England Holy Communion service early on Sunday mornings. Unlike the later-in-the-day and compulsory Morning Prayer service for the whole ship's complement, Holy Communion was voluntary—and sparsely attended. Perhaps two, three, or four worshipers showed up. Being nearly alone was part of the appeal for Charles Stamp: "Just the simple C. of E. service, but it was very nice and took one's mind off their present position. I wondered much when I should be home again." On a boiling hot Sunday morning, with *Astræa* just barely moving over the water at eight knots, "it was nice to be away and quiet for a few moments. Made one think of home and loved ones. But have much to be thankful for—thus health, etc."[4] To the degree that Charles Stamp's diary lets one inside this sailor's head, the pause and quiet meditation of religious services, combined with the emotions stirred by the music of the hymns, brings thoughts of home and family (Stamp was married) and thereby taps some reservoir of inner strength that energizes him and enables him to cope with the difficult and distasteful life in which he finds himself immersed.

But Stamp's is an outsider's perspective. He is a man who will never be at home in the navy, no matter how competently he does his job nor how highly his superiors evaluate him. He is not a *real* sailor, is he? One can dismiss his testimony. This is not so easy to do in the case of Leading Seaman and (subsequently) Petty Officer Philip Powell. This long-service rating was also a lifelong member of the Bristol Citadel of the Salvation Army—and a committed, enthusiastic, and active member of the Army, whether afloat or ashore. At Halifax, Nova Scotia, in September 1914, Powell helped a local Salvation Army officer conduct an evening service: "Not only was my presences [sic] a welcome [one], but the service was beneficial to me." Back on shipboard and eastward bound in the second-class cruiser *Talbot*, with a convoy under escort, Powell participated in a voluntary gathering organized by evangelical kindred-spirits: "A happy Sunday night's service . . . with good singing and a . . . Bible reading by yours truly." There was compulsory Church of England service in the morning, to be sure, but most Sunday evenings, "when it is convenient for the men," there is also "a singing of Sankey's hymns [one of the compilations of *Gospel Hymns* created by the American singing evangelist Ira D. Sankey] and Bible reading given by a few Christians . . . There are sometimes a good gathering." Early in 1916, when motor lighter X152, under Powell's command, was being towed through the Suez Canal by SS *Wheatbury*, a small coaster, *Wheatbury*'s crew invited Powell on board to conduct a Sunday evening service, "so with music, concertina, hymns books and Bible we spent what I believe to be an enjoyable hour and a half." Three and a half months later Powell found himself in Bombay, quickly located the Salvation Army there, and attended Sunday morning service. "This I thoroughly enjoyed. The singing of the hymns and the gospel reading was indeed a pleasure to hear, for it was over eighteen months since I had attended a place of worship, except once at Basra when I found an American mission church." Energized, Powell joined an army friend and led an evening meeting at his friend's barracks: "This was a good success and rather a pity I was not able to come again."

Philip Powell does not let us penetrate much below the surface of his spiritual life. He tells us about the comradeship and enthusiasm of the Salvation Army and the emotions stirred by hymn singing and the gospel message, but there must have been more. He hints at a deeper spirituality when he remembers pre-1914 visits to the Salvation Army Naval and Military Home at Floriana, Malta, "and the little private prayer room that Christian servicemen used to use, surely a place of spiritual blessing to body and soul." For Philip Powell, as for Charles Stamp, religion involves a time to be alone, a time to pray and to think. And he is not going to let anyone intrude upon that personal space.[5]

No doubt about it, Charles Stamp, Philip Powell, and their fellow sailors who found in religious faith the means of dealing with the anxieties, hardships, and dangers of their lives were a minority among their messmates. More typical were the Dardanelles-campaign sailors who appreciated the YMCA canteen at Stavros for its inexpensive tea (no beer, alas!), its tinned fruit, and the piano in the corner: "But today our chaps commenced to play ragtime tunes on the piano while the crowd sang them. The pious old gent in charge of the YMCA was shocked and said 'we were not allowed to sing that in the YMCA' and must stop; but, if we wanted to sing anything, we could sing 'There Is a Green Hill Far Away' or 'Onward Christian Soldiers.' Can one imagine a more ridiculous thing than a crowd of sailors ashore to enjoy themselves sitting down singing hymns?—not out of any disrespect for the hymns, but it's not in keeping with the 'navy on shore.'"[6] One must always behave in accordance with one's stereotypical image!

Beyond those sailors who appeared not to care about religion one way or another were the thoughtful men whose experience of war shattered the unquestioning faith they possessed in childhood and adolescence. One such sailor was twenty-one-year-old Able Seaman Robert L. Fagg, serving in the First World War destroyer *Tirade*. He later recalled the incidents that finally shattered his naive religious belief: "I remember the awe with which on one convoy trip during the night we passed in the distance the burning ships of an earlier convoy that had been attacked by raiding German warships and the British escorting destroyers, *Mary Rose* and *Strongbow*, sunk [October 17, 1917]. Such incidents irrevocably and finally shook my faith in all the religious teaching and brainwashing to which I had been subjected in childhood and throughout my naval career, and the following [event, which happened a few days later,] strengthened that rejection.

"The usual formation of convoys across the North Sea was an echelon of 20 to 30 merchant ships enclosed, as it were, within an imaginary rectangle. One escorting destroyer would be in position just outside the right-hand foremost corner of the rectangle and the other destroyer just outside the left-hand rearmost corner. When we picked up this particular convoy off the east coast of Northumberland *Tirade* took up position on the rearmost corner just outside of the convoy echelon on the port side of it and we began the 500-odd miles journey to Norway. At night I was on duty at the midships searchlight, which was mounted on a raised platform, and had taken over the middle watch at eight bells midnight. The *Tirade* was rolling and pitching horribly, one moment being lifted on waves 20 to 30 feet high and the next plunging down into a trough with the bow cutting through the next oncoming wave with a shudder that shook the vessel from stem to stern. Normally I was not scared of this kind of weather (we certainly had had plenty of it), nor was I during the hour that followed my taking over the watch, but to help wile away the time, and perhaps because I still retained some belief in that all-seeing and all-powerful God whom I had been taught could see us safely through that terrible night—certainly one of the most terrible and awful nights we had ever experienced—I was quietly crooning the hymn 'Eternal Father, Strong to Save.'

"Suddenly, just before 1 A.M. [October 21] (two bells) we crashed into something and, although it was so dark, we could just make out the grey shape of another destroyer which had obviously been hit amidships on her port side in her fuel tanks. Our officer of the watch on the bridge immediately rang the alarm bells for collision stations to bring all hands on deck, and the boatswain's mate piped 'All hands to collision stations on the fo'c'sle.' There was no panic, but an all-pervading feeling of horror that we must have encountered something very terrible. For all we knew at the moment, it could have been [an] enemy ramming us.

"The collision mat was taken forward to the bows of the ship and portholes and watertight doors closed. I distinctly remember that AB Jarvis and I closed the portholes in the engine room and helped the engine-room crew to close the engine-room watertight doors, after which we scrambled up on deck again. We could see in the blackness of the night the other ship's hand-signaling lamp flashing out the message that she was the British destroyer HMS *Marmion* and sinking fast, which she did quite quickly.

"As we were stopped and completely at the mercy of the huge waves we were rolling badly. This made it most difficult to pick up the men who were struggling in the water. Of course we threw out lines and lifebelts, but the drowning men were too exhausted to grasp them and other measure[s] had to be taken. With other seamen I stretched out on the deck on my stomach with Bob Jarvis and other seamen holding my legs and with a line around my chest. As the roll of *Tirade* plunged me down into the water I grasped hold of a man with my arms around his chest and, as the reverse roll of our boat lifted us out of the water, willing hands grasped the rescued man and pulled him inboard. What made the whole operation so ghastly was that the *Marmion*'s men were coated with thick, slimy fuel oil from her damaged fuel tanks into which *Tirade*'s bow had crashed. This made it very difficult to keep a tight hold on a man as we both came up out of the water with the roll, even with our hands tightly clasped behind the man being pulled out of the water. I pulled out four or five in this manner, but several slipped through my arms and just fell back into the oily water and disappeared with a wailing cry, the sound of which remained with me for years afterwards. We pulled out about 17 of the *Marmion*'s crew of about 120, the remainder having perished in the icy waters of the North Sea.

"The extraordinary thing about this tragedy was that the *Marmion*, returning from a previous convoy across the North Sea, must have blindly threaded her way through all those ships in our convoy without mishap and yet was struck by *Tirade*, which was the very last ship of the whole convoy with which she could have collided."[7]

Believers or nonbelievers, zealous Christians or reluctant ones, almost all sailors agreed on one thing: dislike of the compulsory Church of England services in the big ships. During these services, conducted by an ordained chaplain, the ship's complement assembled in hierarchical formations and with the marine band supplying the music for the hymns. Ratings required to attend envied those sailors who had been savvy enough at the time of enlistment to declare themselves to be dissenters or Roman Catholics or atheists and thereby won the right to fall out when it came time for compulsory church services. It was a rare sailor (in this case Acting Leading Signalman William A. D. Bailey) who admitted that he liked and supported required attendance at morning and evening prayer. "Without such the majority would never know a Bible or a higher culture other than pubs and streetwalkers," Bailey remarked. Another man of the lower deck, Chief Ordnance Artificer Leslie Nancarrow, admitted that he dodged mandatory church service whenever he could, "but, on reflection, the beautiful words of the prayerbook did draw us towards home and loved ones. I'm still moved by 'Eternal Father.'"[8] In these sentiments Leslie Nancarrow echoes Charles Stamp: religion and religious services are salutary because they remind sailors of home, of family, and of the sailor's obligations to loved ones—not because they bring the sailor into a closer relationship with his God. Or at least that is as much as these men were willing to admit in writing. A third sailor, James D. Callister, had no use for compulsory church services in barracks but said, "I rather liked the Sunday morning church service on small ships, conducted by the captain, who read the prayers on the quarterdeck."[9] Leading Seaman Callister was not alone in this sentiment. In matters of prayer, as in many other aspects of naval life, the distinction between service in big ships and service in small ones is fundamental.

Callister's preference for his captain over an ordained chaplain as his religious leader reflects his own less-than-positive feelings about men of the cloth at sea. But it is also indicative of the strong opinions—positive or negative—that almost all ratings seemed to hold about chaplains. An obvious factor influencing a sailor's attitude toward his chaplain—the *sin boatswain* or the *sky pilot*, as in "Look out, 'ere comes the old sky pilot"[10]—was the sailor's own degree of religious commitment. "I became an agnostic while I was in the service," said Thomas Thompson, a former seaman. His attitude about chaplains is predictable: "The only service they appeared [to] fill in capital ships during the '14–'18 war was letter censors, outside their other function, which, in my opinion, was mythical, and they served no useful purpose." Listening to Chief Petty Officer Charles Lazenby, a sailor with religious convictions, one hears a different story. Yes, Lazenby could recite in detail all the things men of the lower deck held against chaplains, but he himself judged differently: "You see, I thought the chaplains did a good job, and I knew some of the chaplains intimately."[11]

Ratings who disliked chaplains typically cited two reasons. For one, chaplains were officers. This automatically made them the *other*. Most chaplains seemed to identify with the wardroom more than the messdeck. Another, and perhaps more damning, reason was the question of the sincerity and depth of the chaplain's religious commitment, as well as the genuineness of his concern for the ratings and their personal problems.[12] From the perspective of the lower deck, being a chaplain was an easy job that paid well and provided excellent employment security. Too often the post attracted men of low motivation who were looking for a snug niche in which to settle down. Add to this mix a man whose behavior diverged from the principles he was supposed to profess and the stage was set for lower-deck contempt and alienation. Joiner First Class George Michael Clarkson remembered a Portsmouth-based chaplain who was "just there for the job . . . And I've heard people say to him, 'Oh, have you heard this one, Sir?'

> Mary had a little lamb.
> She kept it in a bucket.
> And every time the lamb got out,
> The dog would try to——put it back.

'Naughty, naughty,' he'd say. Old sods like that, they—the majority of 'em were—the navy was an easy place for them. They had rank and they had the money."[13]

The minority of sailors who valued chaplains did so for a variety of reasons, some of them not strictly religious—at least not in any narrow sense of the word. "They were very brave in wartime!" recollected Petty Officer Phillip Jenkins. "Always happy and sensible sermons, which were good to listen to, and [they were] always ready to listen to your troubles—help your peace of mind." If Jenkins had an opinion regarding the inner resources from which chaplains drew their bravery in combat, their positive outlook on life, or their skills as good advisers in times of personal trouble, the format in which he was asked about padres gave him no opportunity to elaborate. "Chaplains had their place on board," said Roland Purvis, a chief petty officer and twenty-five-year naval veteran. "A good liaison officer between lower deck and the captain in the moral behavior of the crew . . . Especially were they good value in ships with boy seamen and ordinary seamen. Without the chaplain, on shore leave boys and [ordinary seamen] would have been hard pressed what to do." Intriguing here is Purvis's apparent opinion that seamen, leading seamen, petty officers, and chiefs had less need of moral guidance than boys and ordinary seamen when they went ashore. Purvis did not say why he thought this was the case—and he provides no clues to inform speculation.[14]

Chaplains were also valued as the officers most deeply involved in organizing recreational opportunities for the ship—sports, concerts, and the like—and also as advisors and intermediaries in times of trouble. Say a sailor was having family problems. Perhaps his wife was overwhelmed with loneliness and more single-parent challenges than she could well handle. Or maybe the sailor had disabling doubts about his wife's fidelity during his long absences at sea. The chaplain was the man who was supposed to help sort out such problems by sending a letter to someone back home who could put things right or by arranging a short emergency leave for the troubled rating.[15]

Being an effective naval chaplain was (and is) a challenging vocation. What, from the lower deck's perspective, did it take to make a good chaplain? Leslie Nancarrow, who served in the navy for twenty-two years, did not have much esteem for the Church of England naval chaplains. Most were not suited to their responsibilities. A few had joined with good intentions but soon found that Jesus Christ was only a junior officer in the wardroom. By contrast, Roman Catholic chaplains "could box, play soccer, and [in] general got respect that way first."[16] George Michael Clarkson made essentially the same point about what it took to succeed as a naval chaplain, although in Clarkson's story the exemplary man was Church of England: "[Ratings] didn't have any time for [padres], but I'll tell you, the man I've ever had the most respect for was a padre who came out to us in the Red Sea [toward the end of the First World War]. I'd love to see him if he's still alive. Out there our ship's company were comprised of hooligans, jailbirds, mercantile marine reserve—oh, they were a crowd of villains some of 'em. And they decided that we should have a chaplain for our ship and the other small ships there. And this fellow came out from Frimley. His name was Mitchell [William Maurice Harper Mitchell, chaplain of the armed boarding steamer *Suva* from August 30, 1918]. And he dug up an old squeeze box and brought it along and asked me to repair it, which I did. And everybody was prepared to give him the raspberry. They didn't want any parson there. They were going to give him a dog's life. But he persevered in his quiet way. He'd sit down of an evening, get the organ out on a Sunday, and say, 'Now we'll have a prayer or two, but first of all the latest hit from London.' And he'd have that. And he could play that on the organ. And he was a fellow that interested himself in everybody. At night, when they were coming off drunk or anything like that, he'd be there to lead them down below . . . And if anybody was in trouble, he went to enormous lengths, domestic trouble at home or anything like that. And eventually Mitchell, he was the kingpin. He couldn't do wrong. And the biggest villains there, when eventually he left the ship to go home, they . . . collected and they bought him a whole lot of silver stuff, you know, for his altar when he got home. And they cheered him when he left the ship. And the officers pulled him away in the gig. That is the finest parson I've ever come across."[17]

John Davidson, a leading seaman of the Second World War, encapsulated in one succinct paragraph what was, probably, the most typical lower-deck attitude toward both chaplains and religious faith: "One evening, when we were confined to the mess in harbor, a padre visited us. He seemed to have dined only too well in the officers' mess; his face was flushed and he was puffing a cigar. I contemplated a religious discussion with him but decided it would be a waste of time. I would have liked to tell him that I refused to attend a thanksgiving service held for the survivors of the [antiaircraft ship] *Tynwald* [Davidson's previous assignment, sunk by an Italian submarine in November 1942]. If you thank God for saving some, presumably you must blame him for those who lost their lives. I wonder what he would have said?"

Davidson's words are a forceful reminder that one important question remains unasked: *Why* are sailors traditionally not religious people? Irreligious seafarers are hardly unique to the twentieth century and its conventional agnosticism: thoughtful nineteenth-century men of the lower deck also remarked that, as a class, sailors are not religious. Although the informants for *Sober Men and True* are eloquent witnesses on the subjects of twentieth-century agnosticism, loss of faith, and atheism, they offer no particular insights on the reason for lack of religious faith among men of the sea across the centuries. The argument that sailors are typically young, and that the young feel immortal and are consequently less concerned with religious faith than are humans in their more mature years, can quickly be dismissed. This book offers ample testimony that the sailors of the two world wars were keenly aware of their mortality. No, if naval ratings of 1900–1945 became indifferent to, lost or seriously questioned their previously held religious faith, or if they were simply confirmed in agnosticism or atheism, it was because they personally and directly experienced the random, irrational, and overwhelming horrors of war: a battle cruiser hit in its magazine and taking hundreds to their deaths in an instant; a lone torpedo from an unseen U-boat in the dark Arctic night; good men dying and bad ones thriving in self-indulgent comfort. For many, such atrocities could not coexist with the idea of a personal, just, and loving God who cared for each individual human being. Unable to reconcile ideal and experience, such sailors parted company with the idea of a caring, sustaining God. Of hell's existence they had no doubt—they had been there themselves.[18]

⚓

Sailors had more worldly (and more common) alternatives to religious faith for coping with the anxieties and the frustrations of life at sea. One of these was shipboard gambling. "[Gambling] was a time-filler," said Able Seaman Walter Basford, speaking of the men's free hours after the workday ended in the late afternoon. "That was all it was, because there was nothing else to do, bar go up on the upper deck and walk up and down . . . So there was nothing vicious in gambling like that. It was just something to occupy your time, 'cause otherwise you just didn't know what to do."[19] Idle time may be a big part of what motivated men to gamble, but it is certainly not the whole picture. Because gambling was strictly forbidden on shipboard, to play involved the gamblers in a challenging battle of wits as they sought to escape detection by the master-at-arms and the ship's police. Here was an opportunity bound to appeal to the kind of men the navy liked to recruit: men of high spirits—men who wanted to test the rules, push the envelope, live on the edge.

Psychologists, sociologists, and historians who study gamblers and gambling offer additional insights into why gambling is a popular activity with sailors—though the ideas these scholars propose are subject to intense debate among themselves.[20] One study concluded that regular gamblers in Great Britain were typically young, single, skilled working-class men who came from a low-income background. That description is almost a perfect match with the typical profile of men of the lower deck, 1900–1945, but it does not necessarily explain gambling's wide appeal to sailors over several centuries. More general explanations are required, and some of the ideas proposed by those who study gamblers intensely seem especially relevant to naval ratings.

Except for the *bankers* who control the games, gambling is not a rational money-making activity over the long run. A few players may be lucky on particular occasions, but those who manage the games organize them in such a way that the typical player loses money. Consequently, the desire to make extra income should be dismissed as a motivation for shipboard gambling. Not all people are equally attracted to gambling. Some never gamble. Others gamble only occasionally. Still others participate regularly in games of chance but do not become compulsive gamblers. (The latter group, the compulsive gamblers, are not of concern here.) Some studies suggest that gambling as entertainment is more likely to appeal to persons who are typically directed by external sources of motivation than to those who march to their own drummers. This appears to be closely related to the theory that recreational gambling is more likely to attract an extrovert—a social person who craves excitement and enjoys noisy, active environments—than to an introvert. (To test this theory try imagining Charles R. Thomas as a shipboard gambler.) One especially relevant thesis holds that gambling will have less attraction for a potential player who is directed toward a goal (whether habitually or at the moment)—always exempting, of course, the banker—and greater draw for someone who lives in the moment and learns that the excitement of gambling heightens the pleasure of that moment. Excitement (arousal) then becomes a key to understanding gambling. People who are under-aroused, that is, bored—and there is certainly an ample supply of boredom in naval life, whether in peace or in war—can turn to gambling to satisfy that psychological need for arousal. (This, of course, does not explain *why* some people need that shot of adrenaline to survive psychologically and others do not.) A major part of the arousal comes from the risks involved in gambling. Following the sea—a statistically dangerous occupation—and joining a navy, an organization whose ultimate purpose is combat, are life choices more likely to appeal to individuals who are risk-oriented than those who are risk-averse. Finally, gambling is a social activity that promotes bonding—or, to use the word preferred in this book, *comradeship*—the central value in lower-deck ethos. Indeed, one writer argues that the primary reward which regular gamblers find in play is the recognition by others of their courage and strength in the face of great risks, an idea that resonates well with what *Sober Men and True* has discovered about attitudes among naval ratings.[21]

As seen by the master-at-arms, there was gambling and then there was *serious* gambling. Old sailors pretty much agreed with this assessment. In the benign category were games such as tombola (or housey-housey), pontoon, and napoleon, which the master-at-arms and the ship's police tended to tolerate or ignore. The stakes were always small and there was never cash money on the board. Wins and losses were marked on a tally to be settled at the end of the game or—more likely—at the next payday. Comradeship and trust were key here: "Everybody knew who was who and what you owed."[22]

But crown and anchor? Now *that* was serious gambling, and the master-at-arms and the ship's police were on the prowl, looking for any little knot of sailors huddled around a crown-and-anchor board. Strictly speaking, it was not a board at all, but a piece of cloth about the size of a large handkerchief. This cloth was divided into six squares, in each of which either a club, a diamond, a heart, a spade, a crown, or an anchor was painted in gaudy colors against an equally garish background. The banker assembled the players about him and encouraged them to place bets on (or *back*) one or the other of the symbols. Assume, for purposes of illustration, that there are six players, each of whom backs a different symbol with a shilling. The banker shakes three dice, each bearing the six symbols, in a cup, all the while encouraging more bets with silver-tongued guile. When the banker can secure no more bets he rolls the dice or places the cup on the cloth, opening down, and lifts it. Suppose the dice come up one diamond, one spade, and one crown. Each of the players who has backed these symbols gets his own shilling back and the banker pays him a shilling—in reality the three shillings forfeited by the other players; the banker does not make or lose anything on that roll of the dice. If two anchors and a heart come up, the sailor who backed the anchor receives his own shilling plus two additional shillings; the sailor who bet on the heart gets his own shilling plus one; four sailors forfeit a shilling each; and the banker is one shilling to the good. Say the cup is lifted and there are—three crowns! The sailor who chose the crown gets his own shilling back and wins three; the banker pockets two forfeited shillings. The more the banker can get the players to back symbols that do not come up on the dice, the more money he makes. For the players the eternal hope is to have bet heavily on a symbol that comes up on all three dice, as did sometimes happen.[23]

Crown and anchor was a high-stakes game, more complex than the simple example just outlined. Typically, large sums could be wagered; more than one symbol might be backed by the same player; and multiple players could put money down on the same symbol. Leading Signalman Reginald Ashley recalled one sailor walking away from the game £30 richer at the end of the night. "That was a lot of money in those days," and Ashley should have known—he was the man who ran the game and paid out the £30. Ashley was serious about his gaming: "Oh, I don't play for fun." He gambled for the money and he made sure he won by running the game with loaded dice. The trick was to switch one set of loaded dice for another set without being detected. Suppose Ashley, the banker, was using a set loaded for hearts and was subtly encouraging the players to back other symbols. Once the other players realized that hearts were coming up a disproportionate number of times, they would start betting hearts. Ashley would then surreptitiously retire the hearts-loaded dice for ones that favored diamonds or clubs or spades while the other players still had their money on hearts. Even after they realized it was a crooked game, sailors kept playing crown and anchor in the hope that they could outsmart the banker and figure out which way the dice in play were loaded before he switched them.[24]

Chief Petty Officer James Cox said that there was no need for men like Reginald Ashley to use loaded dice at the crown-and-anchor board. The way Cox saw it, the odds were eight to one against any individual player and heavily stacked in favor of the banker. "That's why I wouldn't touch it," he said. "I don't think it's fair."[25] But Reginald Ashley was not taking any chances, because, after all, "I don't play for fun." Upon leaving the navy in 1919, Ashley studied for and passed the civil service examination and went to work for Inland Revenue ferreting out tax delinquents and tax evaders. He must have been excellent at this job.

It is time to get some sense of scale here. Just how prevalent and serious was gambling on the lower deck? Of course there is not, and never will be, any way to get an accurate answer. In the fog surrounding a clandestine activity such as gambling, one can only steer by the impressionistic memories of the old sailors. But broad agreement exists among these veterans. Low-stakes, casual card games aside, serious gambling was confined to a small minority of the sailors in any ship. This minority included, of course, the compulsive gamblers—"perhaps half a dozen in a big ship," according to James Cox's estimate. The great majority of sailors stayed away from the crown-and-anchor boards for good reasons: pay was low, money was scarce, and men could not afford to lose what little they had—whether they were thinking about supporting their families at home or financing their next run ashore. "Here . . . money and sense went together. Sailors are very 'canny' when it comes to parting with 'brass,'" commented Able Seaman Alan Pitt. Engine Room Artificer First Class Philip Robinson echoed his sentiment: "Not interested [in gambling]. Could never see any fun in throwing my hard-earned money away."[26] In particular, crown and anchor was seen as "generally run by a couple of crooked characters that were out to, well, make a bit of money," recalled Albert Heron. When asked if he meant that most of the games were fixed, Bert responded, "I wouldn't say they were fixed, but they were the chaps that you couldn't get, you couldn't—what shall I say?—take over. They were the tough guys . . . They were in command of the crown-and-anchor board and no one else . . . ran a crown-and-anchor board except these two . . . in the one mess . . . Only the stupid chaps would play crown and anchor, because the winner is the same as the bookie. The bookie wins every time . . . I watched it played. I've been fascinated by it. But, no, I wouldn't play it, no."[27]

The Reginald Ashleys of the navy (and their apologists) saw themselves in a more benign light. Did they feel any responsibility for the compulsive gambler who might be losing money that should have been going to his family at home? No. The loser's decision to gamble could be rationalized as a conscious choice: if a man elected to gamble, it was assumed (they said) that he had calculated how much he could afford to lose at the crown-and-anchor board before he started to play. Any loss was softened by the comradeship of messmates. According to Walter Basford, the crown-and-anchor board was never a ruthless environment: "It was never anything vicious—not vicious gambling. 'Cause—say a bloke had £5 . . . and then he'd take his money out and say, 'Well, I've got this,' and he'd keep gambling till he lost the lot—if he was that way inclined . . . Bloke'd get cleaned out and say, 'Well, I'm out.' And the bloke that won the money'd say, 'Well, all right, here's a couple of quid back to go ashore tonight . . . and have a drink.'"[28]

Yes, Reginald Ashley was ready to admit under questioning, there were "quite a lot" of men gambling more than they could afford, but he saw himself as being responsible for those who could not be responsible for themselves: "One bloke particularly, I said to him, I said, 'Well, you're not going to play on my board, because you haven't got the money to play with.' He said, 'I'll borrow some.' I said, 'Well, you're not going to play with borrowed money.'"[29]

Perhaps Ashley really did run a responsible and humane crown-and-anchor board. Apart from asserting that they avoided the game themselves, the old sailors did not have much to say about the dark side of shipboard gambling and the effect it could have on men who were addicted. Crown and anchor? That "could be disastrous," said Bert Heron, who elaborated elsewhere that gambling "led to a great deal of personal stealing on the part of the loser." Raymond Blowers, a petty officer with more than twenty years of service, also noted that "gambling leads to stealing" but added cryptically that stealing was "dealt with heavy by the theifes messmates." These comments stand in contrast to the assertion by most former ratings that there was little theft among sailors and that, when it did occur, it was always reported to the master-at-arms and handled by the ship's justice system, not in any direct manner by the sailors themselves. Petty Officer Blowers's is the sole voice to suggest that direct physical reprisal was also an option for dealing with thieves.[30]

The Royal Navy was dead set against gambling, especially the high-stakes gambling embodied in crown and anchor. Enforcing its prohibition fell to the master-at-arms and the regulating petty officers. The best way to avoid their unwelcome intrusion on a game-in-progress was to play in a locked storeroom. Failing that, the games had to be run in some secluded but public space, such as one of the heads, with a lookout posted to warn of the jaunty's approach. Reginald Ashley paid his lookout £5 a night (by contrast, in 1918 a typical leading signalman's base pay was two shillings nine pence per day)—an indication of just how much Ashley was earning from his crown-and-anchor board and his loaded dice.[31]

When the master-at-arms did catch crown-and-anchor gamblers in the heat of play he was supposed to put the men on report and leave them to suffer whatever punishment the commander and the captain were prepared to assign. But the master-at-arms had another option if he was less than entirely ethical: he could gather up the board, the dice, and the cash, destroy the board and the dice—and keep the money for himself. The culprits were in no position to file a complaint. And that, according to Petty Officer Harry Sowdon, was one of the worst problems created by gambling: it lured the ship's police into corruption. Some of them took bribes to look the other way when gaming was afoot.[32]

Even when the master-at-arms was a man of the strictest integrity, he had a tough time catching the gamblers and proving the case at commander's or captain's report. The odds were definitely not in the MA's favor. Suppose he comes upon a group of men huddled around what he knows must be a crown-and-anchor board. The sailors separate quickly once they sense his approach. The master-at-arms picks out Seaman Jack Jones, the guiltiest looking one in the crowd: "Now you're playing crown and anchor, wasn't you, Jones?" "What *me*, Master? *Never in your life!*"

The master-at-arms decides to search the players, beginning with Jack Jones, for evidence; but while he does this the crown-and-anchor board is being passed surreptitiously from one sailor to another, faster than the men can be searched, before it disappears altogether. Not only is it hard to find evidence to seize, but the master-at-arms knows that group loyalty and comradeship will prevent any sailor from informing on gamblers, no matter how opposed to gambling he himself may be. "I may say," reported one former master-at-arms, "I would give Jack his due, that he is—you don't get a creeper, as the saying is; that they're all for one, and the one who's out of it [and snitches], he *is* really in trouble."[33]

In their hearts some masters-at-arms and some members of the ship's police may have been less than enthusiastic about having to enforce the prohibition against gambling. Ought they really get down on the men for having a little recreation if that was the way they chose to amuse themselves? Many people in the ship saw no harm in permitting gambling for those who chose to participate, and this created an atmosphere hostile to vigorous enforcement of prohibition on the part of the master-at-arms and the regulating petty officers. This was the case not just in the small-stakes card games, but around the crown-and-anchor boards as well. "There used to be a lot of shut-eye," according to Walter Basford. "They could have caught you plenty of times. Duty petty officer could have walked round and caught you times out of number, but they just didn't bother. There was a lot of shut-eye about it . . . because he'd be ostracized by the rest of the ship's company for a start. And 'That so-and-so!' you know, and all that kind of thing, look see. But to some of the petty officers—they weren't what we call *pusser*. That means to say they weren't officious. But there was one or two that, you know—but then if he went—if he was a bit too officious, then [when] he went back in his mess, the other petty officers'd say, 'What'd you want to go and do that for? Why don't you leave 'em alone? They ain't hurting nothing.' You see? So we did get a lot of leeway."[34]

⚓

The best-known palliative to the hardships and anxieties of a sailor's life was far more universal than gambling: it was the daily rum ration, a Royal Navy tradition that continued until 1970. Rum issue was a psychological high point of the lower deck's day, an event rich in tradition and ceremony.

To judge from the written and photographic evidence, although rituals for serving out rum varied in detail from one ship to another, the essential elements were similar. In a big ship rum issue went much like this: at 11 A.M. a boatswain's mate piped "Up spirits," notes sure to provoke a responsive chorus of "Stand fast the Holy Ghost" from wise-cracking sailors. On this cue the petty officer of the day went on the quarterdeck to receive the keys to the spirit room. He then joined a small party made up (typically) of the officer of the day, the sergeant of marines, the chief steward, the cooper (Jimmy Bung), and two marines. With much formality the party went below, unlocked the spirit room, and there, using a hand pump, decanted into a small keg, the barrico or breaker, one-eighth of a pint of rum for every rating in the ship. Or, more correctly, they measured out one-eighth of a pint of rum for every rating in the ship except those who, in the steward's record, were marked "T" for *Temperance*—men commuting their rum ration for a small increase in pay (nine-sixteenths of a pence per day, then one pence per day, in the early years of the century, but three pence per day from 1919)—or "UA" for *Under Age;* that is, ratings nineteen and younger. (U.S. readers will wish to keep in mind that the British pint is one-fifth larger than the American liquid measure of the same name and that naval rum was 95.5 proof [Sykes] or 54.6 percent alcohol, in contrast to the off-the-shelf rum from the liquor store or supermarket, which is typically 40 percent alcohol.)

Once the breaker was filled with the measured amount of rum, the two marines carried it up—"religiously, it was just like taking the Holy Sacrament," said George Michael Clarkson—to the aft deck, where the breaker was set up and guarded by the marines who had carried it there. By now it was 11:10 or perhaps 11:15. The cooks or messmen for petty officer and chief petty officer messes lined up with their jugs, and each in turn called out his mess number: "Number Three Mess, Sir!" The chief steward checked his record, then announced the number of drinking men present for duty in that mess. Thereupon the sergeant of marines served out one-eighth of a pint of rum per drinking man to that mess cook, because petty officers and chief petty officers had the privilege of drawing their rum ration neat—undiluted by water.

After the petty officer and chief petty officer messes were served, the balance of the rum was poured into a large tub bearing the legend GOD BLESS THE KING (or some variant on those words) in big brass letters. To this tub the petty officer of the day or sergeant of marines added three times as much water as there was rum (beginning in 1938 only twice as much water as rum), transforming the resulting mixture into the legendary naval beverage *grog*. At noon the boatswain's mate piped "Muster for your rum" and the designated *rum cooks* for that day from each mess lined up with the mess's fannies (typically oblong metal buckets with a bail-type handle), announced their mess numbers, and were authorized to receive so many tots—that is, a half pint of the mixture for each grog-drawing man in the mess—dipped out by the sergeant of marines, who wielded the half-gallon and quart measures, and the petty officer of the day, assisting with the smaller measures.

Once all the messes had been served, whatever grog remained at the bottom of the tub—typically the equivalent of two or three tots and known as *plushers*—was tipped out of the tub into one of the scuppers by the master-at-arms or one of the regulating petty officers in the presence of the officer of the day—"That was the most awful thing, that was," said George Michael Clarkson—the issuing party secured their gear and dispersed to their messes. Unless he was himself a teetotaler, the petty officer of the day was probably the happiest man in the party, because tradition dictated that he was entitled to an extra tot (neat, of course), a little bribe and thank you to ensure that he did not add an ounce more water to the rum than was required by the regulations.

Before the plushers had gone down the scupper and the gear had been secured, the jugs of neat rum had begun arriving in the petty officer and the chief petty officer messes. Around 11:30 or 11:45 the POs and CPOs who could manage to slip away from the morning's work had begun to trickle in, ready for the dinnertime tot. The far-from-onerous task of being rum bosun rotated among the members of the mess. One former petty officer described the rum bosun's responsibility: "This entailed adding a very small quantity of water to allow for shrinkage and standing by while each member of the mess measured and drank his tot . . . In the meantime the rum bosun was feeling no pain. As each man drew his tot, he offered it to the [rum] bosun first. 'Sipper?' he said. The [rum] bosun would take a small sip and return it to the donor, who would now see it off at one go."

Unlike the petty officers and chief petty officers, lower-rated sailors were not dismissed from work until noon. By the time they reached their messes, the daily tot was waiting for them (or was supposed to be), ladled out equally into their individual basins—or, in later years, glasses—by the leading hand or the cook of the mess. Or at least that was the ideal. John E. Needham, an able seaman from the Second World War, reported how it really happened—at least in his ship: "When the tots were measured out, quite often the leading hand would put his thumb in the measure (which displaced quite a lot of spirit, depending on the size of his thumb) so quite often he would end up with three tots for himself." This abuse was not well received by the *old stripeys*, the regular long-service sailors among Needham's wartime shipmates, men who could get rather paranoid in protection of their fair share of the daily rum ration: "Quite often on board ship when the tots were poured out [they] would get down on their knees, peering along a row of twenty-four glasses to see if all the levels were right. In a rough seaway the whole lot was in danger of slopping over, so these silly old prats would be about as popular as a ham sandwich at a bar mitzvah and many became the recipients of pointed comment—mostly two words, the last of which was 'off.'"

But let some poor member of the mess have his rum stopped as part of a punishment and such self-serving protectiveness went over the side. Each time the leading hand ladled out a tot, he would shake the ladle slightly, slopping some grog back into the fanny and ensuring that, when all the non-punishment members of the mess had been served, there still remained in the bottom of the fanny a tot for the man on 10A.

"Bottoms up," declared the leading hand as soon as all the members of the mess were in their places, drinking his half-pint of grog in one long swallow. His messmates followed his example—or at least they tried to do so, with varying degrees of success, depending on their grog-drinking experience.[35]

When the old sailors looked back and talked about their lives in the navy, they remembered the daily rum issue and its anticipation as one great morale booster in lives that included a copious supply of monotony, hardship, and sometimes danger. George Michael Clarkson said it about as well as any sailor: "Now, I've often noticed . . . you go down at quarter to twelve [to your mess] to have your tot of neaters and everybody would be sitting around gloomy, you know, quiet, nothing at all. By five minutes to twelve they were all arguing the point and thumping the table about football, anything. And then when the dinner came up very often the meat was a little bit off, we'll say, or there was something not very tasty about it. But with that tot . . . you could eat anything, give you a wonderful appetite . . .

"This rum it was wonderful stuff really . . . It's an awful thing coming off leave in the navy, I think. You come back into the dockyard and you get aboard the ship. And everybody is miserable. You're probably sailing that night and going away for another few months . . . You struggle up from the station with your suitcase, you're fed up. You get aboard there. You go down the mess. And your leave is up at twelve o'clock. And the rum has come up. It's there when you get there. And you swallow this tot and you're at peace with the world. You are. It's sort of brought you right back to where you left off before you went . . .

"And rum it has—at times, sometimes I suppose I've had too much—but otherwise it does bring a little bit of light into your life in the navy. The teetotallers are miseries, there's no doubt about that."[36]

Plumber First Class William (Jock) Batters, one of the more reflective of the memoir writers, had his own take on the daily alcohol break: "The rum issue held the navy together. Maybe it wasn't quite the panacea for all our complaints and ailments, but it was the rose-colored spectacles through which things appeared that bit more in perspective and bearable. We inevitably became obsessed at times, but perhaps less so at tot time. Of course passions which had been restrained sometimes were let loose at tot time and no doubt there was more fighting then than at tea time. But it wasn't a bad thing to get it out of your system. After a few days at sea something had to give.

"Despite the popular conception of the sailor which depicts him as a good-drinking type, on one tot of rum a day we were not likely to become alcoholics. They had more latitude for that in the wardroom . . . Our own routine was good enough for us. It made a break, gave us something to look forward to, and one could have too much of a good thing."[37]

Clarkson and Batters hint at a darker side to the daily rum ration, but they come down firmly in support of the tradition as a good thing. John Needham was more ambivalent. He admitted that when he was on duty in the North Atlantic in the destroyer *Montgomery* during the Second World War the rum issue was "the only bright spot of the day and greatly appreciated," and he noted "I wouldn't mind a litre of [navy rum] right now in my wine cabinet." But he also saw plenty that was negative: "RN rum is *strong*. When you have had one tot you are aware of it and after three or four the legs go like stewed rhubarb. Quite a lot of the elder ratings had that typically yellow tinge to their faces which indicated that their liver was starting to rebel and possibly turning up at the edges like a British Railway sandwich . . . In the tropics [the daily rum issue] could lead to some bitter arguments and many a bloke was 'filled in' [beaten up] after tot time."[38]

If the Royal Navy's daily rum issue to the lower deck was so limited and well controlled, how were sailors getting enough alcohol to turn their faces yellow and their legs to rhubarb? By the twentieth century the navy had been successful, thanks to rigid policing and draconian sanctions, in eliminating the problem of alcohol smuggled from shore to the lower deck, a practice that had caused serious disciplinary problems in the eighteenth- and nineteenth-century navies. Among all the ratings whose memoirs, diaries, letters, and interviews have been studied for *Sober Men and True*, only two claimed to have smuggled alcohol from shore on board a ship.

One of these men was—is it any surprise?—Edward Pullen. It was Christmas Day 1912 or 1913 and Pullen's ship, the second-class cruiser *Glasgow*, was at Montevideo. *Glasgow* had a small skiff that ran back and forth to shore, and Pullen had access to it. One of his mates, an AB named Brum Brecknell, said, "What about getting us a bottle of whiskey, Ted?" Ted—himself a non-drinker but clearly a real friend—said, Okay, if Brum arranged the purchase, he'd get it out to *Glasgow* for him. Brum secured the bottle, Ted picked it up ashore, attached a piece of string to it, then pulled the string through the plug hole in the bottom of the skiff and the bottle tight up against the underside of the skiff's hull. Then Ted rowed out to *Glasgow*. Because it was Christmas morning, everyone was singing and no one was keeping a sharp lookout. Pullen tied the skiff alongside the ship and told Brecknell, "It's out there, Brum. It's up to you now to do the rest." By afternoon Brecknell was drunk as a skunk and Pink, the ship's corporal, was busy trying to find out where in the world Brecknell had gotten the liquor. He never did discover the truth.

It almost seems as if Ted Pullen did not believe his own story. When asked if much liquor made it on board this way, he responded: "No, never. Never. Never known—I've never known any to get on board. Every man was searched, you know, in the mornings when he come on board. Officer of the watch used to search him, see? . . . But if you had any liquor on board him, bad day for him anyhow."[39]

Security was so tight and the punishment if caught so severe—loss of rank and good conduct badges, perhaps detention barracks or outright dismissal—that, for all practical purposes, sources for extra alcohol had to be found within the ship or not at all. One scam that Pullen insisted was run during his 1922–1924 service in the battleship *Thunderer* was for the petty officer of the day to add extra water (beyond the regulation 3:1 water to rum dilution) to the rum before grog was served to the messes of the non-petty officers. This resulted in extra—if more diluted— plushers being left over at the end of grog distribution. These were then shared out among the sergeant of marines and the petty officers who had been attending that day's rum issue. A good thing it was until harsh words exchanged over the extra grog blew the fraud into the open, cost a chief stoker his rating, and brought the practice to an end. But were not the plushers always supposed to be poured down the scupper? Pullen was asked. Did not that always happen? "Didn't happen at all . . . They'd just have an extra jug there and put it in, see?"[40]

Or so said Ted Pullen. George T. Weekes, a former master-at-arms, was equally adamant that regulations were much too strict—and strictly observed—to permit such a thing to happen: "There was no chance of it at all. There was no [extra] rum taken below deck from the rum tub . . . [After the issue] the rum tub would then [be] turned upside down, assuring the officer of the day that nobody had been able to touch that rum, if there was any left over. And in all my time I never saw any occasion where there was any impropriety of it." Enough accounts exist in the memoirs describing sailors' long faces when the plushers went into the sea—"I've seen many a dozen old 'regulars' with tears running down their faces at this sacrilege, but it was, after all, tradition" (John E. Needham)—to assure the lower deck's historian that the dump of the plushers was the norm. But in how many laxer ships was the fraud that Pullen describes an established exception to the rule? One can never know for sure.[41]

A different kind of fraud could be practiced in smaller ships when they were in harbor. "Of course, I'm giving away secrets now," said James

Cox when he told the story. Small ships such as destroyers did not carry a master-at-arms; the duties the MA would normally have performed were allocated to the small ship's coxswain. By all accounts the small-ship coxswain was too busy with other responsibilities, and probably too close to his shipmates, to take on the role of chief policeman with enthusiasm. Cox, who had served as coxswain of a destroyer and had been responsible for the rum issue, knew exactly how the scam worked. In port, the number of men who had leave from the ship for a weekend was supposed to be entered in the spirit stoppage book and the amount of rum issued (served neat in small ships) reduced by the number of men ashore. But Cox typically recorded in the spirit stoppage book a smaller number of men ashore than was actually the case. This resulted, obviously, in a larger number of one-eighth pints of rum being issued than the number of ratings on board actually justified—and in extra cheer for all non-teetotalers stuck on board for the weekend.

Other opportunities for acquiring extra alcohol were either built into the system or were traditions that, if not strictly by-the-book, were typically ignored by those in authority. The custom of splicing the mainbrace—an extra issue of grog ordered by the captain or the admiral in honor of a special holiday (perhaps Navy Day or Trafalgar Day) or as a reward for some extraordinary service (say, the Falklands victory in 1914)—is well known to anyone with even a passing knowledge of naval life at sea. There is no need to describe it or linger over it here, though the sailors surely lingered over its memory.[42]

Less well known, if just as celebratory, was the birthday tradition: on a man's birthday he was entitled to as much of the mess's collective rum ration as he wanted. Reginald Ashley described the custom: "Say it's Old Bill's birthday today. Give him the rum and let him have what rum he has. He generally goes underneath the table and sleep[s] for a couple of days and then the rest is dished out to whoever wants it."[43] Clearly, in this case superiors would deliberately avoid asking or investigating why Old Bill was not reporting for duty. But this is only one of several not-by-the-book customs that could only have flourished if those in authority occasionally looked the other way.

In a petty officers' mess in the light cruiser *Dauntless*, George Michael Clarkson reported that the mess members agreed to file one-sixteenth of an inch off the top of the measure used to serve out individual glasses of rum. No one seemed to miss the small quantity of rum he did not get (or so says Clarkson), and the leftovers were set aside for the ship's cook. "Would you like a tot—a nightcap—chef?" "Oh yes." Now the cook was definitely in the mood to perform little extras for that mess's dining pleasure.[44]

But all of these customs, evasions, and abuses could provide only an occasional or meager ration of extra alcohol—small threat here to a man's health or to a ship's efficiency. To find threats more compromising to either, one has to look for widespread and systematic practices.

A major reason for issuing rum mixed with three (or later, two) parts water was to prevent saving or bottling. Grog that was left sitting around forty-five minutes or so after mixing became a flat and tasteless drink. But not so neat rum, which could be bottled up quite nicely. Who had neat rum? Again, chief petty officers and petty officers—*and* all ratings who served in small ships. In a destroyer, a minesweeper, or a submarine much of the formal ritual of the spirit issue, as observed in a battleship or a cruiser, was cut way back. Not only was rum served neat to all hands entitled to draw it; it was served out at whatever time of day the captain decided was appropriate. If a chief or a petty officer in a big ship or any non-teetotaler rating in a small ship was into deferred gratification and was prepared to risk the consequences of being caught, he could simply bottle up his daily issue of neat rum, tuck it away in a safe place, "and," said James Cox, "we'd have a booze-up every now and again, you see?"[45]

But the biggest and best source of extra alcohol on shipboard was the practice of trading neat rum or grog rations for services or favors. "A tot actually is a matter of exchange, we'll say," reported George Michael Clarkson. "It's a currency. It's what tobacco is in the prison. You can get anything done for a tot, where you wouldn't be charged kind of thing. A fellow will—a tot is priceless actually. A man will do anything for a tot. He'll do a job of work for you. You can buy all sorts of things for a tot."

Edward Pullen, aged eighty-nine, elaborated on Clarkson's point for a visitor to his home in Parkstone, a suburb of Poole: "Sometimes I might say, 'I'm just going up and scrub my hammock.' 'I'll do that, Ted.' Now see? He knows tomorrow he'll get my tot of rum . . . I've had anything done for a tot of rum. I've had carpenters has made me picture frames. In fact, there's two there made aboard ship—this one and that one—

that's made aboard ship, all for a tot of rum. You'd never believe what you could get done."[46]

And the rate of exchange? The denominations of liquid currency were sippers, gulpers, and tots—the tot being, of course, the one-eighth pint of rum, diluted or not with water. Three sippers equaled one gulper. Three gulpers equaled one tot. "If someone had done you a great favor, he got a gulper," said Bill Batters. "For doing a night's duty for your chum it was usually a tot." Another sailor (John Needham) remembered a slightly different pay scale: "Some blokes would make you a suit for six tots or do you a week's dhobeying for two or a spell of watchkeeping, if you had an appointment ashore, for the same amount."[47]

Only one sailor, George Michael Clarkson, reported purchasing extra rum with money. He did this by paying a teetotaler more for the non-drinker's daily spirit ration than he would have received if he had commuted it for cash through the paymaster. By this arrangement Clarkson, then a joiner first class in *Dauntless*, 1930–1932, was able to have a quarter of a pint of alcohol midday, day in and day out: one-eighth of a pint at 11:45 and the other at his noon dinner. But Clarkson's story is unique. Most sailors said they were never aware of cash sales of the alcohol ration. Rum (neat or as grog) was almost invariably a barter item.[48]

This barter system clearly gave non-drinkers (or those with the strength of purpose to pass up the daily ration from time to time) the psychological upper hand in their relations with the committed rum-drinkers. There was, at least according to Arthur Ford, no particular prejudice against the non-drinkers who forwent the daily rum ration in favor of cash: "There was no comments about it much. No, no comments about it much. Might be one or two say they was too—'bit tight-fisted,' you know, and wanted the money or something like that. But there wasn't much said if you either drew it or you didn't draw it. And that was the end of it, you see." The navy had more non-drinkers of the daily spirit ration in its ranks than principled teetotalers who commuted the daily alcohol for a cash addition to their pay. The alcohol was, for savvy non-drinkers, much more valuable as an article of barter and a source of power if they drew the ration but did not themselves drink it than if they commuted it for cash—especially when the compensation was nine-sixteenths of a pence or one pence per day. For some non-drinkers there was no issue of principle involved—they just did not like rum. "I never cared for it," admitted Arthur Ford. "No, nor beer or long drink. I like a nice sweet wine." And, perhaps surprisingly—but perhaps not, given his father's problems with alcohol—Ted Pullen, too, was a non-drinker. Both old sailors preferred to give their tots away, sometimes with no expectation of return, at other times in explicit or implicit barter for favors or services.[49]

A sense of the subtle psychological advantage that the non-drinkers had over the drinkers and the resentment this fueled in the drinkers comes to light in George Michael Clarkson's story about the non-drinkers who used their hoarded rum to barter for the coupons that came with Players cigarettes, coupons that the non-drinkers would then sell ashore. "Funny thing, the people [who] used to collect these coupons were nearly all non-smokers. But they used to collect 'em by—they were, as a rule, teetotallers as well. And so people—I've done it myself, I suppose—[who had] gone ashore and had a bit of a night out and the next day come aboard early in the morning and you'd have a terrific fat head. Well, the only thing to cure it was a hair off the dog that had bitten you. And naturally you'd look for a tot. And you always knew where to go—some of these very clean-living people that used to save up their rum. And you'd go along and say, 'Ahem. What is the rate of exchange this morning?' And they knew and they used to push it up, too . . . And so you could go round and get a couple of tots that way by surrendering your coupons."[50]

Most of the former ratings were silent about the cumulative effect of all this sharing and bartering of alcohol on their comrades of the lower deck. Only Arthur Ford spoke up: "Some [shipmates] used to have quite a few [tots], too. And they used to look the worse for it—some of 'em, too—I can assure you, yeah, some of 'em did."[51]

Saving and trading rum issues was contrary to regulations and subject to severe penalties, including disrating and loss of good conduct badges. From time to time there would be crackdowns and draconian enforcement. Acting Leading Telegraphist Donald Goodbrand remembered that during his winter 1942–1943 service in the destroyer *Obdurate*, on a convoy run to one of Russia's arctic ports, "some people bottled their tots secretly for later consumption [or to barter], hiding the bottles in clothes lockers or in shipboard nooks and crannies, known only to themselves." Then he added: "Sometimes the wardroom got wind of these goings-on and all hell broke loose." Goodbrand's account of what happened then may be a bit too self-consciously literary; still, he captures the feel of that dreaded moment: "All non-duty hands were piped to muster on deck and lined up near the torpedo tubes, marshaled into some sort of order by grim-faced bossy POs and leading hands, shivering in the Arctic air and whispering buzzes nineteen to the dozen. Each mess was deserted, illegal brag and pontoon sessions ruthlessly interrupted, with cards left strewn over mess tables as the snap inspection got under way.

"The Skipper [Lieutenant Commander Claude E. L. Sclater], face taut with anger, was observed stalking forward with his entourage of Jimmy-the-One [the first lieutenant], master-at-arms, and Buffer [the chief boatswain's mate], wrapped in his duffle coat against the keen wind. The sailors craned forward, watching the ominous party vanish below. Minutes passed. Old hands groaned at the inconvenience and malefactors inwardly rejoiced in the expertise of their concealment.

"Down in the messdecks the crew's lockers and hammocks were systematically rifled for evidence of the demon rum. A queer feeling of expectancy and foreboding pervaded the silent ranks of guilty and innocent alike freezing on the upper deck. When the inspection party reappeared it was obvious from its dispirited air that the search had been in vain. The sailors relaxed, innocent and guilty alike. The Skipper went aft, the crew reclaimed their quarters. Sly whispers, furtive looks. The last dog watch sounded. Tension lifted. Card games and letter-writing were resumed where they had left off."[52]

As anxiety-provoking as moments like these must have been, no reader of sailor autobiographies and interviews can ever seriously think that the Royal Navy had an effective policy of discovering and punishing saving and trading. These practices were simply too much a part of the fabric of daily shipboard life for the ship's officers not to have known what was going on and to have turned a blind eye to it so long as matters did not get out of hand. The navy's predilection for men of high spirits who liked to test both the limits and their own ability to circumvent the rules was surely a factor here. Officers must have judged that, so long as there was a daily issue of rum, watered or not, it was impossible totally to stop the system of saving and trading, even though it resulted in some ratings having too much alcohol for their own good or the good of the navy's readiness and discipline. But how whole-hearted could enforcement be when alcoholic beverages were regularly served in officer messes and were available in officer quarters, with far fewer systematic structural limits on how much a gentleman might drink—and when the lower deck knew it, too?[53]

⚓

Gambling and drinking were high-profile palliatives for the multiple anxieties and hardships of a sailor's life at sea. Less obvious perhaps, but not to be overlooked, was the relief from the strain of day-to-day discipline provided by rituals that temporarily suspended the hierarchical sailor-officer relationship. The egalitarian mood which existed during coaling, when the convention prevailed that every man's real identity was concealed behind a mask of coal dust, has already been described: "Everybody was brought down to one level there. Everybody was as good as anybody else."[54]

Equator-crossing initiations were a more purely festive occasion when the rating-officer hierarchy was suspended for a few hours. But these are so notorious and have been so often described that they can be bypassed here in favor of a different, if less written about, festival: Christmas on active duty.[55]

The lower deck (and officers as well) took Christmas seriously. Messes began stocking up on special foods and preparing puddings days in advance. "Turkeys, geese, fowls, pigs, etc., are running round the ship and there is crowing and cackling and grunting all day long," one sailor-diarist recorded on the first Christmas after the 1918 Armistice. "Now and again a loud screeching goes on, denoting that some unfortunate bird or animal is 'getting it in the neck.'" Cooks seemed to be working around the clock. Greens, flags, mistletoe, and Chinese lanterns decorated the messdeck. Although customs varied from ship to ship and over time, the day went something like this:

The youngest boy in the ship put on the captain's or the commander's uniform. At the conclusion of the Christmas morning church service, during which he had stood alongside the captain, the boy-commander took over and gave the ship's orders until the ten o'clock "Lights out" that night. "Whatever he said or—he had the bosun's call, he'd blow [on it] and he'd say . . . 'Carry on smoking.' And everybody obeyed him or any other order." Uniform regulations went by the board. Some sailors put on fancy dress. Others switched or mixed uniforms: the sergeant of marines might turn up dressed as an AB. In each mess the junior member donned the uniform and badges of the leading hand and assumed his role for the day. At dinner the captain—escorted by the boy-commander, a jazz or ragtime band from the lower deck, and a clutch of clowns or mummers—made a round of all the messes, wishing each a Merry Christmas and sampling a roast here or a pudding there. Alcohol was more plentiful than usual—or than regulations allowed. Illegally bottled rum appeared mysteriously, and in smaller ships it was not unknown for a senior officer to present each mess with a bottle of whiskey. Here is how one first writer recorded Christmas 1914 in the armored cruiser *Kent*, then in eager pursuit of the fleeing German light cruiser *Dresden* in the eastern Pacific Ocean: "*Xmas Day*. Simply great. Ship's company made up a 'hurrah party' with a tin whistle and mouth-organ band, assisted by the drums. They borrowed various officers' old uniforms and togged themselves up. Stoker Potter got into Commander's clothes. At 10 [A.M.] all officers went round the ship headed by 'Commander' Potter and his tin orchestra; then came the captain and other officers, followed by the funny party. After lunch all the officers were chased and captured, then carried shoulder-high round the upper deck, headed by the band, which caused sport for quite an hour and a half . . . Splendid day under these warlike circumstances. Everything immediately ready for action at any moment although we were having a banyan."

Once the dinner festivities were over, if the ship was in port any sailor who was not on duty was free to go ashore and return when and as he wished—no one was checking up on him. Those who remained on board might spend the rest of the day singing around a piano or organizing an impromptu concert. Or officers and ratings might dance as partners to the music of the marine band. "The officers join in with the men," Charles Thomas, the egalitarian telegraphist with a generally low opinion of the officer class, wrote home, "it being rather strange to anyone who doesn't know the navy to see a lieutenant commander dancing with an AB. These dances are really serious . . . I was quite surprised to find such a lot of relaxing of discipline."

An anthropologist looking at the naval Christmas would call all this a *ritual of status reversal*—a term that would also apply to some aspects of coaling and of equator-crossing ceremonies. Rituals of status reversal typically occur at fixed points in the year (in this case Christmas Day) or in a cyclical manner (as coaling occurred whenever a ship went into port). In such a ritual those who normally occupy low-status positions in a social structure (here ratings) are expected to turn the normal order of things on its head and exercise ritual authority over their superiors (officers), who must accept the situation with as much good will and humor as they can muster. Such rituals often involve what the anthropologist Victor Turner calls "robust verbal and nonverbal behavior in which inferiors revile and even physically maltreat superiors"—an excellent description of the abuse of officers in an equator-crossing ceremony. Or the inferiors may assume the clothing, badges of rank, and style of the superiors, even to the point of organizing a mock hierarchy that parodies the real hierarchy. Rituals of status reversal can also involve the wearing of masks, a practice that has a clear naval parallel in the fictitious convention that coal dust made it impossible to distinguish officer from rating and permitted all participants to treat one another as equals.

According to anthropologists, the effect of rituals of status reversals is, paradoxically, to reinforce the rightness of the normal social structure that has been parodied in a world turned upside-down. Such rituals reinforce that structure rather than weakening it because they dramatize ranks and patterns of behavior that are regarded as the way things *must be*. Victor Turner puts it this way: "Cognitively, nothing underlines regularity so well as absurdity or paradox. Emotionally, nothing satisfies as much as extravagant or temporarily permitted illicit behavior. Rituals of status reversal accommodate both aspects. By making the low high and the high low, they reaffirm the hierarchical principle. By making the low mimic (often to the point of caricature) the behavior of the high, and by restraining the initiatives of the proud, they underline the reasonableness of everyday culturally predictable behavior between the various estates of [a] society."

Rituals of status reversal have another role as well: those who hold positions of authority may use that authority in ways that subordinates in a social structure experience as abusive—as witness lower-deck perceptions of disciplinary excesses in a naval ship. Status reversal gives those holding authority (naval officers) a ritual opportunity to do penance for any such abuses of power and thereby to heal potential or real rifts in the unity that a society (all those who serve in a ship) must have if the society is to function smoothly—or, in a naval world, if the ship is to be an effective operating and fighting unit.[56]

There is much here to help the historian understand the implications of the traditional naval Christmas—and coaling egalitarianism and equator initiations as well. None of these temporary suspensions of the rating-officer hierarchy really changed the underlying power relationship. Once Christmas was over, the officers went back to giving the orders and the ratings to obeying them. By mid-morning of Boxing Day "the messdeck was its old self again—bleak, formal, business-looking. The enchantment of flags and the soft glow of lamps upon the various colors had gone and once more our lives were practical."

True enough, the suspension of the normal order of things had been permitted by those with the power. But did they have any choice other than to honor a tradition that had taken on a life of its own? Witness various futile attempts by officials over the years to suppress equator-crossing initiations—a tradition still alive and in vigorous health. And this makes an important point about naval hierarchy and obedience that bears repeating here. In any naval ship officers are vastly outnumbered by the lower deck. The many obey the few because the few accept the principle, whether consciously or unconsciously, that the officers have the right to give the orders and the ratings consider obedience to those orders necessary for the wellbeing of all. It would be foolish to suppose that, in a modern warship, sailors' obedience is based on fear. (It was not in the eighteenth- or nineteenth-century English-speaking naval world either, though the idea of such fear-based obedience continues to be a firmly established historical myth.) Naval sailors are not galley slaves. Typically, they sign on voluntarily. Both officers and ratings recognize that, should they wish and be strongly motivated to do so, the ratings could simply refuse to obey. If this rebellious resolution is widespread enough in the fleet, there is little that can be done to force the sailors to return to their duty. This is why, although the lower-deck leaders may later suffer draconian sanctions, *mutiny*—the term naval hierarchy prefers to use, though the actual behavior to which the term refers covers a wide range of actions from work stoppage to murderous violence—often does produce real changes to the benefit of the mass of sailors. In the final analysis the leaders are there only because of the willing, if silent, consent of the led.

It is clear that the men of the lower deck valued these traditional episodes of status-reversal and were shrewd enough to see them for what they were. When asked about the custom of the youngest boy wearing the captain's or the commander's uniform and giving the orders for the day, Chief Petty Officer Cook Reginald Willis said simply (if enigmatically), "I don't know—you had to be there to realize what it meant," laughed, and let it go at that.[57] Events that do not happen create no records. Who can say how many instances of insubordination, little or big, did not occur because these safety-valves—Christmas, the egalitarian anonymity of coaling, roughhousing at the equator—existed to release pent-up tensions between the ratings and their officers?

6

A Sailor's Paradise

One escape from the anxieties, frustrations, and hardships of naval life at sea exceeded all others in its appeal. It was far better than gambling; more eagerly anticipated than the daily rum ration; stronger than religious faith; and rewarding beyond the rituals of status reversal or misbehavior. That Great Escape was an opportunity for a run on shore.

An important way in which the coal- and oil-powered navies of 1900–1945 differed from the sailing navies of the eighteenth and nineteenth centuries—and, indeed, from the nuclear-powered navies of the later twentieth century—was that their warships were not (and could not be) at sea for weeks between port calls. Not only could the typical cruising warship of 1900–1945 travel briskly from one destination to the next; it had to go into port frequently to replenish its supplies of fuel (especially coal) and fresh food. Although opportunities for shore leave might be sharply curtailed in time of war, during a peacetime, show-the-flag cruise, sailors could expect to rotate ashore in large numbers at almost every port of call. In a ship's home port in Britain only a portion of the officers and men needed to remain on duty at the end of the ship's normal workday or over a weekend. All others were free—and almost always eager—to get ashore.

In pursuing the sailor ashore one must hack a path through a luxuriant jungle of stereotypes. A passage from the diary of Charles Stamp, a hostilities-only rating who served during the First World War, captures the traditional image of the man of the lower deck on shore leave. Stamp's ship had just reached Capetown: "Went ashore in evening—not many [teetotalers] in navy—most back drunk—it's a rotten life and one wishes for home and decency again. One wonders at men getting so low and yet in a way it can easily [be] explained."[1]

This observation was perhaps true for some, but it was a gross injustice to many other sailors. Even though he may sometimes have thought so, Ordinary Seaman Stamp was not the only decent human being in the navy. When the boats went ashore not every rating made a dash for his favorite pub, tanked up on beer, and then set off in search of the nearest prostitute or brothel. Sailors went to cinemas, to theaters for vaudeville shows, and to dance halls—to dance, let it be noted. They walked and bussed around strange cities abroad or familiar ports at home. They ate in restaurants and hung out at Dame Agnes Weston's Royal Sailors' Rests, even at the price of having to pretend that they bought into Miss Aggie's temperance crusade. They appreciated the hospitality of local people who made them welcome at special parties for the fleet, and they loved it when they were invited into local homes. And, yes, sailors even went to church occasionally. But sailors who stay out of trouble do not attract attention, make news, or (as a consequence) wind up on the written record. Instead, they disappear from the historian's vision, leaving only the miscreants behind to represent all sailors.

Many naval ratings went to sea because they were would-be travelers, eager to see other lands and to meet different peoples. Their diaries and letters document how fully they took advantage of these opportunities. Times beyond counting sailors have entered in their diaries paragraphs similar to this one, penned by Signalman Walter Dawson of the battleship *Albion*, on October 13, 1914, at Pôrto Grande on São Vicente in the Cape Verde islands: "On entering Porto Grande the first thing that meets the eye is a huge rock which rears its lofty summit, which is crowned with a solitary lighthouse, high in the air. The town lies snugly in the eastern corner of the harbor, being only a very small place, (being) for the most part composed of offices and stores. The largest building to be seen is the laundry. All around are high hills and on the southern side is a freak of nature in the form of Napoleon's head, formed—as clearly as if it had been cut by human hands—by the hills. From the crown of the head to the chin is a distance of about a mile. Boats from ships who happen to be in harbor land at the only pier that Porto Grande possesses and that is only a frail wooden structure. Little more can be said, but it is essential that an account should be made of the native 'diving boys.' They are called 'Heave-I-dive' boys by sailors from the fact that they cannot make use of any further English. They come alongside the ship in boats and yelling to the sailors 'Heave, I dive'—meaning 'Throw money and I will dive for it.' Dive! Well, it is nothing for one of these boys to be under for two or three minutes and they dive to a tremendous depth. Very rarely do they come to the surface without the object of their dive."[2]

Enthusiasm for the sights continued on shore. Just a few weeks after Dawson recorded his description of Pôrto Grande, Leading Seaman Philip Powell was at Gibraltar in the cruiser *Talbot:* "It was a thorough treat to have a quiet day. It seemed more natural and certainly like a Sunday. Leave was given at 1 P.M. and almost everyone took advantage of it. Myself, with two shipmates, went for a grand walk up the rocks and spent some time in viewing the scenery, for it was certainly delightful. About 4:30 strolled down to the town and had tea at the Army Salvation Home [the Salvation Army Naval and Military Home, Governor's Square], where the officers in charge's [*sic*] gave us a hearty welcome and prepared for us well. In the evening we went to the service, which was very bright and helpful. Ten P.M., after a little supper, we strolled on board after a very pleasant day, so our sleep was the sleep of the just."[3]

Granted, Powell was in some degree an anomaly: more religious than many sailors and a committed and active member of the Salvation Army. But he was far from alone in avoiding the pubs and the brothels, at least according to Chief Petty Officer Albert Heron: "I managed to save up enough to get myself a civilian suit . . . in Portsmouth, because I preferred to go ashore in civilians—or not go ashore. I kept my civilians in a locker which I booked in the Sailors' Rest, and I had a pal, a shipmate of mine that was serving with me. He did much the same. And I was also able to buy a bicycle, as did my pal, and we would do a lot of cycling. And because I didn't used to drink all that much and I certainly didn't— I hadn't much use for these tarts—I had no use for them, actually—I used to do a lot of sport, like fencing, swimming and boxing, water polo, and the two wouldn't have gone down well—not women and sport."[4]

And here is how Ordinary Seaman Wilfrid Smith, so far as one knows a perfectly typical sailor, spent his forty-eight hours in Capetown in January 1942: "This place proved to be quite a Sailor's Paradise and quite lived up to the many tales I had heard beforehand of its great hospitality to the English sailor . . . These good people (a mixture of English and Dutch) by arrangement met us in the town . . . and whisked us off in twos and threes, usually in large cars, perhaps to a beautiful bungalow or house just out of town or perhaps to a farm in the country. The choice of 'town' or 'country' was ours. My own experience was somewhat mixed [Smith provides no details 'for prudence sake'] . . . Speaking generally, the chaps were entertained royally, with a free run of everything, usually including the sideboard and everything contained therein, also visits to dances, cinemas, etc., with their hosts."[5]

Hospitality and visits to private homes were what Joiner First Class George Michael Clarkson remembered and appreciated about the light cruiser *Dauntless*'s tour up the west coast of the United States in the early 1930s: "All the way up there they did give us a good time, there's no doubt about it. And they seemed anxious to meet you and to take you home. Now that was a great thing, is to take you home to their homes and make you welcome there, even if it's only for a cup of tea or something like that."[6]

In trying to correct one sailor stereotype—that of shiploads of boozy, fight-primed womanizers—the historian must be careful not to create another (and equally misleading) stereotype: ships manned by sober-sided Edwardian gentlemen. After all, the navy wanted men with high spirits. The exploits of sailors from the armored cruiser *Kent*—far from unique in naval annals—demonstrate that negative stereotypes *do* have a foundation in the real world. When *Kent* called at Chatham Island in the Galapagos group in January 1916, roughly one hundred ratings were allowed to land. They headed for a settlement some five miles up in the hills. "There," according to a lower-deck diarist who was on duty that day and did not get to go, "they found a sugar plantation and they sampled the white rum. Consequently, about thirty got left behind [on the island] and at 9 P.M. there were no signs of them.

"Our thirty absentees were retrieved [the next] morning. They were found lying by the roadside in the scrub at various distances from the shore. There they had been all night and a sorry spectacle they looked, too. They had become overcome with the white rum and had simply fallen helpless by the way. The half-savage natives had then come along in bands and robbed them of boots, caps, silk 'kerchiefs, money, etc., and in one or two cases [the] best part of their clothes. They did look a lot of guys when the[y] got on board, half-naked and showing signs of battle with the robbing half-savages."[7]

Scenes such as these were hardly confined to remote islands of the Pacific Ocean. Signalman Edgar R. Baker's First World War diary tells about a party of sailors from the destroyer *Thrasher* who booked seats at a theater one night in June 1917: "As there were five of us [we] booked a box, but the evening was not a success. It was a rotten show and one of our number was half drunk and would keep calling out. Then he found some girls' hats in the box and put them on. As soon as we got out three of us returned to the ship. The one who was drunk went for more beer and 'General' [a shipmate] stayed to look after him. He managed to get him back by 12:30."[8]

Similar incidents, repeated who knows how many times in full public view in the first half of the twentieth century, laid the foundation for the stereotypical image of the drunken sailor. In focusing on the intoxicated rating who wore the girls' hats and behaved raucously in the theater, those—be they members of a different social class looking on with self-comforting disdain or sensation-seeking historians—who want to pigeonhole sailors ignore the four other lower-deck men who conformed to expected standards of behavior. And they ignore the one man who remained behind to see that his shipmate stayed out of serious trouble and got back to the ship safely.

But even the suggestion of a clear dichotomy between good sailors and chronically misbehaving sailors can be seriously misleading. In reality, sailors on shore leave displayed a range of behaviors, from that of sobersided prigs to men whose actions had them habitually flirting with a term in detention barracks or dishonorable discharge. The behavior of most fell somewhere between these two extremes. What the autobiographical records created by the sailor-informants do not reveal is why one sailor went ashore and rented a bicycle while his messmate set course for a brothel. It is easy enough to say that Charles Stamp avoided drinking because of his powerful Methodist convictions or that Bert Heron bypassed prostitutes for fear of compromising his athletic abilities. But this does not explain *why* Stamp was a man of religious faith or Heron preferred sport to women while the sailor in the hammock next to theirs may have been a dedicated hedonist. Many of the sailors whose memories, diaries, and letters have contributed to this book were given to introspection. But they were fundamentally *sailors*—men of action—neither Sigmund Freud nor Marcel Proust. The records they created can take the historian a fair distance into the sailor psyche, but eventually one reaches some critical point in the exploration of behaviors, asks *Why?* and finds no answers in the historical records.

⚓

The diary of Archibald Richards, a leading telegraphist from the Second World War, provides a rare glimpse into the moods that sailors brought with them on shore leave. Richards was disgusted with the spit-and-polish, peacetime way he thought his ship, the aircraft carrier *Formidable*, was being run. In his eyes there was a war that needed to be won so that he could get home alive and start drawing his pension. Why all this traditional navy nonsense of Sunday inspections in dress uniforms when Japanese divebombers might drop from the clouds at any moment? "What a contrast to be on shore [at Mombasa] during the day and away from all the pettifogging trivialities associated with this institution. One experiences a pleasant sensation on stepping ashore, a sense of freedom which is entirely lacking on board. Hemmed in by walls of steel, oppressed by a[n] atmosphere usually guaranteed to weigh one down, life is not too thrilling and, coupled with [un]sympathetic and unsociable superiors, one can imagine why enthusiasm is lacking and efficiency is below standard. It's bad enough for the youngsters, but for the more serious-minded, whose one aim is to get this business over as quickly as possible, it's deadly."[9]

A sailor named Cook, a First World War shipmate of Edgar Baker's in *Thrasher*, was neither as reflective nor as eloquent as Archibald Richards, but he went ashore in a similar mood. Unlike Richards, who chose to vent his frustrations in his diary, Cook acted his out when ashore. He "was a very quiet and decent fellow, but every now and then he would break out and overstay his leave. He told me he felt fed up, got drunk, and, on finding he had broken his leave, went on the spree until his money was gone and then he came back . . . After his breakouts he would go on steadily for months."[10]

"You give me the impression that in foreign ports all sailors mainly did was look for drink and women," a questioner commented to Chief Yeoman of Signals Thomas Wallace. "Well, that mostly, yes," Wallace replied. "I won't say *all* sailors, but a great majority of them."[11] Wallace would certainly have gotten a hearty *Amen* from Telegraphist William

Blamey, whose First World War diary told of a visit to Khaniá in Crete by himself and a group of shipmates: "The town . . . itself is a shake-down affair and of the old cobble type, very interesting as far as old and out-of-fashion civilization goes, but that doesn't interest the average sailor. When on leave after a long period aboard, the streets he likes to see are pub, pub, pub, eating house, restaurant, pub, pub, pub, pub, wine store, lodging house, pub, pub, pub, etc. The town, though not large, runs a street—a whole street—for prostitutes, as is found in practically all countr——." With this final word fragment then ex-Telegraphist Blamey threw the sand of latter-day discretion in the eyes of history by cutting out the bottom quarter of that page of his old diary.[12]

But was it that simple? According to George Michael Clarkson—and his comment would have been heartily seconded by many another sailor or army ranker—the absence of a welcoming attitude by the ratings' own countrymen abroad, whether in the ports of the Empire or in those of foreign nations, encouraged sailors to go off in search of a binge: "You'd think that, say, the white population in some of these places—in our own colonies, Bombay, Colombo, and all those places—you'd think, naturally, 'Oh, a sailor's going to be all right there. The people from the Old Country will look after—' but, no, they don't want to know you. You go in Bombay, for instance, in the Taj Mahal Hotel, and they don't want to serve you there . . . [Sailors] end up by looking for comfort [in] places like brothels and places like that."[13]

The navy itself realized that for some—perhaps most—sailors occasionally drinking to excess or even to the point of oblivion was an essential psychological safety valve, a means of escaping, at least temporarily, from the unavoidably harsh realities of a naval life at sea. Too little noticed amid all the pages that have been written concerning disciplinary actions against intoxicated sailors is an old naval tradition. When sailors returned on board under the influence, the master-at-arms, the duty officer, indeed, everyone in authority, worked strenuously at looking the other way with a silent prayer that, even if a drunken sailor, once safely on board, turned violent or verbally abusive, his messmates would get him under control—knocking him out, if necessary—before events went so far that the ship's disciplinary machinery had to grind into action.

Edgar Baker's First World War diary tells the story of one such return from shore leave at Jarrow: "Two of the party were drunk, one of them almost helpless. By the time we reached the boat he was senseless. Hauled him on board. There is always an inspection on return, but this is the merest of formalities. While waiting, some of the men pushed the drunkard into the PO's head and, watching their chance, took him forward. He was put on the lockers, a blanket thrown over him, and left to sleep it off."[14]

At the end of the day, when their active-duty years were long behind them, the former men of the lower deck had distance and time for reflection about their years at sea. Had sailors drunk too much? Was the Royal Navy a service peopled by alcoholics or its performance compromised by alcoholism? Should more have been done to promote temperance? As on so many other subjects, the answers depended on the man asked.

Yes, there *was* too much drinking and drunken behavior by men of the lower deck, at least according to half of the veterans asked. "The sailor in those days worked hard and played hard," reflected Albert Heron years later, "but believe me he drank hard and very often became most abusive; hence the reason for so many naval patrols having to be landed to help keep the peace, especially in ports such as [Portsmouth], Chatham, and Devonport."[15] The navy should have done more to encourage temperance and been less tolerant of drinking—or so many of the veterans thought as old men. More interesting, at least to this historian, are the voices of the men who answered, "No," drinking was not a problem in the navy.

According to Petty Officer Phillip Jenkins, "It was a treat to drink after weeks, sometimes months, at sea." Leading Seaman James Callister concurred: "Drinking was no problem, especially at sea, and I never met an alcoholic sailor. They liked a pint and knew how to behave except for a fight or two ashore." Signalman William Humphries declared: "Shut up as we were in tin boxes, I reckon a man was entitled to celebrate once or twice a month. Then he was broke."[16]

Many more former sailors could be quoted to the same effect, but on this subject the final word can appropriately be given to Edgar Baker. When he reread his First World War diary forty-odd years later, Baker came to the entry about getting the drunken shipmate back on board *Thrasher* at Jarrow and added a second thought: "I put this down [in 1917] to show how the men help one another. As regard[s] the whole practice of drinking and women one cannot help feeling really ashamed of it. At the time there is no doubt that I felt very bitter, but experience made me a lot more reasonable. Later I realized that the average sailor drank but little; for weeks often he had nothing but his tot of rum. Also it must be realized that when ashore more often than not it was only the pubs that gave him a welcome. Also I overlooked the fact that there were large numbers of thoroughly decent men afloat who would have honored any walk of life."[17]

This historian's choice for one of those "thoroughly decent men afloat" who nevertheless was fond of his beer is Yeoman of Signals John E. Attrill, a married man and father then in his thirties. Attrill's First World War diary provides a two-and-a-half-year chronicle of his drinking. It begins when he is attached to the hired yacht *Lorna*, patrolling the waters around the Hebrides, and ends with his service in the battleship *Marlborough*. January 28, 1915: "We went across to Portree, Isle of Skye . . . Great amusement was caused this day on account of the gig's crew going up to get a haircut and visited the pub instead. They got quite *giddy* and I wrote a few verses on the 'Visit and the Results,' which was quite amusing and can be found at the end of the book." (The verses, sad to report, are no longer to be found at the back of this or any other volume of Attrill's diary.) March 23, 1915: "We laid quiet at Stornoway, a very nice mild day. Went for a couple of hours' walk. Of course no 'booze.' Wasn't allowed to look at a pub, let alone go in one. One of the fortunes of war." July 11, 1915, a Sunday: "Still in Mallaig awaiting orders . . . We laid quiet all day. We had never had such a time in harbor since Christmas. Went for a four-mile walk in the evening through the highlands to a village called Morar. Had a drink and walked back. Very pleasant." September 2, 1915: "[Castlebay] hadn't been a bad place, very small but able to get a nice glass of beer."

September 9, 1915: "Went up to Loch Inchard, anchoring at 5:45 P.M. Went ashore for a walk and a *glass*. Very dark and rocky." October 23, 1916, in *Marlborough* at Invergordon: "Nothing doing, so went for a stroll and a glass in the afternoon. Made up for lost time." January 19, 1917, at Invergordon: "Nothing doing. Had a walk in the afternoon and a couple of glasses. Quite a nice change to meet old ships and old faces again." February 3, 1917, at Invergordon: "Nothing doing of much interest. Went ashore for a *few* glasses. It came on to snow very heavy during the afternoon and the ground was soon covered. When we went off at 6 P.M. all the ships looked lovely, all white and the moon shining." July 8, 1917, at Scapa Flow: "Went ashore for a walk to Kirkwall and back in the afternoon (very dry)."[18]

John Attrill liked his beer. Most of the time he drank in moderation. Occasionally he downed enough pints to become pleasantly intoxicated. He was sufficiently self-aware to be alert to the danger hidden behind his love of beer, and he never drank so much (or at least never got caught drinking so much) that he faced disciplinary problems or jeopardized his career. After his June 1922 discharge from the Royal Navy, in which he had attained the rate of chief yeoman of signals, John Attrill returned to the Isle of Wight, where he had been born in 1885. For about five years he worked at various pick-up jobs until 1927 brought an ideal opportunity for John Attrill to combine work and pleasure by becoming landlord of the Green Dragon public house in Shanklin. He was a popular host, and the Green Dragon provided a good living for Attrill and his family of three boys and two girls until the Second World War put the Isle of Wight off limits for holiday-makers, who were a major part of the Green Dragon's clientele. This cut income at the Green Dragon so seriously that John Attrill gave up the pub-running business in 1941 and went to work in an aircraft factory at Cowes. War's end in 1945 also put an end to factory employment, but John Attrill still loved the sea and being out-of-doors—the latter no surprise to anyone who reads his diary entries describing hikes through the countryside ashore. Beaches on the Isle of Wight were being cleared of their wartime defense obstructions, but not nearly fast enough for Britons bent on a holiday by the sea. John Attrill found a new career as a beach attendant, loved the job, and kept on doing it right up until his death in July 1955.[19]

⚓

Like William Blamey in Crete during the First World War, most ratings found it impossible to talk or write about shore leave and drink without their thoughts and their words wandering off to the subject of sex. Sailors were obsessed with women and sex. At least that is what they themselves said. Edgar Baker, fresh from civilian life, noticed it right away: "I don't know what it is about the life at sea, but it is a fact that it makes women play a much greater part in one's life. Their company becomes almost a necessity. After a time it seems that there are only two courses open. The first is a girl in the best sense of the word. Failing that, a man generally goes in for women. I suppose it is the complete separation that is the cause. Personally, I know I do not run after girls, but I have never wished for a girl's company as much as I have done these last months."[20]

Leading Seaman Arthur Ford, the farm boy who joined the navy in part because he felt it would grant him easy access to women, said much the same thing, if less eloquently. According to Ford, there was a lot of talk of sex in the messes: "I won't say that it's the most popular topic, but it certainly ranks pretty high . . . And the singing and all and the songs they make up and parodies they make up are all based on the same thing." It was not all talk, though there was some of that, too: "When they go ashore . . . not all of 'em, of course—it'd be silly to say they're all the same, but quite a lot of 'em, you see—that's the first thing they do, you see, is go looking for girls . . . I suppose it's only natural, really. I mean, you're away from home. Nobody knows you, do they? I mean, nobody knows what you do when you're away from home in any case. And you don't know anybody. And you don't hardly know the place per-haps. So naturally you just get hold of a girl. And you go out and have a walk and a [*unintelligible word*] . . . you know, and make your own com-pany, you see. You had to."[21]

Edgar Baker's diary puts the choice confronting the sailor in search of females in classic either/or terms. Either one sought "a girl in the best sense of the word"—more usually referred to as a *nice girl*—"or a man goes in for women," by which Baker presumably meant prostitutes. So far as this historian is aware, no man of the lower deck, 1900–1945, left a diary describing his sex life in fresh, contemporary detail. What sailors had to say about their encounters with females was all recorded many years later. As men of a more private era, these sailors—with one excep-tion—were not prepared to describe such encounters in explicit erotic detail. Moreover, in the case of the oral interviews on which much of our knowledge of sailors and women must be based, the interviewers were much too ill at ease to pursue such detail, even if the old sailors had been willing to reveal it. (The same reticence, on both sides of the tape re-corder, inhibits efforts to explore shipboard homoeroticism—of which, more in a few pages. As for masturbation, although its prevalence on board was recognized in the navy's traditional wake-up call, "Hands off cocks, on socks," it was a completely taboo topic among the sailor-informants for *Sober Men and True*, never even mentioned, let alone discussed in diary, letter, memoir, questionnaire, or interview.) Subject to these limitations, much can be teased out about men of the lower deck and their search for female companionship.

There is ample evidence that sailors typically thought of their female companions, actual and potential, in terms of the nice girls/not-nice women dichotomy. *Nice girls.* Everyone had an intuitive sense of what those words signified. But when one tries to confine the term within the limits of a definition, all goes murky. Nice girls were women whom one would consider appropriate as wives and the mothers of one's children. They had obvious ethical values and were committed to monogamous family life. A sailor could take a nice girl to church or out to a museum or home to meet his mother. (Not all sailors married nice girls, of course; but more on that later.) Just how far, sexually speaking, a nice girl could go with a sailor who was her prospective future husband and still remain a nice girl is not revealed in the surviving records. Evidence-free speculation is always dangerous, but most likely the definition of a nice girl was elastic enough to cover a range of behavior, so long as it was in the context of a serious, committed relationship that had marriage as its intended outcome. However, 1900–1945 is a foreign country in terms of the rules and rituals of premarital courtship. Society at that time laid a heavy taboo on premarital sex, and sexual ignorance (fostered with the misguided idea of protecting sexual innocence) inhibited the enjoyment of sex by many young women and ensured a high rate of needless prenuptial pregnancy.[22] The danger of projecting post-1950s sexual mores onto that earlier world is close at hand and insidious.

It is almost certainly safe to assume that nice girls were on Chief Petty Officer James G. Cox's mind as he described the pleasures awaiting sailors when ships of the fleet visited British outports—say Lowestoft, Torquay, or Weymouth: "The ships was always open perhaps at nearly every place you went to. It was always open one or two days to the public . . . And when you got visitors aboard everybody picked up their own visitors, whoever they were. You know, you made the acquaintances. Mostly you had an eye for the girls. I mean, as a young man you'd, say, you'd join perhaps two or three girls and take them round the ship, see if you could make a date and things like that, you see. I mean, because that was the only opportunity you had really of making dates with anybody. Because you got to remember that when a ship leaves a port there used to be an old saying in the service, you know, 'Turn of the screw pays all debts.' I mean, you have your romance there and then you forget all about it. Away you go. You may fall in love with a girl for a couple of weeks and write to her once or twice, and just that, exchange her photograph with you. And, well, that was the last you hear of 'em. I can remember when I first got married I turned out my ditty box and I think I had somewhere about thirty or forty different photographs of girls. And some I couldn't even remember, you see. And I used to put 'em—and I used to say to the wife, 'Now look how happy I could be with any of 'em.'"[23]

At the other end of the traditional nice girl/not-nice woman dichotomy is the detailed narrative of the sexual initiation and erotic maturation of Plumber First Class William (Jock) Batters, in 1937 an acting plumber fourth class attached to the repair ship *Resource* in the Mediterranean—a narrative supported by the key pieces of photographic and written evidence that Batters saved to substantiate his story: "It was in Argostoli, [Cephalonia Island], that I had my first woman, and nothing could have been less premeditated or contrived . . . I decided to go ashore . . . with a handful seeking recreation and local color. Three of us joined forces and went off [exploring the area] . . .

"As the afternoon was wearing on we made our way back into town and, as if by instinct, gravitated to a hotel. We were taken to a large room on the first floor and, on entering, found a goodly number of *Resource*'s men sitting around drinking or playing crown and anchor. A waiter came for our order, which was for a bottle of wine. We filled our glasses and sat back and surveyed the scene.

"Presently the door opened and a young woman entered and looked round. She was about seventeen and quite pretty but seemed a bit tentative and uncertain. She made her way over to me and stood by my shoulder and smiled down at me. There were a couple of dozen men in the room but I had been singled out—for what I had no idea. Anyway, it cost me nothing to smile back and say 'Hello.' That was the start of it. From every corner of the room came the barracking: 'Go on, Jock, fix the lady up.' 'Go on, Jock, have a go.' 'Go on, mate, you know you want it.' I was acutely embarrassed and was rapidly turning beetroot. I turned to my companions, but they offered no advice and were just as amused as the rest. There was only one way out—and that was through the door. I got up and made my way out, accompanied by the girl, with the cheers of the assembly ringing in my ears.

"She took me along the hallway to a room. We entered and she closed and locked the door and started to undress. Well, this was it. At the age of twenty-three I was a long way behind in the sex stakes. I had neither the time nor the money to get involved until I joined the RN and hadn't had the opportunity since then . . . There was a knock at the door and I opened it to find a middle-aged woman with hand held out for my attention. There were 500 drachmas to the pound and, fishing in my pockets, I found that I had fifteen—equivalent to seven pence. I had some British money and gave her the drachmas and a shilling. She was satisfied and went off before I had a chance to ask her if it was enough.

"It was my turn to strip off now and I couldn't have done it with much enthusiasm. I knew, basically, what I had to do, but I had never contemplated doing it with someone whom I had only known for ten minutes and with whom I had exchanged about six words. Anyway, I got on with it—and a disappointing business it was. I was ashamed and a bit disgusted with myself and felt I was somehow letting my family down. In consequence, I got no pleasure from the encounter and my main reaction to the girl was pity at having to debase herself by giving her body to a stranger like me. All this for 1/7 . . .

"When I returned to the large room where it all started I was welcomed like a young lion. 'Good old Jock! Have a drink—you need it.' They were right about that part anyway."

Batters's next opportunity for sex came when *Resource* was ordered to Arzew on the Algerian coast to act as depot ship to two squadrons of flying boats assigned to assist in protecting British and French shipping during the Spanish civil war. On the first chance for shore leave, "I went off at 1 A.M. in company with some shipmates who I knew were lively characters—mostly stoker POs and mechanicians. When we got ashore we decided to go up to Oran, about twenty miles away, in search of adventure in the form of wine, women, and woodbine. Between us we hired a bus which was to take us to Oran, wait for us, and, finally, take us back to Arzew . . .

"After my experience with the Greek girl I had tried to come to terms with this sex skylark and decided that, having had one woman, I might as well try a few more. I figured that it was the particular circumstances, plus the publicity, that had inhibited my first attempt and that, under different conditions, there might be a better reaction. I was not reluctant therefore when, shortly after reaching Oran, I found we were heading for a bagshanty. There were about a dozen of us and we found a hotel of this nature near the main thoroughfare. To my discredit perhaps, I led the way in and found myself at a reception desk. There was a very handsome woman in black at the desk and she, it seemed, was the matron. She counted us and pressed a series of bells on the wall behind the desk, then ushered us into a large lounge where we ordered our drinks.

"The drinks came quickly but nothing else happened for a few minutes, when suddenly the door opened and in came a dozen girls. They were not overdressed and I quickly singled out my fancy and hailed her in French. I had used my schoolboy French for the first time ever in Arzew, an hour or so before, when the bus had been held up for petrol—or the money to buy it. With this newfound confidence I had secured for myself the pick of the bunch and she came quickly over and sat on my knee.

"She wore a skirt, open at the front, under which she wore pants, and, as she sat down, these and her bare legs were fully exposed. She also wore a bolero jacket—but no brassiere—and, as the jacket was open, the goods were on display. I felt myself getting quite excited but restrained myself until I could see what the others were doing.

"They were doing very well—so much so that our sick berth petty officer, who incidentally wasn't involved with the women, decided to take a photograph of the scene. When it was developed and printed later it would have made a good recruiting poster, as the highly polished table, glasses and bottles of wine, half-naked women and laughing sailors portrayed pleasures seldom encountered in civilian life. I still have this photo, as well as the card my girl gave me, which is headed 'LE SÉLECT, 18, Rue de l'Acqueduc, ORAN.' Her name was Sonia and she signed the card."

Batters carefully preserved Le Sélect's business card, with Sonia's signature written boldly across the back, and the snapshot (see photo insert for both)—the latter perhaps a unique photographic record of British sailors in action in a brothel. The anonymous sick-berth petty officer apparently lacked a flash on his camera—this *was* 1937 after all—so the photograph is a bit dark. The picture is also slightly out of focus, suggesting that the PO's hand may have been a little unsteady with the excitement. To the left one young woman, naked to the waist (at least—the table hides the bottom half of her body) has her arms around two happy-looking sailors. In the center another woman presses her cheek against that of yet one more happy sailor. At the right sits Bill Batters, Sonia on his lap with a breast escaping through the open front of her bolero jacket. None of the women looks unhappy about her chosen line of work. All smile broadly for the camera. Aye, who would not a sailor be! "I managed to contain myself for a few minutes," Batters continues, "but eventually I led the exodus from this riotous scene. Sonia took me upstairs and along a passage on each side of which were bedrooms, some of them with open doors. I noticed that each room had its own predominant color. One was blue, one pink, one yellow, and so on. There was a pedestal washbasin and bidet in each room in matching colors with the walls and bed counterpanes and it was quite an elegant setup. Fit for a sheik no less and certainly good enough for a crowd of POs.

"Sonia was a pro and there was no awkwardness or embarrassment such as I had experienced with the Greek girl who, I later realized, must have been an amateur. Only one thing had to be decided: the price. She asked for forty francs and I told her I could only afford twenty. This was a sort of routine to us, as we never really understood the equivalent rates in foreign countries but haggled because it was expected of us. She agreed to twenty, as I promised her forty next time. At 140 francs to the pound she wasn't overcharging for her favors but, at three in the afternoon, every little helps.

"If my session with the Greek girl had been ridiculous, Sonia took me to the sublime. She was a craftsman and I almost adored her before I left. I promised to return on Wednesday. Among other things she sprayed my hair with perfume and for the next few weeks every time I had a shower I was transported in thought to her boudoir, which I smelt like."

Batters definitely wanted more of this kind of experience: A few days later "I came ashore again, but without my former shipmates, and made my way from Arzew to Oran and the Le Sélect. I chatted to the lovely patron and was saucy enough to ask her to do the honors, which she declined. At nearly forty she was not unflattered at the advances of an eager young sailor but [she] handed me over to Sonia.

"We retired to her room and I hoped to repeat the pleasures of Sunday but, like many plans, it misfired somewhat. She wanted forty francs plus the twenty she was short of on Sunday and I wouldn't cough up. I said I'd give her forty for this occasion and no more. I found myself trying to make love to a tigress, but I wouldn't back down. In the end she did, but it took the joy out of things and, although she turned sweet, I had again become disillusioned. So I was back to square one, but I was learning.

"I said I'd see her again, but had no strong intentions and, in fact, never did see her again. However, I had chalked up my second woman in about two weeks which, for a chap who had taken twenty-three years to get started, wasn't bad going."

Batters's next sexual encounter occurred in Alexandria, after he and his companions narrowly escaped more trouble than they could handle through wandering off into a part of the city where even sailors were not safe! Once back in a less-threatening, more sailor-friendly part of Alexandria, "we . . . made our way into the first bagshanty and relaxed with a bottle of beer. The girls soon congregated and that was it. There were about a half dozen of them and I chose one, quite young, with a good figure and, most important, very cheerful demeanor. I always figured that if they looked happy and laughed a lot, they weren't rotten. After a time I made my way upstairs with her, my third woman. She led the way and turned a couple of times and laughed—not a giggle or a chuckle, but a belly laugh. I wondered if she was a head case or, alternatively, if there was something special in store for me. It was the latter in fact, for she had the biggest organ that I ever encountered and the laugh was on me. She must have been on the game since she was about twelve. I could never have guessed, but that's just how it was."

That experience seems to have cooled Bill Batters's newfound sexual enthusiasm for a while. It was not until *Resource* had returned to Britain in November 1937 and had paid off that Batters had his next bedtime adventure. He was on leave, but he was in no great hurry to get home to Scotland, where he would have to be on his best behavior. Batters elected to linger a bit in London: "I was one of the first ones in the Windmill Theatre that afternoon and enjoyed the pulchritude, remembering some recent cabarets and comparing them, much to their detriment, with this polished and titillating performance. I came out eventually and wandered along Piccadilly just drinking in the atmosphere. Stopping at the window of a large store, I was joined quietly by a well-dressed, pretty girl whose stare invited some response on my part. As she moved off I walked beside her and we started to chat. We had traveled but a few yards when we crossed the road and entered Duke Street. A few yards more and we turned into an entrance [Number 29] which led to some flats. On the second floor she took a key from her handbag and opened the door to her flat. We passed through an entrance hall into a room just like the rooms in Le Sélect. Join the navy and see the world!

"Her name was Rosie [Batters preserved her discreet business card: just name, address, and telephone number] and she was Belgian. She had her own maid and a very pleasant setting for a, perhaps, doubtful occupation, but I was now committed to this form of relief and my only problem was price and quality. The price was acceptable and the quality unsurpassable, and I was later privileged to enjoy her favors any time I passed through London . . .

"I reached home eventually, now quite satisfied to sit at the fire and chat, drink tea, or visit my aging relations. My conscience didn't trouble me for having done what came naturally, as I thought it might have done." At which point, sitting guilt-free by the home fires in Scotland, Bill Batters chose to end the narrative of his sexual maturation.[24] Although he stands alone among the informants for *Sober Men and True* in his willingness to reveal his sexual initiation and early experiences with women in explicit detail, there is no reason to think that the events he describes were in any way atypical. If Bill Batters's peers had been less inhibited, many of them could probably have told stories as detailed and informative as his. The early erotic adventures of Plumber First Class Batters are narrated here in such detail precisely because they must be similar to the unrecorded sexual initiations of thousands of sailors.

Unabashed William Batters aside, what, typically, did sailors have to say about women they considered "not nice"? Portsmouth may be just the place to pursue an answer to this question. "Portsmouth used to be alive with sailors when they had the big ships . . . over a thousand men on them," recalled Arthur Ford. "You got the Home Fleet in there. Portsmouth was alive, Commercial Road, with ships, you see—with people."[25] Here it is worth emphasizing a point made by many of the ex-sailors: by no means did all men of the lower deck resort to sex-for-hire. Other options existed for those seeking recreation. "Yes, there were plenty of amenities for a sailor" in Portsmouth, remembered Albert Heron. "There were dance halls. There were an adequate supply of cinemas. There was various nightclubs, if you wanted to become a member of a nightclub . . . There were plenty of eating houses, restaurants. You name it, Portsmouth had it . . .

"I had a very good chum . . . and we made our run ashores together, and we would either have a—well, we'd have a couple of pints in whatever pub we chose . . . The Yorkshire Grey [50 Commercial Road, now 25 Guildhall Walk] was a nice quiet pub and we liked the barmaid there. She was a nice girl and it was a very pleasant pub. No rowdyism. I didn't know of any rowdyism at all. And of course it was opposite the Albert Hall [3 Commercial Road], which was a dance hall, and we were particularly fond, my friend and I—Bert Bloomfield and I—of going to dances. And the jazz age was just coming along and we liked it."[26]

Bert Heron did not seem to have any problem in Portsmouth meeting young women whom he would have identified as nice, whether it was in the pubs or as dance partners at the Albert Hall. But others had a different impression. According to Arthur Ford, respectable young women of Portsmouth had seen too much drunken, antisocial behavior by the sailors who swarmed over the great naval port to want these men as boyfriends or as potential husbands. Moreover, these respectable young women were all too aware that a sailor could be gone on foreign service for two or three years at a time. "It's not much incentive, is there, really, for a girl?"[27] That left prostitutes as the primary source of female companionship for the lonely sailor. This is how many sailors remembered that scene: "Oh *yes*, there was plenty of prostitutes! There was the ramps down right alongside the barracks down there—Drake's Drift it was called—right alongside the barracks down there . . . That was a rare old place up there. Some of the old harridans that used to be up there!" The speaker, Able Seaman Walter Basford, laughed. "Then there'd be all these girls in the pubs ashore and all that. Oh yeah, that was prevalent, that was, yeah."[28]

"Oh, there [were] plenty of pubs there, always full of sailors and prostitutes—prostitutes galore there," echoed Petty Officer Edward Pullen.

"You couldn't pass—you couldn't go to the barracks but what one woman wasn't saying, 'Want a short time, Jack?' See? Or you could sleep with her for five bob for the night. There was all that going on."[29]

If the reader will imagine himself or herself as a sailor in search of sexual adventure, the world of the Portsmouth pubs can be explored with Bert Heron as the initial guide: "I won't stamp all the pubs in Portsmouth as being dens of iniquity. No, certainly not. But in, I would say, seventy percent of the pubs, if you wanted to pick up a woman for the night, then it was quite simple. You'd be talking to your chum and someone would say, 'Oh, she's all right over there.' And it was as simple as that . . .

"They were painted ladies. They were made up like tarts, and you can tell a tart anywhere, all over the world. And, yes, I'm afraid prostitution was flounced, it was quite open in Portsmouth . . .

"Some sailors would go up and say, 'Well, would you like a drink?' And this tart would say, 'Yes,' and that would be the beginning of a romance. On the other hand you might get a tart calling over, 'Hello, Jack, how are you?'—that sort of thing—and sidle over alongside. 'What are you doing?' 'What ship are you on?' 'You just come home from so-and-so?' And she would make the conversation. And the next thing you'd see were Jolly Jack and her having their tipple and then walking off outside."[30]

Here Leading Signalman Reginald Ashley might interrupt to assert that prostitutes were the aggressors in the sexual encounters. Drink and women, "that was [the] downfall of every sailor anyway . . . They're very free-hearted when they're ashore. [Take a pub like the Pelican (186–188 Commercial Road).] You had one side sitting all these prostitutes. You had prostitutes in every pub in Portsmouth. You had to be firm with them . . . They were always in the pubs, 'cause that's—when a sailor has had a few drinks that's the time they say, 'Well, you come home with me. I'll look after you.' That sort of thing . . . You had all these women sitting down there, waiting to pounce on the sailor once he's got a few drinks and especially if he's on a ship that's just come home from abroad with plenty of money. They were the people they were after."[31]

Or Chief Petty Officer Telegraphist William Halter might speak up to point out that the women available included both "professionals" and "amateurs." Not all sailors married "nice girls," and the amateurs were hanging around the pubs, he warns, with long-term mercenary intent: "There was quite a lot of people—it seems incredible to talk like it, but—who had daughters [who would] say, 'You go out and get a sailor, my dear. You go out and find a sailor. When he goes abroad you got your [allotment] book, you know. You get your money whether he's there or whether he isn't. And you'll be certain of that, my dear.' They did. It was the ambition of quite a lot of them was to get hold of a sailor and marry him."[32]

Then Reginald Ashley chimes in to caution against going to the Albany, "the worst pub in Portsmouth," at 106–108 Commercial Road: "Every type of humanity got in there: Nancy boys and girls and prostitutes. And the Albany was always used by foreign seamen visiting the port . . . You'd go in there about seven and you'd be there till about ten and that meantime you'd be arguing the point with women, and possibly a few men as well, as to the merits of these women that are trying to take it out of you, 'cause these women never buy drinks for themselves. They come up and ask you for a drink . . . If you had any sense, you'd walk out, but if you tried to walk out, possibly some burly bloke would get hold of me and say, 'Oh no, you're not going. You're coming home with her. You've been treating her all night and leading her up the garden. You've got to go home with her.' There was a lot of that done in Portsmouth." The Albany? "Well, I wouldn't go in there meself."[33]

Two or three hours have elapsed in the pub, the number of pints consumed is a hazy memory, the bell has rung for last call, and a sailor still has not made a pick-up. Bert Heron points out that there is time to swing by the town hall, Portsmouth's number one outdoor rendezvous: "Round about eleven o'clock you'd see [the prostitutes] congregate round about the town hall. That was quite a reasonable picking up place, if I can use that word *reasonable*, and you'd see the tarts hanging around there. And you knew what they were [there] for, especially at that time of night. Young, old, indifferent, and what-have-you, they were there."[34]

Reginald Ashley speaks: "They'd come up to you and say, 'You're coming home with me for the night.' And, funnily enough, if you had a submarine cap badge on, they would charge you more, because they knew you got more money in the submarine service than the ordinary sailor did." Asked where the woman would take a sailor if she had no place of her own, Ashley replies: "[The place] where you'd go to was

Southsea Common, which at that day was a large open space on The Front. And every time a sailor picked up a girl, they took 'em down there if they couldn't go home with 'em, because that was the place where you could get away with anything."[35]

These eloquent descriptions of sex and the sailor are missing one key element: the voices of the women. Only the men speak. In the 1970s, when the energetic historians whose work made the writing of *Sober Men and True* possible tracked down and interviewed pre-1945 Royal Navy sailors, no one was interested in finding and speaking with the women of Chatham, Portsmouth, and Plymouth who had, at an earlier time in their lives, been commercial sex workers. Although they satisfied the sexual needs of uncounted hordes of sailors, no one thought to get their story—to learn their take on the tipsy, randy men of the lower deck. That window of opportunity has by now almost certainly closed, never to be opened again. History is left with only half the story.

Then, too, the distinction between "nice girls" and "not-nice women" is far too dichotomized to be believable. One has only to join Ted Pullen on a visit to a Portsmouth theater to see a short play entitled *The Girl That Took the Wrong Turning* to discover that there was a substantial gray area between the two extremes. Ted remembered the play for many years after, presumably because the values it preached spoke to something deep in his psyche or his experience: "A sailor comes home . . . He can't find his girl. And he says, 'Where's Sophie?' He got a parrot in a cage and he got his bag on his back, see? 'Oh,' they say, 'We don't know. [We've] lose her. We believe she's gone to London.' Then he's going to find her. And off he goes. And he goes to London and he's passing through different places. And all at once he can see a silhouette on the curtains, you know, of a house. And he looks. It looks like Sophie in there, see? Knocks on the door and finds her, brings her back home, you know, see? And she been carrying on. But as a British tar, you know, they forgive and forget and married the girl that took the wrong turning. Then down come the screen and our evening was finished."[36]

The multiple gray shadings of the world of sex and the sailor are also revealed by James Cox's recollections of Chatham: "If you was inclined to run after women, well, you knew all the notorious places such as Mother Knott's [188 High Street] and the Dover Castle [2 Globe Lane] and all pubs like that where you met the women you wanted to see. In fact, some of 'em [the sailors] had longstanding engagements with prostitutes, you see, were very friendly with 'em. [There were many prostitutes in Chatham], very good women, too . . . They [would] congregate in various pubs such as Mrs. Knott's—Mother Knott's—called the Long Bar, the Dover Castle, the Red Lion [145 High Street]. Oh, I forget the names of the pubs now. I can't remember the pubs. And you'd pick 'em up in the theaters. There was the Gaiety, the old Gaiety [49 High Street]. And there was the Theatre Royal [102 High Street] and Barnard's [Palace of Varieties, 107–111 High Street]. And you'd go in there and you'd sit in the back seat and you'd sit next to a girlfriend. And before long you was holding her hand, you see, or holding her knee. You see, all kind of things like that . . .

"Some of the pubs too in Chatham in those days used to have a little dance hall at the back. And you go in and have a pint and you go into the dance hall. And they was all crowded with prostitutes. But there was never no—or, I say, or very, very seldom you ever heard of a fight or a riot or anything like that over women in the pubs. You see, nearly all these girls knew somebody on the ships. They knew each other. They used to come back to 'em time after time. And I can tell you that I've found among prostitutes, the ones I knew, they were very, very good women. I mean, irrespective of their lapses of propriety, you might as well say, they were good, friendly, honest and would always help you out if you was drunk or anything like that. They'd take you home and look after you and things like that. I very seldom came across a bad prostitute in Chatham.

"And the sailors used to treat them straight. And they used to treat us straight, you see."[37]

Cox went on to tell an autobiographical story which suggests that the division of women into two separate categories was more easily accomplished thirty or forty years after the fact than it was perceptible in the smoky, noisy atmosphere of a pub at 9:30 at night. He had gone up to London from Chatham: "I was up on the booze in those days. And, although I say it myself, I was always tall, fair, and I was always clean looking, always a clean-looking young man, you see. And I was in a pub and I was drinking. And I turned round and found me glass was filled up. So after a little while I got to know who it was. And I got to talking to this girl. And I said 'Good night' to her in the end. I said 'Good night' to her and I went outside. And I was outside, just standing outside getting me bearings as to which way I should go and where I should go, when somebody come out and caught hold of me arm. She said, 'You'd better come home with me. You're not fit to walk about.' So that's all I remember about it. I remember her calling a cab. And that's it. In the morning I woke up and I was in a lovely room, sleeping in a lovely room, and I had a look around. A nice girl were beside me. And I thought to meself, 'Where the hell am I?'

"So the first thing I got up was to—I got up and felt in me pockets to see if me money was there. Never had much, of course, but what I did have was precious to us. And me money was all gone. And I thought to myself, 'Hullo, she's knocked me off.' So I turned round to look at her and was going to go for her when she turned round. She says, 'You better look in your boot as well, where you stuffed it last night.' So I'd evidently taken me money out of me pocket and stuffed it in me boot, you see?

"Now that girl I knew for months and months afterwards. I found out afterwards it was a young suffragette. She came from quite a good family. I spent many weekends with her. She paid for it all the time. And I mean it was bad principle for us as young men to take from a woman. But, as she used to say, 'I've got it. I've got an allowance from my parents.'"[38]

How much the historian wishes it were possible to conjure up this emancipated young woman—by now long since dead—and hear her memories of the affair with the handsome young sailor. One doubts that the nice girl/not-nice woman dichotomy would have had much relevance for either one of them at the time. *Eyewash!* is what James Cox would probably have called it. At the same time that Cox was having his affair with the liberated suffragette, he was also dating his future wife—a relationship that had its physical side, too.

So who was most accurate in describing the world of sailors and non-monogamous sex? Was it Albert Heron, Walter Basford, Reginald Ashley, and William Halter, with their memories of a world divided into nice girls and not-so-nice women? Or was it James Cox, for whom only shades of gray existed? Unfortunately, neither the historian nor the reader has first-hand knowledge with which to judge the accuracy of these descriptions of life in the pubs. There is much to believe and value in both pictures, but to this writer James Cox's view seems truer to the realities of the human condition and the more promising track to be followed by future historians of sailors' encounters with women.

⚓

No discussion of sailors' sexual exploits would be complete without mention of sexually transmitted disease—a source of anxiety as real in 2000 as it was in 1900. For sailors in the first half of the century, the sexually transmitted diseases of concern were gonorrhea (the clap) and the more dreaded (and potentially fatal) syphilis. Before the general use of antibiotics to treat sexually communicated disease during the Second World War there was neither effective treatment nor a cure for gonorrhea. Syphilis—if detected and diagnosed—could only be successfully treated after the German physician and medical scientist Paul Ehrlich's 1910 discovery of the arsenical compound arsphenamine, which he marketed under the trade name Salvarsan. This drug was more popularly known as *606* (it was the six hundred and sixth preparation used in a series of experiments), the name commonly used in Royal Navy sick berths.

The sailor's fear of sexually transmitted disease is captured in a story related by Edward Pullen: "I'll tell you of one man that I was friendly with . . . He courted a girl in the Tottenham Court Road . . . He was a smart chap, bit of a fighting man, now. One night he came down off . . . the upper deck, after we'd been dancing around and a bit of fun and that, see. He said, 'What do you reckon that is, Ted?' . . . He showed me his private parts, see? And on the inside part near the belly part was a black spot. I said, 'How did you get that?' He thought it was a fag end been—see? Well, it went on a bit and he got worried, courting this girl at Tottenham. I said, 'Bill, go in the sick bay. Let the doctor see it before you get too far. Don't want to worry. Let 'em see it.' He went in the sick bay and the doctor said—and he's telling me, quoting—'I'll be a father to you,' he said. 'You've got syphilis. I'll give you these injections.' [Bill] said, 'I don't believe I have, Sir.' He wouldn't believe that he'd been—I don't know where he'd gone, see.

"The doctor said, 'Well, I'll give you these pills, and if a rash don't come out on you tonight, I don't want to see you no more.' So he took it easy and that, see? When he come on the mess deck he took off his flannels then. There was the rash. Bill had syphilis. That broke him up. Smart, awful nice-looking, smart chap."[39]

For Reginald Ashley it was a visit to a sexually transmitted disease ward at Haslar, the big naval hospital at Portsmouth, that made him cautious about casual sexual encounters. While he was recovering from appendicitis at Haslar, Ashley decided to have a look around: "I'd never seen such terrible things in all my life . . . People with scars on their faces and scars all over them from the syphilis disease I think it was in those days. And they say the syphilis, you can't be cured. It produces blindness, deafness, and sometimes death."[40] With Arthur Ford the shock came at an unregulated brothel in Egypt: "In Alexandria there's a street. I think it's called Sister Street [Rue des Sœurs or Sharí as Sabá Banat]. 'Course they've all got 'em out everywhere, but that particular one—and this man . . . say this was the room—he's got a bit of a bar there, sold coffee and odd things. And you sat there and if you wanted a girl he'd call one up, see. And then behind . . . there was [a] room not so big as this. And all these girls were sitting round there rotting to death—about a dozen of 'em, rotting away. Never seen anything like it in all me life. You're not supposed to see that, I suppose. Dreadful, isn't it? That's true. They were sitting there like this, covered in sores, dreadful. I mean to say, a lot of people never seen these things, have they? But that's true what I'm telling you. Oh, shocking."[41]

Whether this experience made Ford's enthusiastic search for women more cautious and prudent he does not say. Certainly there was no shortage of sailors whom no amount of warning and cautionary example could deter. "I remember one in particular, a diver he was," said George Michael Clarkson. "And he was a real slut—a married man, too, with a couple of kids. And he was virile and he was gonna have a good time wherever he went. And he did. He always had something wrong. And I remember the surgeon commander said to him one day, 'Well . . . now you're cured once more. You've had syphilis. You've had gonorrhoea. Let me see, is there anything you haven't had? You haven't had a baby yet, have you? Now,' he said, 'I suppose you will go ashore tonight'—this was at St. Vincent—'and you'll catch something.' And he did. And he was useless. Apart from that, he deserted while we were in Alaska [in *Dauntless*]. Got a job with a diving firm. And then he came back eventually with another dose. And he got slung out [of the navy] when we came home."[42]

Clarkson's diver-shipmate was discharged, not because of his repeated cases of sexually transmitted disease, but for a broader history of unacceptable behavior, including leave-breaking and desertion. The navy's attitude, as seen from the lower deck, was that sex was a physical necessity for men. At least in the opinion of Thomas Wallace, it should have been the navy's or the civil authority's responsibility to provide risk-free sexual outlets for sailors through regulated brothels and medically inspected prostitutes, as found in many of the world's ports. In a neat transference of responsibility for any consequences of his own sexual behavior, Wallace contrasted the medically regulated sex scene in other parts of the world with London, "where you go . . . and get hold of a prostitute and get a present you didn't deserve, you didn't bargain for."[43]

Sexually transmitted disease was not a disciplinary offense. If it had been, there would have been a great temptation for men to hide its presence, with far more serious consequences for the navy's health. The organization's emphasis was on education about the dangers of sexually transmitted disease, encouragement of precautionary measures, promotion of after-the-fact prophylaxis, and medical treatment for the infected. When men with serious cases of infection could not immediately be transferred to a shoreside hospital, they were segregated in a special mess reserved for cases of sexually transmitted disease—the *Rose Cottage*, in sailor talk—with carefully regulated mess kit and other precautions designed to prevent contagion. But shipmates attached no stigma to a man's being confined to this special mess; they were more likely to feel sorry for the patients and sneak them a contraband tot of rum from time to time than to mock them or treat them as pariahs.[44]

Edgar Baker, fresh from civvy street, captured the navy's attitude—or at least the lower deck's perception of the navy's attitude—in his diary entry for January 3, 1917: "During the afternoon the whole ship's company [in *Thrasher*] had a medical inspection. The only thing that seemed to interest them was venereal disease. Afterwards the doctor gave a talk on how to avoid this disease by using a preventative (commonly called Dreadnoughts). From first to last never a word was said about behaving oneself. It was regarded as inevitable. To find what one has regarded as next to a deadly sin now considered as a physical necessity gives one a bit of a shock. On consideration, I suppose there is not a lot of choice."[45]

⚓

Able Seaman Arthur G. Adams contended that lectures about the dangers of sexually transmitted disease, cautionary tours of sexually transmitted disease wards, and veterans' stories about the horrors of being treated with mercury all combined to make young sailors afraid of women and more apt to pursue homosexual encounters. But Adams was a man with far-Left political opinions, deeply disaffected from the navy and naval life, a scofflaw often confined to cells, and a sailor who ended his naval career through desertion. When Adams wrote that "homosexuality was rife" in the navy of his day, 1911–1919, his opinion was surely colored by all the negativity he felt toward the sea service.[46] History needs less obviously biased witnesses than Arthur Adams if it is to sort out the question of homoerotic activity among men of the lower deck.

Whether homoeroticism was widespread in the navy of 1900–1945 depended on who one asked. Did former Master-at-Arms George T. Weekes have to deal with a disciplinary case of homosexual behavior during his years in the navy? "Not on any occasion whatsoever throughout my time."[47] At the other end of the opinion spectrum stood Reginald Ashley and Walter Basford. Homosexuality on the messdeck? "In the big ships, yes, quite a lot," Ashley asserted. "They used to say the carpenter's shop in the *Iron Duke* was a proper whore shop, they used to call it, you know. And all the blokes used to go there that went in for these sorts of things." "Yeah, it was prevalent," responded Walter Basford. "Well, you take perhaps a thousand men in a battleship and you don't go ashore and all that kind of thing, the sexual urge comes on, you see, yeah . . . In the nighttime, when lights out and things like that, that carried— was on quite a great deal."[48]

Other sailors were more equivocal in their responses. "How much? Some," was Arthur Ford's assessment. "It's got its quota, as the same as civilian life. It's got its quota. It's bound to have, isn't it? . . . There was quite a bit of talk about it, I can tell you that much. There was quite a bit of talk about it." But had he ever personally witnessed a homoerotic encounter? "No, I haven't actually seen any of that. No."[49]

To inquire "How common was homoerotic behavior in the Royal

Navy of 1900–1945?" is to ask a question that is impossible to answer. There are not, and there could not possibly be, any objective records from which to draw reliable statistics. Opinion is the sole historical source. When asked about the prevalence of homoerotic activity, individual sailors answer with subjective impressions—"rife," "quite a lot," "prevalent," "got its quota"—not objective assessments. Even George Weekes's apparently straightforward "not on any occasion whatsoever" is less informative than it appears to be. It was a carefully phrased answer to a specific question: Did Weekes, in his official capacity as master-at-arms, ever have to deal with a homoerotic encounter as a disciplinary offense? He was not asked if he was personally aware of any such encounters.

Homosexual encounters were a serious offense in the navy's disciplinary code—a court-martial offense, with detention barracks or dismissal awaiting the convicted defendant. But there is strong evidence that, so long as the encounters were between consenting adult sailors, many of those in authority would just as soon avoid knowledge of them. If one did not know, one could not prosecute. As Master-at-Arms Weekes himself admitted, proving a charge of homosexual behavior was no easy task: "At the time, no doubt, they're in such a secluded spot and, if [an] offense was committed like that or anything, well, they're just two and one wouldn't show the other one up. They would no doubt both deny it and have me for citing [falsely] that they were doing it. But, luckily, I never saw anything to get in that position."[50]

George Weekes makes an important point here: the obstacles to a successful conviction of two consenting adult sailors were substantial, never mind the reluctance one might feel to bring a shipmate up on so damning a charge. Bert Heron elaborated on Weekes's explanation. Homosexual activities between consenting sailors were more common than usual during Heron's service in the light cruiser *Carlisle* in China waters in 1919 and 1920, but the chief petty officers and the master-at-arms "more or less" turned a blind eye "because no one wants to be caught up in a sort of, if I can use the phrase, a *News of the World* case. You see, once you're involved in this—for example, supposing I had seen a case, first of all you've got to prove it. You see, it might be happening. You might be asleep on the upper deck or you woke up and you see this sort of incident going on. Well, unless you get up straight away and go and find a witness and then they're reported and they're actually caught doing—in this act, then of course it's a difficult thing to prove . . . It was such a serious thing.

"You can imagine, say, a petty officer being caught in the act with a boy. Well, he would immediately be court martialled, lose his pension, out of the navy, discharged—dishonorably discharged—and this, that, and the other. It's such an involvement. So I should imagine, I should imagine that people, if and when they ever saw these things happen, they didn't want to get involved and, particularly for that reason, they turned a blind eye: 'It's not my business.'"[51]

Arthur Ford summed it up this way: "There's a lot more goes on than is ever caught. Whether they turn a blind eye or whether it's somebody wants to make a case of it, I don't think the officers welcome a case being made of it. I don't think they do at all, because it reflects on the ship perhaps, you see. But of course once it's taken up by the master-at-arms it has to be gone through with, you see."[52]

Even if one cannot satisfactorily answer quantitative questions about homoerotic behavior in the navy, there is much that can be reported, on the basis of sailors' autobiographical records, about the nature and context of homoeroticism in the lives of the men of the lower deck.

In the forest of words it is easy to take a wrong path. Using the word *homosexual* when speaking about sailors can be misleading. The word typically implies a male who is heavily or exclusively determined toward sexual attraction to other males; he may embrace (and perhaps openly exhibit) a certain lifestyle and behavior culturally associated with men whose primary sexual identification is with other males. There were homosexuals in this sense in the navy, though they appear in the autobiographical records only rarely. William Batters offered this recollection from his Second World War service in the light cruiser *Danae:* "One new arrival [on board] . . . had, reputedly, been a member of 'The Splinters,' a pre-war group of female impersonators. He was a professional alright. That young fellow had more sex appeal than Mae West. Even in uniform he had it, but, when he dressed up for our concert party, the effect was unbelievable. If we had had a few more like him, it would have been a happier ship, as we would have been bound to have turned the concert party to at least once a week to see 'Les Girls.'"[53]

If their fellow sailors can be believed, most men of the lower deck were not homosexuals in the full meaning that word signifies at the beginning of the twenty-first century. As the sailor-informants saw it, typical men of the sea who engaged in homoerotic encounters did so because of the relative unavailability of acceptable female partners ashore.[54] Homoerotic encounters were especially likely to occur when a ship spent a long time on a remote foreign station. Remembering his two-year cruise in Chinese waters in *Carlisle*, Bert Heron said: "Yes, there was a certain amount of this, I suppose they call it *buggery*, going on. But that was throughout the ship in all branches and, unless you was a strong character and clean-minded and that, you could be easily drawn into this sort of thing, because you had no leave ashore and no women and what have you. And, yes, there was a fair amount of it, although I can't think of any time when anyone was caught so that they had a court-martial case."[55]

George Michael Clarkson estimated that during his First World War service in the armed boarding steamer *Suva* in the Red Sea, perhaps three boys among the thirty or so white sailors on the lower deck were actively involved in homoerotic encounters with "another half a dozen or so" adult ratings, "who would be, we'll say, the bucks." Pressed to say whether these individuals were committed homosexuals or heterosexual individuals denied other outlets for their erotic energy, Clarkson answered: "I should say that you could get men who were a little bit weak that way. They could easily overstep the mark, I think."[56]

In listening carefully to the old sailors it is possible to distinguish several different types of homosexual or homoerotic encounters. One type that is often implied but never discussed directly is that between two consenting adults on the lower deck. The historical record is, alas, silent on these relationships, and none of the informants for this book admitted to being involved in such an encounter. Neither did he detail an encounter involving men he knew personally. Fearing possible punishment, the participants would want to be as careful as they could be to avoid detection. They were unlikely to be exposed by knowing shipmates unless one or both of them had made shipboard enemies who might use such exposure as a way of striking back at, or getting rid of, the disliked individual or individuals.

Sailors have traditionally had a strong erotic appeal for shoreside homosexuals. One need look no further than the work of artists Paul

Cadmus, Charles Demuth, Emlen Etting, or Robert Mapplethorpe for ample verification. However, the only extended mention of this side of lower-deck homoeroticism comes from the recollections of James Cox, who described the theater and pub scene at Chatham: "Next door [to the theater, Barnard's Palace of Varieties] used to be a pub—I forget the name of the pub now [the Bull Inn, 115 High Street]—where the artists [that is, the theater performers] used to use. And of course we [sailors] used to get in there with 'em, you see? And, as you know, a good many of these show business artists were the chorus girls who done a little bit of sniping on the quiet, because I mean the pay in those days was very hard for a chorus girl in those days. And, if she could earn five bob or ten bob off a sailor, well and good, you see? And on top of that there was the homosexual people, you see? There was always homosexuals. You got to compare show business people with a sailor, because . . . with show business people and sailors, they're comparatively the same. They're people away from their homes. They're in a strange town and they seek the best company they can. And they seemed to gravitate together."[57]

On shipboard the straight sailor sometimes encountered the problem of unwanted advances and even the potential for homosexual rape. George Michael Clarkson retained vivid memories of his early sea duty as a young man serving in Middle Eastern waters: "And you can take it from me that I had an awful job to retain my virginity there in amongst this crowd. And the only way to do it, you *fought*—you did. I remember on one occasion, before I had been there very long, there was a fellow— he was supposed to be a bit of a tough bird—and he was a homosexual. He was after all he could get. And he went after me one Sunday. [I] remember we were living in the hold and we had a straight iron ladder to get up out of it. And it was on a Sunday morning. And he started feeling me around. And I turned round and I said, 'Now I don't want any of that, see?' 'Get away,' he said. So I promptly drew him off one and I slit his eye right across—nearly carved his eye. And then I thought, 'I'm for the chopping block now.' I flew up that ladder. I sprang halfway up it, not quick enough, and his fists came thundering in my back. Oh I thought he'd broken it. Anyhow, I got away and I nipped into the carpenter shop and locked meself in there. I had to come out at dinner time. And by then he just grinned and said, 'You little bastard, I'll have you one of these days,' see? But, as I say, you had to fight 'em."[58]

Even more difficult to deal with, because of the unequal power relationship, were propositions by officers. "I can tell you another occasion when *the captain of a ship*—" Clarkson continued: "I was taking passage on the *Northbrook* . . . to join the *Suva* when she came from Australia. And while I was there—it was an Indian Marine ship and I was working away at a bench there and I was the only white carpenter rating. There was a couple of Goanese there I remember. Now out came a naval captain to join the *Venus,* a cruiser there. And he also had to take passage for a while on the *Northbrook*. And he came round—the commander there was showing him round. And he stopped when he came to the bench. 'Oh,' he said, 'a joiner,' he said. 'I'd like a joiner on my ship. Would you care to go to the *Venus?*' And I said, 'No, I'm destined for the *Suva*.' 'Oh, you can't have him,' said the commander. 'You can't have him. He's going to the *Suva*.' 'Oh, rather a pity.'" The captain was Lancelot Napier Turton, unaffectionately known as "Shits" Turton to the lower deck. Clarkson went on to tell the story of what happened when Captain Turton joined his new command, the second-class cruiser *Venus*. It was a career experience Clarkson was happy to have missed: "The first thing he done was to send for his coxswain. His coxswain I remember was Sam Langford. A proper big bruiser Sam was. And [Captain Turton] said, 'I'd like you to muster my gig's crew.' And he mustered the gig's crew and they were all blokes with sets. 'Cor, get rid of that lot,' he said. And he had all boys and young ordinary seamen. And he even had 'em fitted out with little short briefs and everything nice. And when the ship went round to Trincomalee he used to like to take his gig's crew ashore camping for the night and all that sort of thing. He nearly caused a mutiny on there. He came out half canned one night and was addressing the ship's company. He said, 'You should think of me as your uncle,' see, and they all started raspberrying him. But luckily he died [on October 13, 1918]."[59]

However, older sailors—men in their twenties and thirties—who sought to gratify their sexual urges with the navy's boy seamen, seventeen years old or younger, stood tallest in the memories of the former men of the lower deck whenever same-sex relations were brought up for discussion. Such offenses were also the principal focus of the navy's disciplinary actions concerning sex. Inexperienced in life, away from home, in strange surroundings, confronted with the physical and psychological demands of life at sea, lonely and often hungry, a boy could be an easy target for an older sailor who lured him to a secluded spot with the promise of bread and jam. Then there was the erotic appeal of young bodies. The quartermaster's pipe "Boys muster through the bath" was almost invariably echoed, here and there, with the quip "Hands to mess for meat." The much-maligned stokers were often blamed as the principal source of such scurrilous comments, but this is probably nothing more than another case of anti-stoker prejudice. Be that as it may, it was all talk: the navy took ample precautions. Bert Heron remembered the petty officer who had supervised the baths when he had been a boy. The older, lusty sailors "daren't come within a cable's length of a boy's naked body whilst our PO was around—and HE would stay with us until the last boy was dried and dressed."

The navy's protective attitude toward the boys did not end there. Bert Heron continues: "Boys were allowed to sleep on the upper deck when you were in the tropics. You took your hammock up and laid it out on the deck. But you had to sleep on one particular side [of the deck] and also the PTI [physical training instructor] would come round at intervals and see that you were all turned in and not straying around with the older hands or, you know, this sort of skylarking business. You know, this winger business. They took a close look at that."

This winger business? What was that? Bert Heron was absolutely correct that "they"—the navy—took wingers seriously. Older seamen—in this context *older* usually meant able seamen, men with two or three good conduct badges, men in their thirties, probably—would seek to establish a mentoring relationship with a young sailor, teach him about naval life, initiate him into nautical skills, and act as his advisor and protector. The older sailor took the young man "under his wing," hence the name *wingers* for the junior member of such pairs. Bert Heron estimated that about half of the older sailors attempted to establish such mentoring relationships with the younger men. Sometimes this happened with boys, but the boy seamen were usually so well segregated by the petty officers that winger relationships were most often established when a boy reached eighteen, was promoted to ordinary seaman, and joined a men's mess.

In the abstract the mentor-winger relationship was a good thing. It was an old tradition at sea—a way for novices to move along the path to becoming skilled seamen. But the reality was that the mentor-winger relationship could become something more than a tuteeship in the lore of naval life. The best-looking young men seemed to be the ones preferred as wingers, which aroused suspicions.[60] These suspicions were strengthened by the behavior of some of the mentors toward their wingers. "It got to this stage," said George Michael Clarkson. "I can remember an older man, if he could get hold of a younger one for—what did they call 'em?—his raggy [another (and perhaps slightly pejorative) term for a winger], he'd buy him things and look after him just like a—as if it was a girlfriend. And then sometimes—I don't think anything happened between 'em—it was just that feeling that he'd got somebody who he could worship and spend all his money on and that sort of thing." "But with some elderly chaps," Bert Heron elaborated, "there was this feeling of—what shall I say?—possessiveness. When they got this particular fellow under their wing they wanted to possess him mind, body, soul. You name it—the lot!"[61]

As to possessing his winger's body, there was little opportunity for that on shipboard, although it was known to happen. But when the time for shore leave came, the mentor and his winger might head off drinking and then, as Ted Pullen put it, "What happened between [them] I didn't know." According to Bert Heron at least 30 percent of the winger-mentor relationships became homosexual affairs.[62]

Winger relationships, even if they were never physically consummated, were fraught with potential to disrupt the comradeship and harmony of the messes: "I remember a stoker PO once," recalled George Michael Clarkson, "because his winger . . . wouldn't speak to him—and somebody else had been paying him attention—and this stoker PO went and threw his own kit bag over the side with all his kit in it to get his own back. Daft things like that. You'd be surprised that men would be dafter over another man than they would over a woman."[63]

Bert Heron could top that story: "I can think of two cases where young lads were taken under the wing of elderly fellows and these young lads rather got tired of being mothered and fathered. They wanted to stretch their own wings and go under their own steam. And it caused quite a kefuffle between the two particular lads in question and the two elderlies—you know, the old salts. And there were some nasty scenes. In one case one of the elderly, you know, chaps, I think was going to stab his youngster. You know, it was a case of extreme jealousy."[64]

How did messmates view the young men who allowed themselves to become the lovers of older sailors? "They were more or less despised [by their messmates], we'll say," reported George Michael Clarkson. "But they were like tarts. They could see no shame in it or anything like that." Arthur Adams, the bitter SNLR-discharge man who claimed that homosexuality was rife in the navy—an ex-sailor whose view of naval life needs to be taken cautiously—offered this analysis: "Those who bucked authority somewhat kept clear of the elder ratings, but it was a full-time job . . . I found that the youngsters who had no spunk to talk about their conditions linked up with older ratings and became homos."[65]

There was no looking the other way when an older sailor was caught in a homosexual act with a boy seaman. In what proportions homophobia was mixed with a healthy conviction that it was wrong to exploit a power relationship for one's sexual benefit is impossible to say. To this historian it appears that the latter was the fundamental issue, even though the often-covert presence of homophobia can never be ignored. Here, as related by Chief Petty Officer Cook Reginald Willis, a second cook's mate at the time of the incident, is how Merton, a ship's corporal in the training ship *Lion*, fared when he was discovered in a homosexual encounter with a boy seaman named Smith: "The first class boys, when they finished their training, they were kitted out to go to sea. That would mean to say the clothes they'd been wearing in the training ship was all done away with and they were kitted out with new stuff to go to a ship already—some here, some there, and some somewhere else. And [Merton] was in charge of this place, what they used to call the *hat room*. And this Boy Smith was the one that was helping. He used to have him in there to help him, stow the stuff away and sort this out, sort that out. Yes, and that was the place where he was using him as a woman. And he got caught. [*Willis paused for a long time.*] Un huh, that was that. They went up before the commander of the ship or the captain of the ship. They went separately, of course. Boy Smith was the first one. He got his punishment [birching and dismissal from the navy].

"When he'd gone Mr. Merton was stood there. They took his cap off. And he took the—up in the front there, the anchor and crown on a cap ribbon—well, they took that off. Give him his hat back. They took all his buttons off. Took his first class PO [badge] off on this arm and the NP and the crown on this arm [the naval police insignia: a crown flanked by *N* and *P*]; took all that off and that. And all he had on was just his hat, coat, trousers, and boots.

"And then he was told what he was being punished for and what he was going to suffer and that he was going to be put ashore with disgrace and ignominy. And the top right-hand corner [of his Certificate of Service] in that case was cut off. [The upper right-hand corner of a Certificate of Service, the official record of a man's naval career, which he retained, carried these words: "The corner of this Certificate is to be cut off whenever it is considered that the man's antecedents and character are such as to render his re-entry at any future time undesirable."] That was that. And that was a sight that sickened me. I mean to say, I was only a youngster . . . I was only about less than a year in the navy . . .

"Every living soul in the ship was up on the middle deck or where the mizzenmast was . . . And when that was—he was led aft, took down to the steam pinnace, and sent ashore. And that was the end of him. Hardly before he got in the boat there was 'Ship's company: Attention. About turn. Dismiss.' That was that . . .

"I thought to meself, 'What's his wife and children gonna think?' Then again, I felt more for the boy than anything, because—in my opinion—the poor little devil was coerced or threatened, whichever you like, because naturally I don't suppose he didn't seem that type of boy. I knew him before ever that happened, Boy Smith. And he seemed to be a very nice little boy. *But* how nice can you be when you get hold of a swine like that that'l—going to muck you up."[66]

So far as is known, none of the informants whose diaries, letters, memoirs, and interviews have shaped *Sober Men and True* was himself homosexual or had a consensual homoerotic encounter. It may be badly misleading to try to tease out the informants' attitudes toward homosexuals and homoerotic activity from the scanty evidence, but some such attempt is demanded. All roundly condemned seduction of boys by adult sailors. The issue here was older men taking unfair advantage of youth, inexperience, loneliness, and an unequal power relationship. Bert Heron had no tolerance for homoeroticism: "In my early days [he joined the navy in 1918] there was an awful lot of sodomy in the RN—a most distasteful subject. This was ALWAYS punished by IMMEDIATE dismissal from the service—and rightly so, to my mind."[67]

Heron aside, only one informant—a hostilities-only rating from the Second World War—was openly homophobic.[68] Even in this case it is not clear that the memoir-writer's late-in-life opinions truly represent what he thought in the 1940s, and they may speak more to civilian attitudes toward homoeroticism than they do to the mindset of career ratings. George Michael Clarkson, the former long-service rating who had the most to say about homoeroticism in the navy and who, by his own account, had to resist the unwelcome advances of both lower-deck peers and officers, was more condescending than homophobic: "Well, take it this way. I suppose later on [after the repelled advances] I more or less thought to myself, 'Well, they are built that way and, in some ways, you ought to feel sorry for them.'" Walter Basford was even more blasé. Asked about straight sailors' attitudes to homosexuals and homoerotic encounters, he responded: "They knew and would just laugh about it."[69]

The lower deck's typically relaxed attitude toward, and ambiguity about, homoeroticism is captured in a song, popular in the Royal Navy, that simultaneously asserts the prevalence of homoerotic acts in the service and protests that the singer himself is, of course, a non-participant:

> Backside rules the navy.
> Backside rules the sea.
> If you wanna get some bum,
> better get it from your chum,
> 'cause you'll get no bum from me.[70]

Laughter was the key, too, in Bill Batters's take on shipboard homoeroticism. He repeated the old joke about Nelson's dying words: "Kiss me, Hardy, and make it le---, le---, le---"—the admiral dying before he could finish the sentence. Then Batters offered this exegesis of the joke: "Being deprived of women's company for long spells, messdeck conversation often refers to homosexuality . . . It is crude, a smokescreen, and means nothing."[71] Or does it? Isolated as they were in a society of men, homoeroticism may have had more appeal for some sailors than they were prepared to admit openly to messmates—or even to themselves.

One final form of evidence supporting the idea of a tolerant lower-deck attitude toward homoeroticism is difficult to evaluate, but it should not be ignored. Though it is little mentioned in letters, diaries, questionnaires, or interviews, the surviving photographic record shows that young, attractive sailors, dressed and made up as women, were a staple of shipboard concert parties. No necessary link between cross-dressing and homoeroticism is here suggested. Indeed, cross-dressing has had different cultural meanings and practical uses at various times in recent human history. But it is at least *possible* that repeated exposure to attractive men *en femme* may have conditioned some—many?—sailors to tolerate (or even enjoy) the idea of sex with another man and tempted certain of the cross-dressers themselves to think about crossing sex roles as well. If they existed, such thoughts were sufficiently taboo to ensure that they remained highly private, unlikely to be confided even to the pages of a diary. The historian can only speculate—not document.

The temptation is strong to seek an analogy between the homoerotic encounters of sailors and homosexual acts in a men's prison. On examination, however, the analogy offers little useful insight about the sexual world of the sailor—at least the sexual world of the twentieth-century sailor. Granted, most prisoners and most sailors are heterosexual by preference, although whether that preference is grounded in biology or cultural conditioning is contested ground. When prisoners and sailors seek out other men as sex partners, these typically heterosexual men are perhaps best described as *situational homosexuals*. Beyond that point the prisoner-sailor analogy breaks down. Most obviously, sailors enter the navy voluntarily; prisoners go to jails, reformatories, and penitentiaries under duress. Typically, men are imprisoned for long periods of time, without furlough, during which their sources for sexual gratification are almost wholly limited to masturbation or other men. In the first half of the twentieth century, naval ships made numerous port calls or were based in port for extended periods of time. Sailors of heterosexual preference had frequent opportunities to seek female sexual partners on shore. But perhaps the most fundamental difference between sexual encounters among men in prison and those in the navy is that the former take place under conditions of dominance (the *pitchers*) versus submission (the *catchers*). Rape and psychological and physical coercion set the tone of sexual encounters among inmates, and prison authorities are unable (and often unwilling) to protect the victimized. The situation was, by every account, far different in the twentieth-century Royal Navy. Homosexual rape was abhorrent to the navy's shared values; the naval disciplinary machinery stood ready to punish it with the most draconian of sanctions if it occurred. Similarly, any sort of psychological coercion of younger ratings by older sailors was generally reprobated and severely punished when it was discovered. Consensual sex between two adults (and perhaps between boy peers as well) is the primary theme in the story of naval homoeroticism, but it is only a subordinate (and minor) theme in same-sex encounters in prison.[72]

⚓

As they grew older and advanced in rank to petty officer or chief petty officer, many sailors were drawn more to the stability and emotional satisfactions of marriage and family than to pubs and pick-ups. Responding to these needs, they chose the marriage option.

Because of the nature of the surviving sources, it would be easy to create an overly optimistic picture of lower-deck marriages. Little about their dark side comes out in the autobiographical records, although Chief Stoker James Dunn sketches briefly some of the marital problems facing sailors in his day: "In naval ports you got a great deal of troubles between wives, men's wives that had gone off the rails while their husband was away and this sort of thing . . . Naval men at that time in my career—early career—very often married what you would call nothing else but prostitutes. We've seen 'em do it. We've know 'em that—there's been men on a ship—one man has gone and married a woman that every—half the ship has been with and we'd *know* it, but, you know, they'd be a weak-minded type. And that's happened. And then, on the other hand, you get like one chap that was away on the [light cruiser] *Curlew* with me [1923–1925] and he was sending money home—and this very often happened, that chaps'd send money home or make an allotment [of pay] to a girl, ready for getting married, and she would go and blow it with somebody else. And that's happened over and over and over again."

Charles Stamp recorded just such a tale in his First World War diary: "Court martial on [the armored cruiser] *Kent*. Three-badge AB for striking PO. Man had sent £170 to his girl. She wrote two months after and said she had spent it all (was for their home). Man went ashore—drunk—words, on returning, to PO. Sentence: ninety days cells, three badges. He had done eighteen years. Of course this knocks his pension. They always do their best to kill a man's pension and the last few years are always difficult, as faults are looked for and made."[73]

Perhaps it was one of these steaming-toward-disaster unions that John Attrill described in his diary when he wrote about a shipmate who planned to marry while on leave: "It was all the more amusing to us as we all thought he was a 'wee bit soft' and he had to borrow money to go home, and also he had no house or furniture, and I reckon a cow knew more about dancing than he knew about a woman, let alone getting married. Still we gave him a ton of sympathy, and I hope he'll soon get out of debt."[74]

These few references to naval-marriage-as-shipwreck aside, the surviving autobiographical records of lower-deck marriages all come from stable, prudent men who made choices that were apparently happy and satisfying. But even stories of enduring and strong marriages are less plentiful in the historical record than one might wish. With one or two exceptions, all that is known about these marriages comes from the male partner. Some of the old sailors were widowers when they were interviewed. In a small number of other cases wives were briefly and almost casually included in the interviews. But by-and-large the opportunity to interview lower-deck wives of the battleship-era navy was not taken up. Now that lost opportunity can never be recaptured.

The men whose marriage stories we do know in some detail all waited until they had made petty officer or were about to be promoted before they married. Saying only that much can be deceptive, though, because it suggests a mid-career maturity that would be misleading in many instances. Albert Lilley, already a petty officer, married when he was twenty-four. James G. Cox, twenty-three at the time of his marriage, was then a leading seaman about to be promoted to petty officer. Of course, not every naval bridegroom was that young. Some took more time. Officers' Chief Steward Ernest George Fox met his future wife in 1921 when he was twenty-eight or twenty-nine, but they delayed marriage until 1929, when Fox was approaching the end of his active-duty service and could be assured of desirable home-port billets for the years of service that remained.[75]

Money was a major disincentive to early marriage. "I certainly couldn't have kept a wife and did not marry whilst in the service," reported one sailor who spent fourteen years in the navy.[76] Marriage and children's allowances for ratings were first introduced in the Royal Navy as a temporary measure, called *separation allowances*, during the First World War and were not made a permanent entitlement until 1920—and then only for sailors who had reached the age of twenty-five. Before the First World War, single and married sailors were expected to live on the same pay. In the years before the marriage allowance, even for relatively well-off men such as petty officers and chief petty officers, affording marriage and a family was a stretch. For sailors earning less, it was a huge financial strain. Indeed, it was impossible unless a sailor actively pursued extra income as a member of a shipboard firm—dhobeying, tailoring, or mending shoes perhaps—or was one of the fortunate few who controlled an undetected crown-and-anchor board.

Add to the financial strain the knowledge that the navy did not provide married quarters for sailors in the home ports. Neither did it allow wives and families to follow sailors to foreign stations—and this in a time when a foreign commission to China or Latin America might last two or three years with no leave home. Imagine, too, the loneliness of separation, concern for an absent spouse's well-being—had she perhaps become pregnant on that last leave home?—and the anxieties about a wife's fidelity, sometimes fueled by guilt over one's own infidelities. Take all these factors into consideration and it is easy to understand why men of the lower deck were convinced that the navy did not want married sailors on its rolls. The Royal Navy desired single men, not ratings with loyalties divided between home and ship; the latter was seen as a job that demanded 100 percent of a man—as long as he was not an officer. Or so the lower deck appraised the situation. James Cox was emphatic: "In those days a man was not expected to marry. There wasn't such a thing as a married sailor recognized. A captain used to expect a man, when he joined a ship, to marry his ship. And that's the only wife he wants. His ship should be his greatest interest. That was the theme of most captains in the service. And if a man put in to marry, they try and stop it if they possibly could and put everything in the way. But eventually a man's got his freedom. He do as he like. But, if he did get married, he got no recognition whatever, no money whatever."[77] One could be a married sailor in spite of the Royal Navy, but not with its help.

Chief Petty Officer Telegraphist William Halter, who admitted that "my pay was fairly good compared to most people," summed up the financial and emotional predicament of the married man of the lower deck: "The two years I was in Singapore [1931–1933], when I was married, I could go down to Singapore [from Kranji, the wireless station] once a month, that's all—go down and go to the pictures and probably have a couple of stingo whiskeys in [the] Raffles [Hotel]. Once a month, that's all I could go down. I couldn't afford any more . . .

"[Because of the allotment of my pay to support my family in England, by] the time I'd paid my dues on the station, having a pint occasionally . . . and sharing a taxi or getting a taxi to go down for something and buying odds and ends that you must have, like writing paper and things, I didn't have enough money to be able to do more than one run ashore a month . . .

"I went a go at the commanding officer in Kranji about it. I said, 'Why should they give you a bungalow and have your wife and child out here and not me?' He said, 'Well . . . because I'm an officer, I suppose.' I said, 'Why should that be? I'm the technical head of this station. You're the disciplinary head, it's true. But you can go away for a couple of months and the station still goes on.'"[78]

Was the Royal Navy correct? Were married sailors really men of divided loyalties, men less useful to the navy than single men? The evidence in the autobiographical records leaves the question undecided. William Halter said that marriage and family changed his attitude toward the navy, and not for the better: "It took all the gloss off the navy, that did. I always used to say I'd never get married while I was in the navy. And from thoroughly enjoying the navy I went down to spending most of me time thinking, 'Why should this be. Why shouldn't I be at home?'"[79]

But George Michael Clarkson felt that marriage made him a better man for the navy. When he joined the aircraft carrier *Courageous* in May 1933 he was greeted by his new department head with "Oh, Clarkson, I've heard all about you." "'Oh,' I said, 'well, in what way?' He said, 'Well, you know, sometimes you don't like to come aboard to the time.

If you feel that you're enjoying yourself ashore, you stop. You're not particular about that sort of thing. I'd like to tell you that on this ship they come down on you pretty heavily for it.' . . . And I said, 'Now look, whatever I've done in the navy, if I've done wrong, I've been punished for it . . . But now I'm a married man, a respectable married man. I've got to think of my behavior. I can't afford to step over the lines.'"[80]

Both Halter and Clarkson were right—from their own perspectives. For some men being a married sailor was too fraught with stresses and conflicts to be tolerated. For others—maybe a smaller number, maybe not—enjoying the pleasures of marriage and family *and* relishing time away from that family met conflicting psychological needs. That appears to be the attitude James Cox was trying to express when he spoke about his own marriage: "If you're a married man and you've got a wife who wants you at home and you're still in love, you naturally want to stay at home and get there as often as possible. But I don't think that ever worried me, really, because I think I liked the service. I liked going about. And I married on those conditions, that if I was going on foreign service—and I always believed in Providence. I never believed in trying to maneuver my—where I should go. I used to say, 'I don't often volunteer for anything—if possible, never.' But I tried never to volunteer for anything, but go wherever I was sent. And I believed in what they used to called a wheelbarrow religion: go where you're pushed."[81]

When it came to describing the courtship that led to marriage, the former sailors provided little detail. Men of their times, they were typically reluctant to talk about the role of sexual attraction in the events that led up to marriage, let alone sex in or before marriage. Neither were the interviewers who coaxed out these life stories prepared to explore, more than superficially, sexuality in naval marriage. Call it the mores of their times; call it a sense of what was private and personal; call it inhibition: all parties to these interviews tacitly understood that there was a line they were not going to cross. James Cox was more open, in degree at least, than most of his contemporaries in talking about the role of sexual attraction in his life, both in and out of marriage. When asked how he met his wife, he responded, "Now that is a romance. I met my first wife by chance when I was a boy, when I came home from the Mediterranean, from the [armored cruiser] *Sutlej* [about January 1909, when Cox was sixteen]. I had a friend named Jack Hearn . . . His mother was lying in an asylum and his father was living on his own in a little boot shop in Hackney. 'Course, I was comfortably off. My parents had shops, you see, greengrocery shops and all like that. And I said to him, 'Well, come home and stay with me. My mother won't mind.' So I told him my mother always welcomed any of our friends. And so I took Jack home to my house.

"While we was on leave he said to me one day, he said, 'I'd like to go over and see my aunt.' I said, 'All right. I'll come with you, Jack.' So he said, 'Well, there's two girls there. My cousin is about our age,' he said. 'And she's got a friend,' he says. 'Now,' he said, 'her friend I'm going to date.' We didn't use that particular word. I forget what we used to say. 'I'm going to line her up' or something like that. And he said, 'You can have my cousin.' See, just for the holiday. Just for while we was on ten days leave. Just to pass the time away. Somebody to take out, see? So I said, 'Righto.'

"So we went over to this party. And we started playing Postman's Knock . . . Well, this girl [Alice Elizabeth Rose], who was his cousin's friend, was a very nice singer. She used to sing lovely, and sit down at the piano and play and sing. And I remember the first song I heard her sing was 'Following in Father's Footsteps,' which I sing meself at the present day when I go out anywhere, with other songs. And she'd sing all those lovely songs, you know, the old-fashioned songs which the present-day population don't like. 'In Old Madrid' and all those kind of things. 'I'll Meet You Tonight, Love,' and all that stuff. Well, anyhow, she sang. This is my friend's girl, don't forget—married after, nice-looking girl. She sang and she played the piano and that. And then we played Postman's Knock, you know, all the old stuff. And then we played Murder. And I got her in a corner somewhere and 'murdered' her. I started kissing and cuddling and all that kind of thing in the dark, you know, see? Anyhow, my chum didn't get a look in. I left him with his cousin. [*Cox laughed.*] We made an appointment. Well, we remained friends over several years before we married [during which time Cox had his affair with the suffragette and, presumably, sexual encounters with other women as well], but on and off, you know, we used to . . ." Cox's voice trailed off and both men, old sailor and interviewer, changed the subject.[82]

The men and their wives were more forthcoming about what it meant psychologically to be a married sailor. James Cox described a naval marriage at its best. Asked if the long separations put an emotional strain on the union, Cox replied: "No, I don't think so, because I always kept in— I was always a good correspondent. I always wrote my wife, letter by letter, perhaps once a week perhaps one week, twice a week next week, and so on, according to how the letters came. And we was both good writers. She could talk well. She could write well. And we didn't write a lot of silly gossip or anything like that. But we did write opinions and exchange views, things that were happening, even taste and dislike, where we went to, and all kind of thing. And we were both very descriptive . . .

"My wife and I were very well suited. We both understood each other. We never rowed or anything like that. We knew what we wanted, both of us, you see? But of course I will say this, that every man don't get the wife he wants. I've come across many difficulties with other people who I've had to sort out to 'em."[83]

But for others—perhaps for most sailors—the psychological task of sorting out a naval marriage was more challenging. With the husband/father's long absences at sea and the wife/mother's experience of having to operate and make decisions on her own, it was all but inevitable that the latter would assume the dominant role in the home and surrender it with reluctance. This can only be speculation, but it seems likely that women who wanted (or at least were not unhappy with) independence and authority in their lives, but who still wished to marry, might choose an active-duty sailor for just that reason. At least that is what Reginald Willis seemed to imply when he said, "When [women] married a sailor, they knew what to expect." Then he went on to talk about long absences from home.[84]

Many a petty officer and chief petty officer, accustomed to giving orders and having them obeyed without question on shipboard, had to learn that such behavior did not go down within the walls of his home. "I was rather a little bit of a disciplinarian, I suppose, in my way," recalled Chief Stoker Albert Lilley: "And if I happened to speak sharply to the children when I came home, Mother never used to like it. She said, 'You can talk to the men in the navy whichever way you like, but you're not talking to my children and doing that.' So I used to pack up and I left everything to Mother then, 'cause she brought them up and she brought them up well . . . But I told her, I said, 'I think sometimes you ought to

allow me just to speak to them and just tell them where they are wrong.'
But it was a way Mother had with them—she had a very good way with
them—so I let her go in the end . . . She had a will of her own, you know,
a very good, stubborn wife. And she looked after them well and brought
them up well."[85]

Yes, the most difficult thing for the sailor-father was his role as a parent—a role diminished almost to the vanishing point by his long absences. The Coxes made the arrangement work for them. While James
was away Alice put up a steady and imaginative effort to keep their two
young sons aware of their father and his role, an effort assisted by
James's ability to get home on leave fairly frequently and by his active efforts to stay involved in the boys' lives while he was away. "I used to
leave them questions to answer, see? And they used to think I knew
everything—which I do! But . . . they used to think out things and look
out things, questions that they think I couldn't answer. They'd say, oh,
'Where does the light go when it goes out?' . . . And so on like that, see?
. . . When I used to go back [to active duty], I'd leave a list of what they'd
got to do . . . I taught 'em to mend boots, for instance, sole and heel
boots. I taught 'em different things, knots and splices and all kinds of
things, you see, concreting. They always used to have to join me any job
I was doing, see?"[86]

At least by his own account James Cox was more successful at managing the role of part-time parent than most of his sailor-contemporaries.
More typical, it seems, was the experience of William Halter: "The wife
has been used to being the big noise. And she still wants to be the big
noise. And the children, they acknowledge her as the big noise of the
house. They don't acknowledge their father. You see, you've come and
upset quite a lot of their pet ideas . . . You felt that they resented your
presence. In fact, they did. They used to say, you know, 'Oh, it'll be all
right when you go back. We're all right when you're—what do you
come home for?' . . . Oh yes, it is difficult to adjust to."[87]

And, Kathleen Halter interjected, it became more difficult the older
the children grew: "They could come and go more or less as they liked
until Father came home and [said], 'Where are you going? And what
time will you be back?' And they said, 'We're not children. We don't
want to be told when to be back or tell when we're going.'"[88]

Then there was the tension between what the sailors saw as the or-
derly (male) world of the navy and the chaotic (female) world of family
living. The dialogue between the Halters, husband and wife, continues:

WILLIAM: The lack of order. I suppose Kit's heard it over and over again.
For instance, most of the women that I've come in contact with—
sisters and mothers and wives and that—and daughters—say they use
a pair of scissors to cut their nails or to cut a piece of cotton. They lay
the scissors down where they've got 'em and that's the last they have
them. And five minutes afterwards they want them and they've not
the slightest idea where they are. Ask Kit how many hours she has to
spend looking for her glasses, for instance.
KATHLEEN: I never lose anything, but I never know where anything is.
WILLIAM: And that kind of thing, after—. And I do a lot of work in the
kitchen, you see. Well, it did come to the point once when I said,
"Look, Kit, if this goes on, I shall have to leave my work in the
kitchen. I can't stand going in the kitchen and having to search round
for something, a little knife or a something." You come along and you
say, "Coo, you must be blind. There it is." You see . . .
   Oh, that proper places for the right thing[s as it was in a ship's
mess]. I'll never get over it. I'll never get out of it. I don't want to get
out of it, actually. I can go in my shed in the dark—if you ask me for a
screw of a certain size, I can go out there in the dark and I can get it.
You ask Kit where her long-range glasses are now. Do you know?
KATHLEEN: No, I went out without them this afternoon.
WILLIAM: No. There, you see?[89]

This glimpse of married life in the Halter home comes from the years
after William had retired from the navy. It reminds us that, unless they
died while in service, sailors eventually reached the end of their active-
duty careers and had to deal with returning to the civilian world. Now is
the time to follow them on that journey.

7

Traveling with an Oar on My Shoulder

If things had gone as planned, July 17, 1942, would have been Leading Telegraphist Archibald Richards's last day as an active-duty member of the Royal Navy. But a World War had intervened and he found his enlistment involuntarily extended until the war was over—and who knew when that might be? "Every day from now on will be like years—not that it hasn't been like it so far," Richards complained to his diary: "I had hoped to throw off the yoke of the Royal Navy, sever my connection completely, and wash my hands of the whole business. But, alas, here I am bound hands and foot, firmly entrenched till the end of the war—and what a navy! It was at least tolerable in the pre-1932 days, although I was always eager to get out. But now, in wartime, it's the most detestable institution I can think of. Everything connected with it is, to my mind, exactly opposed to what we're supposed to be fighting for. Well, I'm out for the first quiet job going on shore, and may it be in England, and I fervently hope that 'ere another year passes I shall be back in civvy street, an attractive and peaceful one."[1]

Whether Archibald Richards still felt that way when he was finally released in November 1945 history does not know. But the odds are that when that final day came, his mood was more like that of Edgar Baker, a destroyerman who served during the First World War: "The last night [in *Thrasher*] remains very distinct in my memory. I was really miserable. For weeks I had been doing my best to get away, but that night, as I looked round the mess and realized that I was leaving the old *Thrasher* forever, [that] I truly loved her long before that day and that I should never see any of my old pals again, I regretted my haste [to be demobilized]."[2]

Happy moment or sad, the day came when the ratings whose writings and memories are the foundation of this book—save those who died in combat—finally severed their active-duty connection with the Royal Navy and returned to civvy street.

In 1930 Able Seaman Walter Basford decided to pack it in at the end of his initial twelve-year enlistment: "Yeah, I'd had enough of it . . . I'd done twelve years, and I thought to meself, 'That's enough for any man, in that line anyhow.' 'Cause the discipline was so rigid the whole time, that when you were free it was just like, you know, breathing again sort of thing, yeah. You didn't have to stand to attention when you walked by a policeman or anything like that—or salute him."[3] Discharge papers in his pocket, Basford headed out the gate of the Portsmouth dockyard for what he hoped was the last time, only to be stopped by the guard on duty: "Where's your pass?" (A man had to be rated leading hand or petty officer before he could leave the yard without a pass.)

"Do you think I wants a pass with these?" Basford flourished his discharge papers.

"Oh Christ! Go on."

Basford's first stop was a nearby pub for a couple of pints. Those downed, he walked on, past the Portsmouth and Southsea railway station, along Raglan Street to Number 31, The Raglan, his favorite Portsmouth pub, where he was enthusiastically welcomed by the publican: "There he is, home from the sea! Go on." More pints—then a room for a couple of weeks. Basford's parents had both died while he was in the navy and he was at loose ends. He needed time to get his land bearings. Besides, he had £63 in wartime prize money and pay in his pocket, and that dulled any sense of urgency.

But soon enough reality began to intrude. The vacation at The Raglan had to end, and thirty-year-old Walter Basford needed to decide what to do with the rest of his life. He chose to return to his roots, to the place he knew, to Southampton. There he took a room, paid a month in advance, hung out a bit, and then noticed that the £63 was fast dwindling toward zero. Time to find work! Basford did one or two pick-up assignments for a builder, who then asked him if he would like a regular, full-time job as a painter. Absolutely. In this way Basford's civilian career was decided upon. He worked as a painter for various builders around Southampton for many years, then decided to set out on his own as a painting contractor, but with only mixed success.

This is, however, getting ahead of the story. Back in 1930, when Walter Basford came home to Southampton to resume civilian life, he met his future wife almost immediately. They dated—nights out at the theater and things like that—but not for long. In 1931 they married and soon thereafter began a family that eventually numbered six children and many more grandchildren and great-grandchildren.

Did Walter Basford find it hard leaving the navy and adjusting to civilian life? "No," he replied, "because, you see, when you first come out of the navy like that into a new life—I didn't know this life, civilian life, not as a boy very well, but I—everything to me was new and there was always something to occupy my mind at the time, so I didn't feel like, you know, lost or anything like that. And I was always a bloke that could put me hand to anything pretty well . . . I was always a sort of a bloke, you know, that [could] push along a bit. I wasn't lost at all. I accepted things as they came, like, you know, and took what opportunities that came along . . . I was a big, tall, strongish kind of a lad, like, you know, a chap then, and I could adapt meself to things . . . You always got your ups and downs, you know, in civilian life, same as you did in the navy. There was always times when you're in civilian life when you're up in the air, you know—pocket full of money. Then perhaps you'd go a week and have nothing; and things like that, you know, till you can get another job."[4]

Chief Petty Officer James Cox always knew, somewhere deep down, that when he left the navy he would rejoin his father's businesses—still based on Turner's Road, but now managed by three of James's brothers and grown into George Cox & Sons, Bonded Carmen, Motor Haulage and Removal Contractors, Wheelwrights, and Motor Body Builders, an operation with forty employees. But when Cox retired on his pension in 1932, he resisted the inevitable for a while. He really wanted to go into electrical work, preferably in a power station, but the best he could do was an offer of work as a jointer with the London Electricity Board. The trouble with the job was that he was expected to help in digging up the cables: "And that didn't suit me. I said, 'I've never done digging in my life and I'm not going to start at the age of forty.'" Frustrated in his power-station ambitions, Cox joined London's Metropolitan Police Force for a few months; however, the family pull was getting stronger. When James first came out of the navy and was looking for a permanent job, his brothers had employed him in various short-term assignments as a driver and a laborer. In the end they got him back full time, in the over-the-road end of the business: "I liked the job—road transport at that time . . . I liked going out with them. I liked the free atmosphere. And I liked the power, too, because I was one of the firm, you see?" James's wife, Alice, fought the idea of his being drawn back into the family business as a lorry driver: "You're worth something better than that." "Well, I'm going to stick it for a time anyhow. It's a cert job," James replied. Soon he was working in the family garage, where the firm built and repaired their own lorries. Then one day one of James's brothers said, "I think you'd better come into the office. You can handle this office [work] better than we can." His brothers had occasionally left James to mind the office in the afternoons. "While I was there I used to get the books out. I was a little bit more quicker on the books than what they were." And so James Cox moved into the office permanently, became general manager and a director of the family business, and earned in the 1930s and 1940s a typical yearly income of about £1000. After the Labour government nationalized George Cox & Sons in 1949, James, then in his late fifties, took up managing a pub, an occupation he pursued until he was seventy-five, when he finally retired from his third career—still voting Conservative, as he had all his life, and complaining about the money he had lost under Labour's compulsory nationalization.[5]

When Petty Officer Edward Pullen retired from the navy in 1926 he settled in the Poole area, his wife's home. He came out during tough times, when it was "awfully difficult" to get work. At least that is how Ted remembered it in the 1970s. His actual experience was not so grim, however. In Wareham they were advertising for ex-sailors to do overhead electrical wiring. Ted applied. "Leave your name and address. We will be in touch." Before he left the navy Pullen had taken a pre-discharge vocational training course as a professional driver. In Bournemouth the Royal Blues, a motor coach line, was looking for bus drivers for the summer holidays. Pullen went and saw the boss. "Yes, we've got a bus going to London on such-and-such a day. I'll send for you." Then there was the so-called floating bridge at Sand Banks—actually a chain ferry across the narrow entrance to Poole harbor. A skipper was needed for the ferry.

"I'm only taking navy men on here," said the man doing the hiring.

"Well, I just done twenty-five year there."

"Where's your papers?" Pullen showed him.

"How much a week do you want?"

Pullen paused. He had heard that the pay was only thirty shillings a week. "Two pound ten."

"Leave your name and address."

Then on the same day—at least that is how Ted Pullen remembered it—three telegrams arrived offering him the three jobs. He was at his father-in-law's house, helping with some construction. "Which would you take?" Ted asked his father-in-law. "Well, you been used to the sea. I should take the bridge." That is just what Edward Pullen did, and he held the job for twenty years. Whenever there were openings at the floating bridge—ticket collectors and jobs such as that—he tried to help ex-sailors get the positions. They were fellow navy men, and—his own job-finding experience to the contrary notwithstanding—Pullen remained convinced that former sailors competed at a disadvantage with civilian applicants in the world of work when jobs were scarce.[6]

Was Edward Pullen correct? Were former ratings at a disadvantage when it came to finding jobs in civvy street? As with much else concerning the old sailors, the answer depended on whom one asked. Sailors who ended their active-duty naval careers during economic slumps could encounter truly rough times. "Pretty terrible" was the assessment of Officers' Chief Steward Ernest Fox of the experience of retiring in 1932, right into the worst of the Depression: "There's 5000 unemployed in Portsmouth. I couldn't get work." For twelve months Fox and his family eked out a living on his pension until his naval connections finally landed him a job as a club steward at Exmouth.[7] Others had it worse yet. "Yes," said former Yeoman of Signals Phillip Jenkins, "I was one of [those ex-sailors who could not find decent jobs] for years. There were three million unemployed in 1931. Irish and North Country were pouring into London at that time." "I think I could write a book about that maudlin period between the wars," recalled former Able Seaman Thomas Thompson.[8]

Everyone recognized the special handicaps imposed by hard times, but some former sailors were more analytical about who did or did not find work easily. Electricians, ship's writers, telegraphists, and sick-berth attendants came out of the navy with training and experience that were more or less directly transferable to civilian jobs. "*My trade* can always get work (electrician)," was Leading Electrical Mechanic Kenneth Oke's terse but optimistic assessment. For gunners, seamen, and stokers it was a different story. "Most of my training consisted only in the art of how to destroy, how to kill," lamented Alan Pitt, a seaman gunner. Such men might be looking for work for a long time when the economy was bad. At least one ex-rating thought that former soldiers and marines had a leg up on sailors when it came to finding a civvy-street job: "Their smart appearance qualifies them for commissionaires at large hotels and banks. These are really good jobs which needed looking after. Also warders at prisons, etc. A matelot['s] chance is secondary to others." Chief Petty Officer Arthur Crosby thought that navy men "were inclined to aim too high and, because of inexperience, were unable to give satisfaction to their employers. This situation gets known. If one feel[s] very capable and can pass exams (as always) there is work for them. Non-tradesmen find it rather hard. Common sense is a big factor in this one."[9]

But most ex-sailors were more upbeat about the experience of transferring from guaranteed employment in the Royal Navy to the more problematic experience of finding and keeping work in a world of civilians. "It usually helped, knowing one had been in the navy," Chief Petty Officer James J. Eames commented, echoing Ted Pullen's experience at the floating bridge. This assessment especially applied to the many kinds of civil service employment open to former naval men, whether that employment was in the Post Office, the Inland Revenue, the Admiralty, the London Fire Brigade, or in government work abroad in one of the colonies or protectorates. "I joined the colonial service and did fourteen years in Zambia with the Ministry of Labour and got the appointment partly because I was ex-RN," reported Chief Ordnance Artificer Leslie Nancarrow.[10]

Others, equally successful in the transition to civilian life, had a different take on the relationship between former naval service and finding employment in civvy street. "Did sailors have trouble getting decent jobs in civilian life?" a questioner asked Chief Petty Officer Ronald Watts. "Provided they 'forgot' the navy, no difficulties at all," he replied. Chief Petty Officer Roland Purvis provided the exegesis to understand—if, in the end, partly to contradict—Ronald Watts's cryptic statement: "Once [former sailors] left the naval ports they became disciplined civilians, with a dedication to the works, and were always welcome[d] by employers. The difficulties [in finding civilian employment] were experienced in naval dockyard ports, where sailors were at a premium. When I was a young sailor, the Fleet saying was 'I will travel with an oar on my shoulder and when someone asks what it was, there will I stay and anchor and [seek] to find work.'" And Chief Purvis's own experience in applying this saying? "The first six months of retirement the UTTER LONELINESS of civilian life was chilling," he admitted, "but when you found that civilian works were run on service routine, then you were at 'home' and soon became a CPO of the working class."[11]

Forget the navy. Could they—did they—really? Many a sailor was of the same mindset as Walter Basford: happy to be out of the navy and done with that way of life. The self-disrating former yeoman of signals who earlier described how his decision to join the navy had been a terrible mistake based on a lack of self-knowledge finally arrived home for good one evening late in 1950. Came time for bath and bed, and "I did what I had been promising myself for years: instead of struggling to take my jumper off over my head, I tore it down the front and took it off as if it was a coat."[12] (Even in these two cases the Royal Navy was still very much a part of who both men had become and was less easily discarded than the uniform jumper. Basford recorded a five-hour interview about his sailor days in 1975, and the former yeoman of signals wrote a 112-page memoir entirely devoted to his life in the navy.) For others it was a sad parting with a life they had come to love—the best years of their lives (at least in retrospect) and something they never got over. "Well, yes, you miss the shipboard life, really, after twenty-two years," said Ernest Fox, speaking as a man of eighty-three in 1976. "See, you're bound to miss that association with the sea, aren't you? I mean, I still do."[13]

For Leading Stoker Richard Rose the sense of loss was more intense than it was for Fox: regret for a life he had never really wanted to abandon. Rose left the navy prematurely in 1920 because his wife's emotional illness demanded his presence at home. He was, in a way (he said), glad to be home, but "a little bit sad in leaving the navy. It got into my blood then, and ever since then I've always had that yearning . . . I couldn't get used to civilian life . . . I think [I had] the wanderlust, I think more than anything. I think the spirit of adventure hadn't left you and was one of those things that, I don't know, [no matter] how old in life, you always wanted to do something adventurous. And I felt I hadn't seen all I wanted to of the world. The moment a chance came to see the world [because of the end of the First World War and the resumption of distant-seas cruising by the navy], I came out of the navy. You couldn't see it during the war. And the farthest I went during the war that way—east—was Port Said . . . And whenever I got a chance—Navy Week was down there—the wife will tell you, I dragged her down there and her sister. But I still do it, you know. Warship to me is still home. I mean, I'll watch a warship on the television there . . . and I'm home . . . You seem to associate [with] each other [in the navy] as totally different persons than you do in the outside life. You don't feel antagonistic towards anyone . . . [In civvy street] you're climbing on top of each other to get somewhere, where in the navy it didn't seem that way."[14]

Leading Signalman Reginald Ashley added his own fervent *Amen* to Rose's last point: "I found difficulty in finding friends, making friends [outside the navy]. Great difficulty. I could never seem to get the same companionship outside the service I did within . . . I think the comradeship you get in the service is something out of this world. I mean it doesn't seem to, well, be on a par anywhere."[15]

No matter how far they carried that oar, the ex-sailors never really forgot the navy. When asked about the negative aspects of their naval experience, the men responded with answers that seem, on first reading, as individual as their colorful personalities:

"Can be very unhappy if unlucky to be drafted to a low-character crew."

"Just being IN."

"The bullying and childishness of some of the ratings."

"At times wasted years—like for me—nearly three years on the Red Sea patrol—mostly a matter of showing the flag. There is no place on the Red Sea worth going on shore. Aden perhaps, on the few occasions we called there."

"Seasickness."

"Always returning from leave. That awful feeling as the train entered Portsmouth station. The patrol waiting to check that you had a liberty ticket. I don't think anyone really liked the navy. It was a living of a kind, and when you had completed the first twelve [years], you signed on for the next ten to get something back in the way of a pension."[16]

But on a careful reading the ex-sailors' negative evaluations begin to sort themselves into three broad categories of complaint, all of which a wiser and less tradition-bound Royal Navy might have ameliorated.

The least common of the three major complaints was the slowness of promotion to petty officer and chief petty officer and the almost absolute inability to advance to officer rank, no matter how capable a sailor might be.[17] Then there was the range of frustrations that should be placed under the rubric *Irritations, big and small, of a military life.* These might be stated as "too much saluting and standing to attention" or "morning divisions and evening quarters." Perhaps the complaint was about "the odd 'lunatic' officer that one always finds on a ship and one always manages to come under." Or it might be expressed as "lack of home comforts"—more bluntly, bad food and bad accommodation— and most tellingly as loss of freedom. This might be called "not being able—or, I should say, not allowed—to use one's own mind; everything according to rules and regulations—all things prearranged." Or it might be identified as "never being able to plan ahead, as drafting [to a ship] could knock a hole in all the best-laid plans." In either case it added up to forfeited freedom to do as one pleased and thought best.[18]

By far the single most common complaint about naval life was the long foreign commissions: two and three years (and occasionally longer) away from home, with no extended leaves and (for the married) no opportunity for one's family to follow to a distant foreign station, although there is evidence that some PO and CPO wives did join their husbands at Mediterranean bases such as Malta. The worst liability of naval service was "being away from family life." In this lament the sailor voices are a mighty chorus: "Being up to 10,000 miles away from everything and everybody you had been brought up with." "Saying 'Bye-bye' to loved ones . . . The navy never ever had married accommodation for lower deck [on] foreign stations." "Separation. Two-and-a-half years abroad not much fun. Come home and a month's leave flew by." "In my day being separated from my family for long periods such as two-and-a-half year[s] in China, etc. Nowadays it's a piece a cake with butter both sides." "As a married man too long away on foreign commission—

wrecked many marriages." "Long separating from home and relations. Seventy-five percent of service was foreign, two-and-a-half years on most station[s] and three years on China station. As a single man this suited me. I would volunteer to take the place of a married man."[19]

Add to this the not-infrequent allegation that some men did an unfair share of difficult foreign service during their years in the navy while others managed to secure snug assignments close to home. "I DID have cause to complain" about excessive foreign service, asserted Chief Petty Officer Albert Heron, who was still angry forty years after the fact, "when I found myself being sent abroad AGAIN, having only had three months at home after serving foreign for two and a half years! Then, to my amazement, I was sent abroad AGAIN when I should have been sent to the HOME FLEET, and on this occasion I spent THREE and a HALF YEARS in the destroyer *Delight* on the China Station—from February 1932 [to] January 1936!!! The excuse given me when I saw the captain (the fifth captain during the commission) was 'Regret NO Portsmouth relief available.'"[20]

Memories of the best aspects of life in the navy initially appear highly individual, too: "A healthy life." "From a sixteen-year-old boy to a strong all-round athlete." "A man's job . . . A man's life"—concepts unfortunately not elaborated by these two former ratings. "The chance I got to learn all things, educational and professional." "No pressures of a job card or the bottom line in the ledger." "A great respect for the sea. The loveliness of dawn, of sunrise and sunset. The clear bugle call of the R[oyal] Marines at the ceremony of sunset echoing across the harbor."[21]

But here also a close reading reveals patterns in the responses. Two minor themes stand out: the security gained through being a member of the Royal Navy (an assured job, regular pay, food, clothing, and a pension on retirement); and, more important to most ratings, a sense of pride in the work they were doing and in doing it well:[22] "Giving an order that would be carried out to the T. Receiving an order that would be carried out to the T." "In the war years doing a good job for England." "I was aware I was in the finest navy in the world."[23]

Anyone who has listened attentively to the old sailors up to this point will have no difficulty guessing the two things that most former ratings held to be the best aspects of their years as members of the Royal Navy. Alan Pitt spoke to one of these: "Seeing the world, its people, its customs. The sea itself, its moods, its changes. The free, open-air life. Never in the same place very long. Sailing into a new port; exploring the place; leaving and sailing home again to 'See the other seas we've never seen.'" Leslie Nancarrow shared this opinion, instancing his desire for "travel, which I love but couldn't otherwise afford." "Well, I suppose seeing different countries of the world," echoed Armorer Petty Officer Arthur Lewis. "I did two-and-a-half years in Mesopotamia in river gunboats during [the] First World War on the Euphrates and Tigris rivers, visited Baghdad [and] traveled through India four times . . . I went out to China on HMS *Carlisle* from 1919 to 1921. I visited Vladivostok in Siberia, and we were frozen in for three months after we got in harbor, and of course that was during the revolution in Russia, but we got on with the Russians very well. They treated us with respect. We paid visits to Shanghai in China, Tokyo, Nagasaki, Kyoto, Yokohama in Japan."[24]

These three old sailors spoke for many other former ratings in citing the opportunity for travel and for wider personal horizons as one of the two best aspects of being in the navy. But there was a positive aspect of naval service that was mentioned even more often than travel to foreign lands with their strange peoples and customs: *comradeship*, that is, loyalty to, and fellowship with, messmates and shipmates. The point is central to understanding the enlisted experience. To miss this is to overlook the key that is essential to unlocking the lower-deck world. The former ratings testify best to comradeship's vital role as they crowd onto the stage to speak: "You served with men who were men and acted as such at all times. No petty squabbles that I found when I joined civvy street." "There is no one like a naval man. I mix with no one other than that even today. And I know them before they speak." "It was the men of the lower deck that I missed [after I was invalided out] and shall always remember. They were great fellows . . . They were true comrades, always ready to help one another." "Lack of humbug, good companionship, cleanliness, straightforward dealings, and team spirit. With these assets hardships became easyships." "The marvelous comradeship and lasting loyalties one encountered. So deep a feeling among pals that could never be understood by a landlubber." The best thing about naval life? "Laughs and tears—but more laughs—comradeship." "A great brotherhood of men which you never experience in civilian life."[25]

When they were asked what personal assets they took away with them

at the end of twenty-two or twelve or some lesser number of years of active-duty service, two of the old sailors' answers stood out strongly.
First, naval discipline had instilled a strong habit of self-discipline—a
decided advantage in personal life and in the civilian workplace. Walter
Basford, the seaman-turned-builder's painter, reported that, because of
his Royal Navy experience, "I could adapt meself to things. And to do
things that wouldn't irritate me, after the discipline I'd had, you know,
where blokes—perhaps the builder would say 'Well, go on up there and
paint all round that guttering up there.' And he [the bloke] would say,
'*NNNNNNN!* Blimey! I got to do that again.' Where I wouldn't. I'd go
on up and do it. I was amenable to discipline, you see."[26]

The second great benefit which former ratings perceived from naval
service was a broadened and more enlightened outlook—cosmopolitan-
ism and, yes, sophistication gained from their experience of other places
and different cultures. They found they possessed an absolute feeling of
superiority over their stay-at-home civilian peers: "When I worked at
the colliery [after leaving the navy], their outlook was completely paro-
chial. It was the only thing they [knew] or could talk about. They had
never been anywhere else."[27]

Chief Petty Officer Telegraphist William Halter explained that sense
of superiority in more detail: "The type of men outside the service in all
the places I worked in are nothing like of the standard that naval men
are. All the while I was in the service I was like most naval men. I
thought we were rather inferior beings compared to the people in civilian life. But when I came out and worked with them, no. It's entirely, absolutely the other way . . . For one thing [the] moral status of the men
had disgusted me. Whatever you've heard about the navy, and I know
the navy [has a reputation for profanity and obscenity, but it's nothing
compared to civvy street.] The language! I said to one fellow in the beet
factory [where I worked after leaving the navy] one time, I said, 'Blimey,'
I said, 'you're always on about the Royal Navy.' I said, 'You know what
they'd do with you in the Royal Navy?' I said, 'They'd get you on the
upper deck and they'd put a deck scrubber through your mouth and
then pitch you over the side if you came out with anything like that in
front of them.' And then their loyalty. There isn't the loyalty among
workers outside that there is in the navy. I mean, they'll cut each other's
throat for an hour's overtime, won't they? I don't know if you've run
into it, but I have."[28]

"Oh yes, I've got a pension," said Joiner First Class George Michael Clarkson, who as a young boy had known acute hunger and unheated living spaces after his mother's death and for whom the promise of future financial security was a major motivation to join the Royal Navy. "I also . . . learnt to be—I was disciplined for one thing . . . Then again, if I hadn't gone in the navy, I should have been like some of the village idiots where I came from, who've worked, who've been born, gone to school there, stayed there, and go to work and know nothing. They talk about nothing. Now I've spent a lot of time in the Mediterranean and I've been to [the] Riviera. And I've been all [through] Palestine. I've been to India. I've been to Ceylon. I've been right from Alaska down into the antarctic. I've been all up one side of America and down the other."[29]

"Do you think you were better off in the navy than you would have been in civvy street?" a questioner asked Bert Heron. "A very difficult question, really," Heron replied. "However, I THINK, looking back over the years, I never would have been so happy and contented as I have been in the navy—nor would I have seen the world twice over at the public's expense. I always had itchy feet—that is, wanting to be on the move—so WOULD I have settled for a monotonous job at the bench or sticking on labels all day? I doubt it. Neither would I have been given a 'reasonable' pension at forty, having served for twenty-two years in a factory."[30]

When Bert Heron exits, the last old sailor left on stage is Mechanician First Class Raymond Dutton, who served between 1934 and 1946. He speaks best the sailors' final evaluation of lower-deck life in his memoir, "What! No Isambard? or, A Sort of Autobiography": "I felt then and still do now that I owed the [navy] a debt for taking me out of the rut of the depressive years of the 1930s [and] transforming me from a rather shy and introspective individual who had no real aim in life except to make the most of what I had—which wasn't much! I was taught discipline, a trade, and a pride in achievement. I enjoyed comradeship to a degree I believe unavailable in any other walk of life. I was fed, clothed and housed, and traveled to many parts of the world that I otherwise would never have been able to visit . . .

"A present-day recruiting leaflet proclaims: 'Everybody's somebody in the Royal Navy.' That was as true in my day. *King's Rules and Admiralty Instructions* was the bible upon which your life revolved around.

One knew exactly the consequence of any transgression or meritorious behavior. There was always an answer—you might not have liked it—but it was decreed . . . Promotion wasn't gained by fear or favor, but by examination and honest endeavor . . .

"In case it appears that my nostalgia verges on smugness and sentimentality, I would add that it was not all sweetness and light. Many times I felt lonely, afraid, bored, homesick and seasick, but never to the extent that it seriously affected my desire to serve in what I regarded as a privileged fraternity."[31]

To which this historian, seated in the audience and having heard all the former sailors speak their lines, can only reply: "Righto!"

⚓

Sober Men and True is an essay in the fundamental meaning of that word: a trial or an attempt. It is one historian's interpretation of the autobiographical records created by more than eighty sailors who served in Britain's Royal Navy between 1900 and 1945. Far from being the last word on this subject, *Sober Men and True* is intended to contribute to, and perhaps help to shape, historians' ongoing exploration of the lives of the naval working class: sailors. If it provokes informed disagreement and debate, whether polite or acerbic, and if other historians carry on the story from here, many of my primary goals will have been accomplished.

More and different types of Royal Navy personnel records will be released for study within the next few years. These will permit other kinds of questions to be asked and answered—questions which demand for their resolution documents not now available for research. Additional sailor letters, diaries, and autobiographies will be deposited in libraries and archives. The life stories they tell may justify revisiting some of the ideas I have proposed. Every chapter of this book offers subjects that deserve fuller investigation: social origins of naval sailors; desire for upward mobility into the officer class—and the experiences and life-satisfaction of those who did succeed in making the climb; health threats inherent in naval life and sailors' attitudes in the face of those threats; lower-deck homoeroticism; naval marriages; and managing family life on the pay of an absentee husband and father.

Then, too, fundamental psychological questions remain on the table.

Are seafarers typically irreligious? And, if this is so, why? For another, sailors occasionally spoke of their naval experience as *a man's job* or *a man's life* or said they had *served with men who were men and acted as such at all times.* But the 1970s, when the former sailors were completing questionnaires or participating in oral interviews, was not a time when comments such as those automatically provoked probing follow-up questions concerning perceived gender roles: What is it about naval life that makes it a man's world? What does it mean to say one *acted as a man?* If the former ratings could have imagined a twenty-first century navy in which women serve at sea alongside men, they would surely have had some things to say that would have illuminated their understanding of what it meant to be a man. I have been unwilling, on the basis of the fragments of evidence I saw, to imagine what the old sailors might have said. Others may be bold enough to tease out the concept of the ship and sea as a man's world from casual references in sources that I encountered and others which I overlooked.

What about the public's conflicting images of the sailor? The sailor was the heroic icon of the poster, the china figurine, the postcard, and the cigarette box—not to mention those ubiquitous sailor suits for boys. These valorizing icons coexisted in time and the public consciousness with the image of the real-life sailor as someone to be treated with aversion: illiterate, foul-mouthed, hard-drinking, and over-sexed—perhaps even involved *sexually* with other men! How did these conflicting images influence the way the sailor saw himself? Did he modify his public behavior because of an expectation of how sailors were supposed to act?

Many navies and several centuries of naval seafaring are open to investigation. Much remains to be accomplished before full justice has been done to the histories of the people of the naval lower deck.

Appendixes

Informants for *Sober Men and True*

Abbreviations

Notes

Acknowledgments

Index

⚓

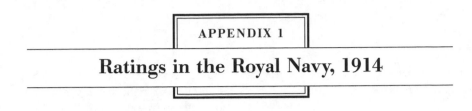

Ratings in the Royal Navy, 1914

This list, adapted from *The King's Regulations and Admiralty Instructions for the Government of His Majesty's Naval Service*, vol. 2 (1914) (London: Eyre and Spottiswoode, 1914), pp. 234–304, is intended primarily to assist readers in identifying ratings mentioned in the text and understanding the relationships among them. Those who wish to learn more complete details about these ratings and changes in them over time should consult this and subsequent editions of *The King's Regulations and Admiralty Instructions*.

Military Branch

Seaman

Chief Petty Officer	Boy, 1st Class
Petty Officer	Boy, 2nd Class
Leading Seaman	Sailmaker
Able Seaman (A.B.)	Sailmaker's Mate
Ordinary Seaman	

Signal

Chief Yeoman of Signals	Signalman
Yeoman of Signals	Ordinary Signalman
Leading Signalman	Signal Boy

Wireless Telegraphy

Chief Petty Officer Telegraphist	Telegraphist
Petty Officer Telegraphist	Ordinary Telegraphist
Leading Telegraphist	Boy Telegraphist

Engineer Branch

Engine Room Artificer (E.R.A.)

Chief Engine Room Artificer, 1st Class	Engine Room Artificer, 3rd Class
	Engine Room Artificer, 4th Class
Chief Engine Room Artificer, 2nd Class	Acting Engine Room Artificer, 4th Class
Engine Room Artificer, 1st Class	Engine Room Artificer, 5th Class
Engine Room Artificer, 2nd Class	Boy Artificer

Stoker

Mechanician	Acting Leading Stoker
Chief Stoker	Stoker, 1st Class
Stoker Petty Officer	Stoker, 2nd Class
Leading Stoker	

Artisan Branch

Electrical Artificer

Chief Electrical Artificer, 1st Class	Electrical Artificer, 3rd Class
Chief Electrical Artificer, 2nd Class	Electrical Artificer, 4th Class
Electrical Artificer, 1st Class	Acting Electrical Artificer, 4th Class
Electrical Artificer, 2nd Class	

Armourer

Chief Armourer	Armourer's Mate
Armourer	Armourer's Crew

Carpenter and Shipwright

Chief Carpenter's Mate	Boy Shipwright
Carpenter's Mate	Leading Carpenter's Crew
Shipwright	Carpenter's Crew

Blacksmith, Plumber, Painter, Cooper

Blacksmith
Blacksmith's Mate
Painter, 1st Class
Painter, 2nd Class
Cooper

Plumber
Plumber's Mate
Second Cooper
Cooper's Crew
Boy Cooper

Miscellaneous

Sick Berth

Chief Sick-Berth Steward
Sick-Berth Steward
Second Sick-Berth Steward

Sick-Berth Attendant
Sick-Berth Attendant (Probationer)

Naval Schoolmaster, Writer, Ship's Steward

Naval Schoolmaster
Chief Writer
First Writer
Second Writer
Third Writer

Boy Writer
Ship's Steward
Second Ship's Steward
Ship's Steward's Assistant
Ship's Steward's Boy

Police

Master-at-Arms
Ship's Corporal, 1st Class

Ship's Corporal, 2nd Class

Cook

Chief Ship's Cook
Ship's Cook
Leading Cook's Mate

Cook's Mate
Second Cook's Mate

Officers' Steward and Cook

Officers' Chief Steward or Cook	Officers' Steward or Cook, 3rd Class
Officers' Steward or Cook, 1st Class	Boy Servant
Officers' Steward or Cook, 2nd Class	

In addition to this basic system of ratings there were numerous "non-substantive" ratings such as Diver, Gunlayer, Seaman Torpedo Man, and Physical Training Instructor. Conferral of these ratings typically required a man to have attained a particular rate and received prescribed special training. Thus Seaman Torpedo Man was "open to A.B.'s and Leading Seamen only. Must have passed in Torpedo in accordance with the prescribed course of instruction in the Torpedo Schools, and at the end of every 3 years (or as soon after as opportunity offers) must re-qualify in a Torpedo School." Non-substantive ratings did not modify the basic rank structure outlined above, but they did confer extra pay. The Seaman Torpedo Man earned three pence per day in addition to his regular pay. For a complete list of the non-substantive ratings, the qualifications required, and the extra pay awarded, see *The King's Regulations and Admiralty Instructions*, vol. 2 (1914), pp. 289–304.

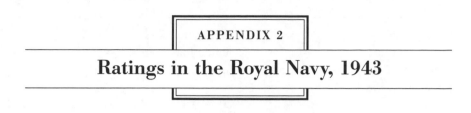

Ratings in the Royal Navy, 1943

Adapted from *The King's Regulations and Admiralty Instructions for the Government of His Majesty's Naval Service*, vol. 2 (1943) (London: His Majesty's Stationery Office, 1944), pp. 150–151, to show the principal changes in the structure of ratings since 1914. Ratings that remained the same as they had been in 1914 are not included. Listed are the principal new ratings that had been introduced since 1914 and older ratings, the names of which had been significantly changed.

Sailmaker

Chief Sailmaker
Sailmaker

Sailmaker's Mate

Mechanician

Mechanician, 1st Class

Mechanician, 2nd Class

Ordnance Artificer

Ordnance Artificer, 1st Class
Ordnance Artificer, 2nd Class
Ordnance Artificer, 3rd Class
Ordnance Artificer, 4th Class

Acting Ordnance Artificer, 4th Class
Ordnance Artificer, 5th Class
Ordnance Artificer Apprentice

Shipwright

Chief Shipwright, 1st Class
Chief Shipwright, 2nd Class
Shipwright, 1st Class
Shipwright, 2nd Class
Shipwright, 3rd Class

Shipwright, 4th Class
Acting Shipwright, 4th Class
Shipwright, 5th Class
Naval Shipwright Apprentice

Joiner

Chief Joiner	Joiner, 4th Class
Joiner, 1st Class	Acting Joiner, 4th Class
Joiner, 2nd Class	Joiner, 5th Class
Joiner, 3rd Class	

Blacksmith

Chief Blacksmith	Blacksmith, 4th Class
Blacksmith, 1st Class	Acting Blacksmith, 4th Class
Blacksmith, 2nd Class	Blacksmith, 5th Class
Blacksmith, 3rd Class	

Plumber

Chief Plumber	Plumber, 4th Class
Plumber, 1st Class	Acting Plumber, 4th Class
Plumber, 2nd Class	Plumber, 5th Class
Plumber, 3rd Class	

Painter

Chief Painter	Painter, 4th Class
Painter, 1st Class	Acting Painter, 4th Class
Painter, 2nd Class	Painter, 5th Class
Painter, 3rd Class	

Cooper

Chief Cooper	Cooper, 3rd Class
Cooper, 1st Class	Cooper, 4th Class
Cooper, 2nd Class	

Photographer

Chief Petty Officer Photographer	Leading Photographer
Petty Officer Photographer	Photographer

Sick Berth

Sick-Berth Chief Petty Officer
Leading Sick-Berth Attendant
Sick-Berth Attendant

Sick-Berth Petty Officer
Sick-Berth Attendant Probationer

Writer

Chief Petty Officer Writer
Petty Officer Writer
Leading Writer

Writer
Writer Probationer
Boy Writer

Supply

Supply Chief Petty Officer
Supply Petty Officer
Leading Supply Assistant

Supply Assistant
Supply Probationer
Supply Boy

Regulating

Master-at-Arms

Regulating Petty Officer

Ship's Cook

Chief Petty Officer Cook
Petty Officer Cook
Leading Cook

Cook
Assistant Cook

Officers' Steward

Chief Petty Officer Steward
Petty Officer Steward
Leading Steward

Steward
Assistant Steward
Boy Steward

Daily Standard Naval Rations, 1914

Slightly adapted from *The King's Regulations and Admiralty Instructions for the Government of His Majesty's Naval Service*, vol. 2 (1914) (London: Eyre and Spottiswoode, 1914), pp. 305–306.

(a) Service Afloat

1 lb. Bread (or ¾ lb. Bread and ¼ lb. Flour)
½ lb. Fresh Meat
1 lb. Fresh Vegetables
1/8 pt. Spirit
4 oz. Sugar
½ oz. Tea (or 1 oz. Coffee for every ¼ oz. Tea)
½ oz. Chocolate (or 1 oz. Coffee)
¾ oz. Condensed Milk
1 oz. Jam, Marmalade, or Pickles
4 oz. Preserved Meat on one day of the week in Harbour, or on two days at Sea
    (*See* Note *f*)
Mustard, Pepper, Vinegar and Salt, as required

Substitute for Soft Bread when the latter is not available:
    ½ lb. Biscuit or 1 lb. Flour

Substitutes for the Fresh Meat and Fresh Vegetable Rations, when these are not available (on alternate days):

Salt Pork Day:
    ½ lb. Salt Pork
    ¼ lb. Split Peas
    Celery Seed, ½ oz. to every 8 lbs. of Split Peas put into the Coppers
    ½ lb. Potatoes

Preserved Meat Day:

6 oz. Preserved Meat
8 oz. Flour
¾ oz. Suet } or 4 oz. Rice
2 oz. Raisins or 2 oz. Jam
½ lb. Potatoes

Substitutes for Potatoes when the latter are not available:

2 oz. Haricot Beans, or
2 oz. Marrowfat Peas

In addition to the Daily Standard Ration outlined above, persons included in (a) receive a Daily Messing Allowance of 4 pence a day.

(b) Shore Establishments and Stationary Depôt Ships

The same Ration as for the Service Afloat, except:
a. ½ pint Fresh Milk is to be issued in lieu of ¾ oz. Condensed Milk.
b. The Weekly Ration of Preserved Meat is not to be issued.

(c) Men in Cells

Men in Cells are to receive the following Dietary:
a. Low Diet: 1 lb. of Biscuit, or
b. Full Diet: 10 oz. Biscuit
        8 oz. Fresh Vegetables or 1 oz. Preserved Vegetables
        ⅛ oz. Tea
        ½ oz. Chocolate
        1½ oz. Sugar

NOTES [selected]

b. Sea-going Ships, when alongside or in the Basins, are allowed to draw Fresh Milk (¼ pt.) in lieu of the Condensed Milk Ration, subject to reasonable notice being given.
f. 4 oz. Salmon or Rabbit, as desired, may be substituted for Preserved Meat on alternate issues of Breakfast or Supper ration.
g. One tin (¾ lb.) of Condensed Milk or 1 quart of Fresh Milk may, at the option of the Messes, be drawn in lieu of 2 lbs. of Sugar or 1 lb. of Jam.

Informants for *Sober Men and True*

Department of Documents, Imperial War Museum, London

Attrill, John Edward. Diaries, October 21, 1913–November 12, 1918; 6 volumes (87/20/1).

Baker, Edgar Robert. Diary, with retrospective additions, March 4, 1916–December 18, 1918 (68/6/1).

Batters, William. "Harry Tate's Navy" and "The Confessions of a Sewage Works Manager"; memoirs (82/10/1)).

Blamey, William James Henry. "Log of The Great War as a British Bluejacket, including a few Months spent in 'Harry Tates' Navy on Patrol duties"; diary/narrative (86/53/1).

Boyd, Henry Bamford. "Diary of Events During 6 weeks In The Baltic Nov.26.1918–Jan.7th.1919 HMTBD Windsor" (73/4/1).

Davidson, H. John. Memoir, May 26, 1941–February 1946 (85/6/1); published as *Between Decks: The World War II Memoirs of Lieutenant John Davidson, R.N.V.R.* (Newlees Farm, Stirlingshire, Scotland: Newlees Press, 1996).

Dutton, Raymond. "What! No Isambard? or, A Sort of Autobiography" (85/49/1).

Eames, James John. "My Life in a Nutshell"; diary, January 20, 1914–June 9, 1920 (PP/MCR/122).

Goodbrand, Donald S. "'Hurrah for the Life of an H.O.!'; A Nautical Ambience"; memoir (91/17/1).

Goodwin, J. A. Letters, November 21–December 28, 1918, and January 28, 1926 (76/3/1).

Green, William Antony. Diary, August 3, 1914–May 8, 1915; also attributed to William Percy Killen (99/75/1).

Hawkes, William Thomas Charles. "Log of H.M.S. Glasgow During the War 1914–15–16"; diary (85/25/1).

Heron, Albert Arthur. "Synopsis of Life in the R.N."; memoir (76/4/1).

Kelleher, James F. "H.M.S. Carlisle: The Fighting Ship of the Mediteranean [*sic*]"; memoir (PP/MCR/114).

Knight, John. "Memories of a Miscreant"; memoir (87/15/1).

McNamara, Thomas P. F. Letters, December 30, 1915–December 9, 1918 (76/233/1).

Mullins, John Patrick. "Naval Memoirs" (92/27/1).

Needham, John Edward. Memoir (92/27/1).

Nicholls, J. "Diary of the *Ajax*'s 2nd Commission. America & W. Indies Station (South American Division)," January 11, 1938–May 7, 1940 (79/53/1).

Osborne, Harold. "My Diary of Naval Life," [May] 3, 1941–April 18, 1942 (87/15/1).

Powell, Philip. "My Diary," August 2, 1914–December 25, 1918, with a postscript carrying his narrative through to demobilization in April 1919 (77/93/1).

Questionnaires completed by former ratings, Royal Navy, about 1973 (Misc 101/1583):

Adams, Arthur George

Ainsworth, Lewis Alexander

Bailey, William Arthur David

Blowers, Raymond W.

Boyle, Francis

Bull, Victor Stanley

Callister, James D.

Clarkson, George Michael (in Sound Archive, Imperial War Museum, contributors' files)

Cole, Samuel John

Cox, James George (in Sound Archive, contributors' files)

Crosby, Arthur Gordon

Dusting, Joseph

Eames, James John (in Department of Documents correspondence file)

Heron, Albert Arthur (in Sound Archive, contributors' files)

Horton, Leslie B.

Humphries, William Charles

Jenkins, Phillip Thomas

Lewis, Arthur

Long, Bertram Napier

Moore, Frederick

Nancarrow, Leslie

Oke, Kenneth Leigh

Orritt, Ronald B.

Pitt, Alan Edward
Purslow, Sidney
Purvis, Roland
Robinson, Philip Edward
Smith, Edward Lewis
Sowdon, Harry Wilson
Thompson, Thomas
Walton, Charles William
Watson, Robert James Daniel
Watts, Ronald George
Weyell, Gilbert Stanley (in Weyell Papers [66/64/1])
Whittingham, Alban George Jackson

Read, William F. Diary, July 17–November 21, 1939 (65/35/1). Read was a master-at-arms. His diary and the George T. Weekes interview (below) provide much-needed correctives to the customary lower-deck view of the regulating branch.

Richards, Archibald Victor. Diaries, February 17–September 25, [1942], October 30, 1942–October 18, [1943] (65/35/1).

Rooke, Percy. Diary, August 4, 1914–October 17, 1915 (76/235/1).

Smith, Wilfrid S. Letters to his mother, December 7, 1941–April 2, 1942, and one undated, but earlier, letter (82/33/1).

Stamp, Charles Alfred. Diary, June 23, 1916–August 9, 1917 (PP/MCR/148).

Thomas, Charles Richard. Letters, September 14, 1934–April 4, 1942; typescript extracts (79/13/1).

Turpin, Frederick William. Diaries, January 10, 1917–February 14, 1919 (91/11/1).

Welch, Henry Stanley. Diary, April 19–December 20, 1910, March 13, 1911, July 29, 1914–June 10, 1918 (Con Shelf).

Weyell, Gilbert Stanley. Papers, March–June 1973 (66/64/1).

Wilkins, Walter George Raymond. Letters to his parents, July 19, 1940–May 3, 1941 (01/2/1).

Sound Archive, Imperial War Museum, London

Interviews, conducted in 1975 and 1976, with former Royal Navy ratings. For a full description, see the catalog published under the Sound Archive's previous name: Imperial War Museum, Department of Sound Records, *Lower Deck, 1910–1922* (London, [1977]). Transcripts exist for many of these interviews, but the researcher is well advised to compare the transcripts' texts with the actual recordings. History and historians are indeed fortunate that the program of interviewing these old sailors was undertaken when it was—just in the nick of time. Some former ratings whom the Imperial War Museum wished to interview died before they could be recorded or were too ill to be interviewed. Edward Pullen, one of the oldest sailors in the group and a most valuable informant, was interviewed in September 1975; he died three months later on December 25.

Ashley, Reginald Claude (#661/10)
Basford, Walter Nicholson (#669/19)
Boin, Henry William (#666/03)
Bunter, Thomas William (#782/03)
Clarkson, George Michael (#679/48)
Cox, James George (#728/21)
Dunn, James (#769/09)
Ford, Arthur William (#719/23)
Fox, Ernest George (#751/08)
Halter, William (#721/20)
Heron, Albert Arthur (#681/20)
Jeffery, Robert John (#757/04)
Lazenby, Charles Henry (#664/12)
Leary, James (#553/18)
Lilley, Albert Ernest Edward (#750/08)
Pullen, Edward (#692/27)
Rose, Richard Frank (#754/13)
Vine, Joseph Harry (#730/06)
Wallace, Thomas (#731/08)
Weekes, George Thomas (#778/05)
Willis, Reginald (#758/15)

Modern Records Centre, University of Warwick Library, Coventry

Fagg, Robert Leonard. "A Man of Kent: The Autobiography of Len Fagg"; memoir (Mss 120).

Royal Naval Museum, Portsmouth

Dawson, Walter. "The Log of H.M.S. Albion: The Great War of 1914–18"; diary/narrative (RNM 1980/82).

"Potmess: Ship's Rag," no. 1–no. 6; manuscript magazine circulated in the cutter HMS *Totland* during the Second World War (RNM 1994/64).

Williams, William. "A commission with the Cape Squadron, Sybille & Barracouta, 1900–04"; diary/narrative (RNM 1976/65).

Abbreviations

DOC Department of Documents, Imperial War Museum, London

MRC Modern Records Centre, University of Warwick Library, Coventry

PRO Public Record Office, Kew

RNM Royal Naval Museum, Portsmouth

SND Sound Archive, Imperial War Museum, London

Notes

Introduction

1. DOC: Osborne diary, May 15 and 25, 1941.
2. DOC: Nancarrow questionnaire.
3. DOC: Pitt questionnaire; Orritt questionnaire.
4. DOC: Pitt questionnaire.
5. An exceptionally insightful analysis of the evolution of naval warfare during the past one hundred years, one with a strong emphasis on the human factor, is Ronald H. Spector, *At War at Sea: Sailors and Naval Combat in the Twentieth Century* (New York: Viking, 2001).
6. For a splendid and suggestive start on this topic see Andrew Gordon's *The Rules of the Game: Jutland and British Naval Command* (London: John Murray, 1996), pp. 328–339; lower-deck comments on the role of Freemasonry can be found in SND: Clarkson interview, reel 38, and Clarkson questionnaire; DOC: Weyell questionnaire.
7. A recent book on this subject is David Phillipson, *Band of Brothers: Boy Seamen in the Royal Navy, 1800–1956* (Annapolis: Naval Institute Press, 1996).
8. Anthony Carew, *The Lower Deck of the Royal Navy, 1900–39: The Invergordon Mutiny in Perspective* (Manchester: Manchester University Press, 1981). A related work is Henry Baynham, *Men from the Dreadnoughts* (London: Hutchinson, 1976). This is essentially an anthology of autobiographical statements, woven together by limited commentary from the author. Baynham's work was heavily based on his interviews with fifty-one former Royal Navy ratings and Royal Marines, only one of whom (Robert L. Fagg) was also an informant for *Sober Men and True*. Those who have worked with tape-recorded interviews will recognize that Baynham must have done an unknown amount of editorial clean-up on the quoted texts. The book does not include any record of the questions Baynham asked his interviewees. These limitations aside, *Men from the Dreadnoughts* is a potentially valuable source for historians of

the lower deck, but I have preferred to work with records in which I had direct access to the former ratings' own words as they wrote or spoke them.

9. I am here summarizing ideas that recur throughout Daniel L. Schachter's book *Searching for Memory: The Brain, the Mind, and the Past* (New York: Basic Books, 1996). For the three levels of memories see especially pp. 88–97; regarding the enhanced memories of late adolescence and early adulthood in older adults, see pp. 297–300.

10. An expert, extended evaluation of these concerns and a classic advocacy of the value of structured interviews as historical sources is Paul Thompson, *The Voice of the Past: Oral History* (Oxford: Oxford University Press, 1978), especially the fourth chapter, "Evidence" (pp. 91–137).

11. Carew, *Lower Deck of the Royal Navy*, p. xvii.

12. Wilfrid Pym Trotter, *The Royal Navy in Old Photographs* (London: Dent, 1975), is the most readily accessible compilation of pictures for the period.

13. SND: Leary interview, reel 7, with the sequence of the sentences rearranged for clarity; Chris Robinson, *The "Prince George" and a Hundred Other Plymouth Pubs, Past & Present* (Plymouth: Pen & Ink Publishing, 1997), pp. iii, 10.

1. I Went Away to Join the Navy

1. These books offer a superb general introduction to the world of Edwardian working-class life: Paul Thompson, *The Edwardians: The Remaking of British Society* (London: Weidenfeld and Nicolson, 1975); Standish Meacham, *A Life Apart: The English Working Class, 1890–1914* (London: Thames and Hudson, 1977); Stephen Humphries, *Hooligans or Rebels? An Oral History of Working-Class Childhood and Youth, 1889–1939* (Oxford: Blackwell, 1981); and Elizabeth Roberts, *A Woman's Place: An Oral History of Working-Class Women, 1890–1940* (Oxford: Blackwell, 1984).

2. SND: Halter interview, reel 1.

3. Thompson, *The Edwardians*, pp. 15–17.

4. SND: Ashley interview, reel 1.

5. SND: Cox interview, reel 1.

6. SND: Pullen interview, reel 1, with the sequence of the paragraphs rearranged in the long quotation.

7. SND: Boin interview, reel 1.

8. SND: Cox interview, reel 1.

9. SND: Dunn interview, reel 1.

10. SND: Rose interview, reel 1.

11. SND: Fox interview, reel 1.

12. SND: Ford interview, reel 1; see also Vine interview, reel 1.

13. SND: Wallace interview, reel 1.

14. SND: Clarkson interview, reel 1; information about the Clarkson family supplied by Geoffrey Clarkson, the son of George Michael Clarkson.

15. SND: Cox interview, reel 2.

16. To view the future sailors' educational experiences in a larger context see Jonathan Rose's "Willingly to School: The Working-Class Response to Elementary Education in Britain, 1875–1918," *Journal of British Studies* 32 (1993): 114–138.

17. SND: Clarkson interview, reel 1.

18. SND: Pullen interview, reel 1.

19. SND: Cox interview, reel 1.

20. SND: Heron interview, reel 1.

21. For instance Anthony Carew's notice in the *East Kent Times & Broadstairs Mail*, March 28, 1973, seeking informants for what subsequently became his book *The Lower Deck of the Royal Navy, 1900–39: The Invergordon Mutiny in Perspective* (Manchester: Manchester University Press, 1981).

22. SND: Dunn interview, reel 2.

23. SND: Pullen interview, reel 1.

24. SND: Clarkson interview, reels 1–3.

25. DOC: Watts questionnaire; SND: Rose interview, reel 1.

26. SND: Clarkson interview, reel 1.

27. SND: Dunn interview, reels 1–2.

28. DOC: Blowers questionnaire; confidential informant.

29. SND: Bunter interview, reel 1, with the order of the sentences changed for clarity.

30. SND: Clarkson interview, reels 2–3.

31. SND: Ashley interview, reel 1.

32. SND: Ford interview, reel 1, with the sequence of the paragraphs rearranged.

33. SND: Ford interview, reels 1–2.

2. They Were Officers and You Were Not

1. SND: Rose interview, reel 2.

2. SND: Dunn interview, reel 3.

3. DOC: Needham memoir, Glossary, p. 2.

4. *The King's Regulations and Admiralty Instructions for the Government of His*

Majesty's Naval Service (London: Eyre and Spottiswoode, 1906), pp. 243–245. This was the edition current at the time that many of the informants for this book entered the navy.

5. *King's Regulations and Admiralty Instructions*, p. 247.

6. Sidney Knock, *"Clear Lower Deck": An Intimate Study of the Men of the Royal Navy* (2d ed.; London: Philip Allan, 1933), pp. 61–62.

7. SND: Pullen interview, reels 6–7.

8. SND: Pullen interview, reel 7, with two instances of "he said" silently suppressed.

9. DOC: Needham memoir, "1942," p. 4.

10. SND: Wallace interview, reel 5.

11. DOC: Ainsworth questionnaire; Knock, *"Clear Lower Deck,"* pp. 68–69.

12. DOC: Crosby questionnaire.

13. For a similar interpretation of bare-bottom canings in British schools of the period see Stephen Humphries, *Hooligans or Rebels? An Oral History of Working-Class Childhood and Youth, 1889–1939* (Oxford: Blackwell, 1981), p. 73.

14. Anthony Carew, *The Lower Deck of the Royal Navy, 1900–39: The Invergordon Mutiny in Perspective* (Manchester: Manchester University Press, 1981), p. 31.

15. SND: Wallace interview, reel 2.

16. Myra C. Glenn, *Campaigns against Corporal Punishment: Prisoners, Sailors, Women, and Children in Antebellum America* (Albany: State University of New York Press, 1984); Harold D. Langley, *Social Reform in the United States Navy, 1798–1862* (Urbana: University of Illinois Press, 1967); Dudley Pope, *The Black Ship* (London: Weidenfeld and Nicolson, 1963), and the wealth of contemporary polemical literature cited by them.

17. Christopher McKee, *A Gentlemanly and Honorable Profession: The Creation of the U.S. Naval Officer Corps, 1794–1815* (Annapolis: Naval Institute Press, 1991).

18. DOC: Orritt questionnaire.

19. SND: Heron interview, reel 8.

20. SND: Basford interview, reels 11–12.

21. DOC: Crosby questionnaire.

22. SND: Cox interview, reel 6.

23. DOC: Pitt questionnaire; Walton questionnaire; Callister questionnaire; Nancarrow questionnaire.

24. DOC: Purslow questionnaire; Robinson questionnaire; Jenkins questionnaire; Sowdon questionnaire. See also SND: Cox questionnaire.

25. SND: Dunn interview, reels 4 and 3.

26. DOC: Horton questionnaire.

27. SND: Ford interview, reel 18.

28. SND: Dunn interview, reel 8.

29. SND: Ford interview, reel 17.

30. SND: Jeffery interview, reel 1.

31. DOC: Needham memoir, Glossary, p. 3.

32. DOC: Read diary, July 29, 1939.

33. SND: Rose interview, reel 3.

34. Paul Thompson, *The Edwardians: The Remaking of British Society* (London: Weidenfeld and Nicolson, 1975), pp. 11–13.

35. Carew, *Lower Deck of the Royal Navy*, pp. 47–53.

36. SND: Ford interview, reel 11.

37. Loose sheets, apparently from a diary-letter, dated July 20, 1917, in the possession of the Stamp family.

38. RNM: Williams diary, May 8, 1901.

39. SND: Pullen interview, reel 7.

40. DOC: Rooke diary, December 27, 1914, February 2, 3, 7–10, 1915. See also Green diary, February 2, 10, 1915.

41. SND: Dunn interview, reel 7.

42. SND: Dunn interview, reel 7.

43. DOC: Rooke diary, December 25, 1914.

44. Confidential informant.

45. DOC: Orritt questionnaire; Green diary, January 1, 1915.

46. SND: Basford interview, reel 12.

47. DOC: Orritt questionnaire.

48. SND: Clarkson interview, reel 25.

49. SND: Rose interview, reel 11.

50. DOC: Attrill diary, October 28, 1914, February 10, 12–13, March 6, May 22, 1915.

51. DOC: Attrill diary, July 10, 12, August 10, undated summary entry following October 21, November 7, 1918.

52. Arthur Marder, *From the Dreadnought to Scapa Flow: The Royal Navy in the Fisher Era, 1904–1919* (London: Oxford University Press, 1961–1978), 2:14, 440–441, 3(2d ed.):42, 338.

53. DOC: Attrill diary, November 28, 1916.

54. DOC: Mullins memoir, pp. 8–9; for a similar comment concerning Captain George Arthur Scott of *Belfast* see DOC: Read diary, September 3, 1939.

55. DOC: Goodwin letters, December 28, 1918.

56. SND: Ford interview, reel 12.

57. For example, SND: Ford interview, reel 11; DOC: Boyle questionnaire.

58. RNM: Dawson diary, May 23, 1915.
59. DOC: Pitt questionnaire.
60. DOC: Crosby questionnaire.
61. For example, DOC: Eames, Smith, Sowdon, and Walton questionnaires; SND: Clarkson and Heron questionnaires. None of the rating-informants discussed why he thought officer relations with the lower deck improved over the 1900–1945 period.
62. DOC: Robinson questionnaire. See also Nancarrow and Watson questionnaires.
63. SND: Heron questionnaire.
64. DOC: Oke questionnaire.
65. DOC: Boyle questionnaire.
66. SND: Ford interview, reel 11.
67. DOC: Thomas letters. This sketch of Thomas's life and opinions is a composite woven from letters dated October 24, 1936, November 25, 1936, March 3, 1937, August 20, 1938, October 15, 1938, January 11, 1939, October 11, 1940, December 26, 1940, and the "Biographical Note" by R. T.

3. The Finest and Most Sincere Crowd of Men

1. William H. McNeill, *Keeping Together in Time: Dance and Drill in Human History* (Cambridge, Mass.: Harvard University Press, 1995).
2. DOC: Smith questionnaire; Dutton memoir, p. 89.
3. DOC: Baker diary, July 15, 1916.
4. SND: Rose interview, reel 11.
5. SND: Pullen interview, reel 23. No vessel commanded by Alfred G. Peace was lost at the Dardanelles; the almost always accurate Pullen must have misremembered what Peace said.
6. DOC: Batters, "Tate's Navy," p. 26.
7. SND: Ashley interview, reel 2; Ford interview, reel 18. See also Wallace interview, reel 3.
8. SND: Ashley interview, reel 2; Basford interview, reel 6.
9. SND: Basford interview, reel 6; Wallace interview, reel 3; DOC: Kelleher memoir, p. 58; SND: Pullen interview, reel 4.
10. SND: Wallace interview, reel 3.
11. SND: Weekes interview, reel 5, with the sequence of the sentences reordered for clarity.
12. SND: Ford interview, reel 11.
13. DOC: Thomas letters, January 22, 1935.

14. SND: Wallace interview, reel 6.

15. SND: Ashley interview, reel 4.

16. SND: Pullen interview, reel 23.

17. SND: Wallace interview, reel 7; Cox interview, reel 17.

18. SND: Ashley interview, reel 4.

19. SND: Basford interview, reel 10; Clarkson interview, reels 12 and 17; Ford interview, reel 13; Heron interview, reel 14; Pullen interview, reel 12; Sidney Knock, *"Clear Lower Deck": An Intimate Study of the Men of the Royal Navy* (2d ed.; London: Philip Allan, 1933), pp. 90–92, 94.

20. SND: Basford interview, reels 6–7.

21. SND: Clarkson interview, reel 12.

22. SND: Ford interview, reel 15.

23. SND: Cox interview, reel 15.

24. SND: Heron interview, reel 17; Ford interview, reel 14.

25. SND: Heron interview, reel 16; Pullen interview, reel 6, with the order of the sentences in the second paragraph rearranged and with Pullen's description of decorating the crust inserted in Heron's description of toad-in-the-hole.

26. SND: Heron interview, reel 17.

27. SND: Cox interview, reel 15; also Heron interview, reel 16.

28. SND: Basford interview, reel 7; Ford interview, reel 14; Cox interview, reel 15.

29. DOC: Smith letters, February 2, [1942].

30. RNM: Dawson diary, December 3, 1914.

31. SND: Rose interview, reel 9; Heron interview, reel 16.

32. DOC: Hawkes diary, September 4, 1914.

33. DOC: Blamey diary, pp. 86–87, 89.

34. DOC: Read diary, August 22, 1939.

35. DOC: Baker diary, February 4, 1917; SND: Basford interview, reel 10; Cox interview, reel 11; Pullen interview, reels 12, 13, and 20; Wallace interview, reel 2.

36. SND: Pullen interview, reel 13.

37. DOC: Smith letters, December 7, 1941; Wilkins letters, November 29, 1940.

38. SND: Ford interview, reel 11; Cox interview, reel 9.

39. DOC: Smith letters, January 18, 1942.

40. SND: Heron interview, reel 15; MRC: Fagg memoir, pp. 77–78.

41. SND: Cox interview, reel 12; Boin interview, reel 2.

42. SND: Cox interview, reel 12.

43. SND: Rose interview, reel 10.

44. SND: Ford interview, reel 13.

45. SND: Cox interview, reel 16.

46. John Davidson, *Between Decks: World War II Memoirs* (Newlees Farm, Stirlingshire: Newlees Press, 1996), p. 19.

47. DOC: Needham memoir, "Introduction," p. 2.

48. DOC: Baker diary, June 9, 1917.

49. DOC: Mullins memoir, p. 19.

50. DOC: Thomas letters, January 12, 1938.

51. DOC: Needham memoir, "1942," p. 13.

52. DOC: Thomas letters, September 11, 1939.

53. DOC: Needham memoir, "1942," p. 14.

54. DOC: Thomas letters, June 12, 1935; Davidson, *Between Decks*, p. 22; SND: Cox interview, reel 17; Basford interview, reel 9.

55. SND: Clarkson interview, reel 18; Ford interview, reel 13, with the order of the sentences rearranged.

56. SND: Clarkson interview, reel 18; Basford interview, reel 9.

57. SND: Ford interview, reel 13; Clarkson interview, reel 18.

58. SND: Rose interview, reel 10.

59. DOC: Batters, "Tate's Navy," p. 30.

60. SND: Basford interview, reel 8.

61. Davidson, *Between Decks*, pp. 50–51.

62. SND: Pullen interview, reels 8–9.

63. DOC: Jenkins questionnaire.

64. Right-oriented lower deck: DOC: Eames questionnaire; Horton questionnaire; Moore questionnaire; Purslow questionnaire; Robinson questionnaire; Sowdon questionnaire; Whittingham questionnaire; SND: Clarkson questionnaire; Heron questionnaire. Left-oriented lower deck: DOC: Crosby questionnaire; Oke questionnaire; Orritt questionnaire; Pitt questionnaire; Walton questionnaire; Watts questionnaire.

65. DOC: Crosby questionnaire; Humphries questionnaire; Jenkins questionnaire; Nancarrow questionnaire; Pitt questionnaire; Robinson questionnaire; Sowdon questionnaire; Weyell questionnaire. There is an excellent discussion of working-class Conservative loyalties in Paul Thompson, *The Edwardians: The Remaking of British Society* (London: Weidenfeld and Nicolson, 1975), chapter 15, "Politics."

66. DOC: Bailey questionnaire; Nancarrow questionnaire; Purvis questionnaire; Watson questionnaire; Watts questionnaire; Whittingham questionnaire.

67. DOC: Adams questionnaire; PRO: Adm 188/677/J15140.

68. DOC: Stamp diary, August 14, 1916; Richards diary, March 16, 1942.

69. DOC: Sowdon questionnaire; Watts questionnaire; Robinson questionnaire.
70. DOC: Bull questionnaire.
71. DOC: Orritt questionnaire; SND: Ashley interview, reel 3.
72. DOC: Humphries questionnaire; SND: Cox interview, reel 18; DOC: Purslow questionnaire.
73. SND: Boin interview, reel 2.
74. SND: Clarkson interview, reel 3.
75. SND: Dunn interview, reel 4.
76. DOC: Bailey questionnaire; SND: Cox interview, reel 17.
77. SND: Willis interview, reels 9–10.
78. DOC: Thomas letters, January 11, 1939.
79. There is a rich literature on this point, most of which traces its intellectual roots to the classic article by Edward A. Shils and Morris Janowitz, "Cohesion and Disintegration in the Wehrmacht in World War II," *Public Opinion Quarterly* 12 (1948/49): 280–315.

4. I Never Thought I'd See Daylight Again

1. DOC: Welch diary, December 8, 1914 (written on December 9). For general accounts of the Falkland Islands battle see Julian S. Corbett and Henry Newbolt, *Naval Operations* (London: Longmans, Green, 1920–1931), 1:414–436; Arthur J. Marder, *From the Dreadnought to Scapa Flow: The Royal Navy in the Fisher Era, 1904–1919* (London: Oxford University Press, 1961–1978), 2:118–129; Geoffrey Bennett, *Coronel and the Falklands* (London: Batsford, 1962). Another contemporary lower-deck narrative of the Falklands battle, and especially the duel between *Glasgow* and *Leipzig*, is in DOC: Hawkes diary, December 8–9, 1914.
2. DOC: Osborne diary, November 25–26, 28, 1941.
3. DOC: Rooke diary, March 11, 1915.
4. Confidential informant.
5. SND: Dunn interview, reel 9.
6. DOC: Pullen interview, reel 10.
7. DOC: Stamp diary, August 30, 1916.
8. DOC: Eames diary.
9. This account of coaling is constructed from SND: Clarkson interview, reels 8–10; Dunn interview, reel 3; Lilley interview, reels 3–4; Rose interview, reels 7–8; Wallace interview, reel 5; DOC: Read diary, September 16, 1939; Stamp diary, July 31, August 29, 1916; Sidney Knock, *"Clear Lower Deck":*

An Intimate Study of the Men of the Royal Navy (2d ed.; London: Philip Allan, 1933), p. 91; Christopher Cradock, *Whispers from the Fleet* (2d ed.; Portsmouth: Gieve's, 1908), pp. 139–157. For typical coaling accidents see DOC: Attrill diary, November 6, 1918; Green diary, November 8, 1914.

10. DOC: Stamp diary, May 5, June 3, 1917.
11. RNM: Dawson diary, February 1, 1915; PRO: Adm 53/33214: *Albion* log, February 1, 1915.
12. SND: Clarkson interview, reel 22.
13. SND: Cox interview, reel 20.
14. DOC: Weyell questionnaire; Watts questionnaire.
15. DOC: Bailey questionnaire; Needham memoir, "1941," pp. 8–9, "Introduction," p. 1.
16. John Davidson, *Between Decks: World War II Memoirs* (Newlees Farm, Stirlingshire: Newlees Press, 1996), p. 20.
17. SND: Cox interview, reel 17; confidential informant.

5. This Rum It Was Wonderful Stuff

1. SND: Ford interview, reel 19.
2. DOC: Kelleher memoir, pp. 64–65.
3. SND: Heron questionnaire.
4. DOC: Stamp diary, July 2, July 16, August 20, 1916, May 6, 1917.
5. DOC: Powell diary, September 22, October 11, October 25, 1914, February 27, June 11, 1916, and retrospective postscript following December 25, 1918.
6. DOC: Blamey diary, p. 108 (second page with this number).
7. MRC: Fagg memoir, pp. 81–83. Fagg erroneously says that the destroyer sunk in the collision was HMS *Sarpedon;* I have substituted the name of the correct destroyer throughout the quotation.
8. DOC: Bailey questionnaire; Nancarrow questionnaire.
9. DOC: Callister questionnaire.
10. DOC: Sowdon questionnaire; SND: Basford interview, reel 14.
11. DOC: Thompson questionnaire; SND: Lazenby interview, reel 12.
12. DOC: Pitt questionnaire.
13. SND: Clarkson interview, reel 36.
14. DOC: Jenkins questionnaire; Purvis questionnaire.
15. SND: Lazenby interview, reel 12; Ashley interview, reel 6.
16. DOC: Nancarrow questionnaire.
17. SND: Clarkson interview, reel 35.

18. John Davidson, *Between Decks: World War II Memoirs* (Newlees Farm, Stirlingshire: Newlees Press, 1996), p. 51. For ratings' loss of religious faith see, in addition to the previously quoted words of Robert Fagg and Thomas Thompson, DOC: Needham memoir, "Sundry Recollections and Afterthoughts," p. 11, and Sidney Knock, *"Clear Lower Deck": An Intimate Study of the Men of the Royal Navy* (2d ed.; London: Philip Allan, 1933), p. 181.

19. SND: Basford interview, reel 11, with the order of the sentences rearranged. See also Ashley interview, reel 4.

20. Those who wish to pursue this subject to a greater depth may find the following books useful places to begin: Michael B. Walker, *The Psychology of Gambling* (Oxford: Pergamon Press, 1992); Gerda Reith, *The Age of Chance: Gambling in Western Culture* (London: Routledge, 1999). Much of my argument here is summarized from Walker.

21. Erving Goffman, *Interaction Ritual: Essays in Face-to-Face Behavior* (Chicago: Aldine, 1967), as cited in Walker, *Psychology of Gambling*, p. 127.

22. DOC: Whittingham questionnaire; SND: Ashley interview, reel 4; Wallace interview, reel 5.

23. See Frank Richards, *Old Soldier Sahib* (New York: Harrison Smith and Robert Haas, 1936), pp. 69–71, for the best description of crown and anchor; also SND: Heron interview, reel 15, and Knock, *"Clear Lower Deck,"* pp. 125–127.

24. SND: Ashley interview, reel 4.

25. SND: Cox interview, reel 12.

26. SND: Cox interview, reel 12; DOC: Pitt questionnaire; Robinson questionnaire. See also Orritt questionnaire.

27. SND: Heron interview, reel 15.

28. SND: Basford interview, reel 10, with the order of the sentences rearranged.

29. SND: Ashley interview, reel 4.

30. SND: Heron interview, reel 15; Heron questionnaire; DOC: Blowers questionnaire.

31. SND: Cox interview, reel 12; Ashley interview, reel 4.

32. SND: Cox interview, reel 12; DOC: Sowdon questionnaire.

33. SND: Weekes interview, reel 4.

34. SND: Basford interview, reel 10.

35. The daily routine of issuing and consuming the rum ration has been reconstructed from DOC: Batters, "Tate's Navy," pp. 57–58; Dutton memoir, p. 13; Goodbrand memoir, pp. 22–24; Needham memoir, "1942," p. 12; SND: Basford interview, reel 7; Clarkson interview, reels 14–15; Ford interview, reel 15; Pullen interview, reels 12–13; Weekes interview, reel 3. All

these details have been checked against, and in some cases supplemented by, A. J. Pack, *Nelson's Blood: The Story of Naval Rum* (Annapolis: Naval Institute Press, [1982]), especially pp. 145–154, and Knock, *"Clear Lower Deck,"* pp. 83, 159–161.

36. SND: Clarkson interview, reels 14–15.

37. DOC: Batters, "Tate's Navy," pp. 57–58.

38. DOC: Needham memoir, "1942," p. 13.

39. SND: Pullen interview, reel 13. *Glasgow* was at Montevideo December 20, 1912–January 2, 1913, and December 18, 1913–January 13, 1914, according to the summary of the ship's movements in DOC: Hawkes diary (four pages at the end of the volume). The other sailor who asserted that there was successful smuggling was Robert L. Fagg; see MRC: Fagg memoir, pp. 70–71A.

40. SND: Pullen interview, reel 13.

41. SND: Weekes interview, reel 3; DOC: Needham memoir, "1942," p. 12. See also Pack, *Nelson's Blood*, pp. 157–159.

42. SND: Cox interview, reel 16.

43. SND: Ashley interview, reel 5.

44. SND: Clarkson interview, reel 14.

45. DOC: Goodbrand memoir, p. 23; Kelleher memoir, p. 56; Knight memoir, pp. 70–71; Needham memoir, Glossary, p. 4; SND: Ashley interview, reel 5; Cox interview, reel 16; Ford interview, reel 15.

46. SND: Clarkson interview, reel 15; Pullen interview, reel 13.

47. DOC: Batters, "Tate's Navy," p. 57; Needham memoir, "1942," p. 12.

48. SND: Clarkson interview, reel 14; Ford interview, reel 15.

49. SND: Ford interview, reel 15; Pullen interview, reel 13.

50. SND: Clarkson interview, reel 15.

51. SND: Ford interview, reel 15.

52. DOC: Goodbrand memoir, pp. 23–24.

53. DOC: Knight memoir, p. 37, for example.

54. SND: Clarkson interview, reel 10.

55. For instance, Henning Henningson, *Crossing the Equator: Sailors' Baptism and Other Initiation Rites* (Copenhagen: Munksgaard, 1961); for homoerotic aspects of equator-crossings, see Steven Zeeland, *Sailors and Sexual Identity: Crossing the Line between "Straight" and "Gay" in the U.S. Navy* (New York: Harrington Park Press, 1995), *passim*. Accounts of equator-crossing ceremonies by informants for this book can be found in DOC: Nicholls diary, August 17–18, 1938, August 2, 1939; Osborne diary, May 29, 1941; RNM: Dawson diary, October 15–19, 1914, January 24, 1915; Williams diary, December 11–12, 1900.

56. I am here recapitulating ideas presented in chapter 5, "Humility and Hierarchy: The Liminality of Status Elevation and Reversal," of Victor Turner's *The Ritual Process: Structure and Anti-Structure* (Chicago: Aldine, 1969).

57. Sources for the naval Christmas: DOC: Attrill diary, December 23–25, 1914, December 25, 1916; Baker diary, December 25, 1916; Boyd diary, December 25, 1918; Goodwin letters, December 28, 1918; McNamara letters, December 30, 1915; Nicholls diary, December 25, 1938, December 24–25, 1939; Powell diary, December 23–26, 1914, December 25, 1917; Thomas letters, December 27, 1935; Turpin diary, December 23–25, 1918; Welch diary, December 24–25, 1914, December 20, 25, 1915, December 25, 1916, December 25, 1917; RNM: Williams diary, December 25, 1900, December 22, 1901, and entry following December 20, 1902; SND: Willis interview, reels 8–9.

6. A Sailor's Paradise

1. DOC: Stamp diary, July 13, 1916.
2. RNM: Dawson diary, October 13, 1914.
3. DOC: Powell diary, December 20, 1914.
4. SND: Heron interview, reel 20.
5. DOC: Smith letters, January 27, 1942.
6. SND: Clarkson interview, reel 44.
7. DOC: Welch diary, January 14–15, 1916.
8. DOC: Baker diary, June 4, 1917.
9. DOC: Richards diary, July 14, 1942.
10. DOC: Baker diary, July 13, 1917.
11. SND: Wallace interview, reel 4.
12. DOC: Blamey diary, p. 102.
13. SND: Clarkson interview, reel 43.
14. DOC: Baker diary, January 16, 1917.
15. SND: Heron questionnaire.
16. DOC: Jenkins questionnaire; Callister questionnaire; Humphries questionnaire.
17. DOC: Baker diary, January 16, 1917.
18. DOC: Attrill diary.
19. Information about John E. Attrill's later life generously supplied by his son, Leslie Attrill.
20. DOC: Baker diary, June 5, 1917.
21. SND: Ford interview, reels 7 and 13.

22. For an appreciation of the sexual mores and realities of this period, the best place to begin is Stephen Humphries, *A Secret World of Sex—Forbidden Fruit: The British Experience, 1900–1950* (London: Sidgwick and Jackson, 1988).
23. SND: Cox interview, reel 13.
24. DOC: Batters, "Confessions," pp. 34–47. Batters recorded Rosie's family name in his narrative. I have omitted it in deference to her living relatives, if any.
25. SND: Ford interview, reel 10.
26. SND: Heron interview, reel 19.
27. SND: Ford interview, reel 10.
28. SND: Basford interview, reel 15.
29. SND: Pullen interview, reel 15.
30. SND: Heron interview, reel 19.
31. SND: Ashley interview, reel 7, with the order of the sentences rearranged.
32. SND: Halter interview, reel 8.
33. SND: Ashley interview, reel 7.
34. SND: Heron interview, reel 20.
35. SND: Ashley interview, reel 7.
36. SND: Pullen interview, reel 15.
37. SND: Cox interview, reels 13–14.
38. SND: Cox interview, reel 14.
39. SND: Pullen interview, reel 16, with "I said" and "he said" silently omitted in several places.
40. SND: Ashley interview, reel 7.
41. SND: Ford interview, reel 7.
42. SND: Clarkson interview, reel 20, with "he said" silently omitted in several places.
43. SND: Wallace interview, reel 4.
44. SND: Basford interview, reel 9; Clarkson interview, reel 20; Ford interview, reel 7; DOC: Needham memoir, Glossary, p. 3.
45. DOC: Baker diary, January 3, 1917.
46. DOC: Adams questionnaire; PRO: Adm 188/677/J15140.
47. SND: Weekes interview, reel 4.
48. SND: Ashley interview, reel 4; Basford interview, reel 8, with the order of the sentences rearranged.
49. SND: Ford interview, reel 7.
50. SND: Weekes interview, reel 4.
51. SND: Heron interview, reel 10.
52. SND: Ford interview, reel 14.

53. DOC: Batters, "Tate's Navy," p. 67. See also Needham memoir, "1941," p. 15.

54. SND: Ashley interview, reel 4.

55. SND: Heron interview, reel 10.

56. SND: Clarkson interview, reel 21.

57. SND: Cox interview, reel 13.

58. SND: Clarkson interview, reel 21.

59. SND: Clarkson interview, reel 21.

60. DOC: Heron memoir, pp. 13, 14–15; SND: Heron interview, reels 8, 10, 14. For a somewhat more benign view of winger relationships see Sidney Knock, *"Clear Lower Deck": An Intimate Study of the Men of the Royal Navy* (2d ed.; London: Philip Allan, 1933), pp. 161–162.

61. SND: Clarkson interview, reel 21; Heron interview, reel 10.

62. SND: Basford interview, reel 8; Pullen interview, reel 21; Heron interview, reel 10.

63. SND: Clarkson interview, reel 21.

64. SND: Heron interview, reel 10.

65. SND: Clarkson interview, reel 21; DOC: Adams questionnaire.

66. SND: Willis interview, reel 6.

67. SND: Heron questionnaire.

68. DOC: Needham memoir, "Introduction," pp. 2–3; but compare "1941," p. 15.

69. SND: Clarkson interview, reel 21; Basford interview, reel 8. For civvy-street hostility to homoeroticism as contrasted with the navy's (and the army's) "greater tolerance of it and a greater interest in sexual experimentation," see also Humphries, *A Secret World of Sex*, pp. 202, 204, a judgment of which I was unaware until after I had already reached the same conclusion.

70. *Encyclopedia of Homosexuality*, Wayne R. Dynes, ed. (New York: Garland Publishing, 1990), 2:1173. Oscar Brand and Dave Sear recorded "Backside Rules the Navy" (with slightly different words) on their *Bawdy Sea Shanties*, Audio Fidelity AFLP 1884, subsequently reissued as a compact disc with varying titles and publishers.

71. DOC: Batters, "Tate's Navy," p. 73.

72. Especially useful introductions to the subject of homosexuality in prison are Stephen Donaldson's entry "Prisons, Jails, and Reformatories" in the *Encyclopedia of Homosexuality*, 2:1035–1048, and his web-published lecture "A Million Jockers, Punks, and Queens: Sex among American Male Prisoners and Its Implications for Concepts of Sexual Orientation," February 4, 1993, <http://www.spr.org/docs/prison-sex-lecture> (January 25, 2001). Donaldson's writings, and especially the latter, have good bibliographies to

guide those who wish to explore this subject more extensively. See also Donaldson's entry "Seafaring," *Encyclopedia of Homosexuality*, 2:1172–1175, a right-on-target overview, provocative for further research. Donaldson, a first-rate independent scholar and activist, wrote of prison, the navy, and homoeroticism in both settings with the insights of personal experience.

73. SND: Dunn interview, reel 6; DOC: Stamp diary, July 24, 1916.
74. DOC: Attrill diary, April 4, 1915.
75. SND: Lilley interview, reel 8; Cox interview, reel 20; Fox interview, reel 8.
76. DOC: Whittingham questionnaire.
77. SND: Cox interview, reel 21.
78. SND: Halter interview, reel 20, with the sequence of the paragraphs rearranged and several instances of "I said" silently suppressed in the final paragraph.
79. SND: Halter interview, reel 20.
80. SND: Clarkson interview, reel 38, with a number of instances of "he said" silently omitted.
81. SND: Cox interview, reel 21.
82. SND: Cox interview, reel 21.
83. SND: Cox interview, reel 21.
84. SND: Willis interview, reel 15.
85. SND: Lilley interview, reel 8.
86. SND: Cox interview, reel 21.
87. SND: Halter interview, reels 20 and 2.
88. SND: Halter interview, reel 2.
89. SND: Halter interview, reel 20.

7. Traveling with an Oar on My Shoulder

1. DOC: Richards diary, July 17–18, 1942.
2. DOC: Baker diary, postscript written in 1960 (p. 187).
3. SND: Basford interview, reel 19.
4. SND: Basford interview, reels 18–19, with the sequence of the sentences in the quotation changed.
5. SND: Cox interview, reels 12 and 21; Cox questionnaire.
6. SND: Pullen interview, reel 27.
7. SND: Fox interview, reel 8.
8. DOC: Jenkins questionnaire; Thompson questionnaire.
9. DOC: Oke questionnaire; Pitt questionnaire; Adams questionnaire; Crosby questionnaire.

10. DOC: Eames questionnaire; Nancarrow questionnaire.

11. DOC: Watts questionnaire; Purvis questionnaire.

12. Confidential informant.

13. SND: Fox interview, reel 8.

14. SND: Rose interview, reel 13.

15. SND: Ashley interview, reel 10.

16. DOC: Bailey questionnaire; Walton questionnaire; Humphries questionnaire; Boyle questionnaire; Nancarrow questionnaire; SND: Clarkson questionnaire.

17. DOC: Jenkins questionnaire; Nancarrow questionnaire; Weyell questionnaire.

18. DOC: Lewis questionnaire; Horton questionnaire; Pitt questionnaire; Watts questionnaire; Moore questionnaire; Callister questionnaire; Boyle questionnaire; Ainsworth questionnaire.

19. DOC: Whittingham questionnaire; Jenkins questionnaire; Pitt questionnaire; Robinson questionnaire; Watts questionnaire; Nancarrow questionnaire; Sowdon questionnaire.

20. SND: Heron questionnaire.

21. DOC: Callister questionnaire; Jenkins questionnaire; Watson questionnaire; Boyle questionnaire; Nancarrow questionnaire; Purvis questionnaire.

22. DOC: Ainsworth questionnaire; Eames questionnaire; Sowdon questionnaire.

23. DOC: Crosby questionnaire; Bull questionnaire; Callister questionnaire; Dusting questionnaire.

24. DOC: Pitt questionnaire; Nancarrow questionnaire; Lewis questionnaire.

25. DOC: Horton questionnaire; Blowers questionnaire; Thompson questionnaire; Crosby questionnaire; Moore questionnaire; Watts questionnaire; SND: Cox questionnaire.

26. SND: Basford interview, reel 19.

27. DOC: Robinson questionnaire.

28. SND: Halter interview, reel 20.

29. SND: Clarkson interview, reel 22.

30. SND: Heron questionnaire.

31. DOC: Dutton memoir, p. 89.

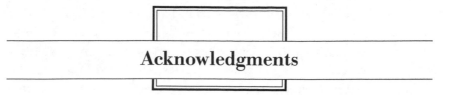

Acknowledgments

Although the manuscript of *Sober Men and True* traveled with me in my briefcase to many locations—parts of the book were written in places as diverse as Oakland, California, Mitchell, South Dakota, and Washington, D.C.—its spiritual and intellectual home has always been London's Imperial War Museum, whose splendid collections of primary documents on all aspects of twentieth-century conflict and military forces form so large a part of the sources on which it is based. The real treasure of the Imperial War Museum is not its collections, fine as these are, but the capable, friendly, and enthusiastic staff who facilitate the use of the museum's resources and make that experience such a happy one.

Foremost among those at the Imperial War Museum who helped to make *Sober Men and True* a reality is Roderick Suddaby, Keeper of the Department of Documents. When we first met in the museum's reading room ten years ago he could not have foreseen how much of the coming decade he was going to spend with this project. Not only has Roderick Suddaby been a constant source of encouragement; he has guided me to the most useful sources in the Department of Documents' rich holdings, pointed me in the direction of sources of which I was unaware in other IWM departments, made the necessary introductions in those departments, troubleshot the occasional problem on my behalf, guided me to just the right people in Her Majesty's ministries, and answered by letter and e-mail transatlantic questions beyond counting.

At the Department of Documents I have benefited often over the years from the good-humored assistance of archivist Stephen Walton. Across the reading room, in the Department of Printed Books, my reliance was on Mary Wilkinson, who always knew the correct answer to my questions and guided me through the complexities of the Imperial War Museum's print-based resources. This book draws heavily on the text collections of the Department of Documents, but it was equally dependent on the audio riches of the museum's Sound Archive, where for many weeks I was supported by the warm hospitality and keen helpfulness of keeper Margaret Brooks and senior interviewer Conrad Wood as I listened, hour after hour, to the recorded voices of my book's informants. In the Department of Art, Jenny Wood helped me to find the best possible image for my dust jacket with astonishing efficiency.

If the Imperial War Museum was my book's spiritual and intellectual home, its home away from home was the Royal Naval Museum in Portsmouth. Here I benefited from the knowledge and friendly support of Stephen Courtney and Matthew Sheldon, curators of photographs and manuscripts respectively. I cannot imagine another mile they could have gone beyond what they did to facilitate my work.

During successive visits to the Plymouth Naval Base Museum, I was guided through the museum's rich material resources by Andy Endacott and Michael Phillips. Andy Endacott also shared with me his fabulous personal collection of Royal Navy postcards. Peter Hore introduced me to the Plymouth Naval Base Museum, the treasures of which I might otherwise have overlooked, and guided my first visit to that city.

Gillian Hughes was a skillful and much appreciated guide to the mysteries of the Admiralty archives at the Public Record Office, Kew. She also undertook a number of last-minute research assignments on my behalf as my book neared completion and I needed this name or that service record in short order.

Research for *Sober Men and True* involved extended annual residencies in London for the better part of a decade. Alison Lurie and Charles Weis made those annual visits possible by leasing me their London flats at rates which I could afford in London's terrifyingly expensive rental market. Christine Quayle kept both flats tidy and found me a replacement flat when one of them was sold.

Grinnell College, through its two successive vice-presidents for academic affairs, Charles Duke and James Swartz, and my colleagues on the Committee for the Support of Faculty Scholarship, provided the financial aid that made most of my London research trips possible. In 1995–96 I was awarded the Newberry Library/British Academy Fellowship for Study in Great Britain; this enabled me to extend that year's stay from my customary four or five weeks to a full three months. To all three institutions I am indeed grateful, because without their financial support I could never have afforded the travel and extended residencies that enabled me to write *Sober Men and True*. In 1990–91 I held the Secretary of the Navy's Research Chair in Naval History at the Naval Historical Center in Washington. Although the present book was not part of the work I undertook at the Naval Historical Center, I value highly the opportunity that year gave me to think about the problems of, and sources for, writing naval enlisted history—an opportunity I hope to continue to repay in my future work.

My 1997–98 sabbatical leave was spent at the Obermann Center for Advanced Studies of the University of Iowa, where I began the actual writing of the manuscript that eventually evolved into *Sober Men and True*. Director Jay Semel and his assistant Lorna Olson worked hard to make the Obermann Center an ideal setting for serious thought and productive writing—and they succeeded admirably!

For permission to reproduce in this book materials in their collections I am most grateful to Leslie H. Attrill, Geoffrey Clarkson, the Imperial War Museum, the National Maritime Museum, and the Royal Naval Museum. Similarly, the following individuals kindly granted me permission to quote material for which they hold the copyright: Leslie H. Attrill, Beryl Batters, Geoffrey Clarkson, Roger Davidson, Joan Dutton, Alan Eames, David Eames, Patricia L. Goatman, Donald S. Goodbrand, Audrey M. Green, A. W. Hawkes, Carole Jackson, Lillian McWilliam, Joy Mullins, Peggy W. Nancarrow, Harry Osborne, P. Read, Maisie M. Redhead, Alfred J. Rooke, B. H. Stamp, Gavin Stamp, Robert Thomas, J. M. Wainwright, Alan J. Welch, and one informant who asked that he not be identified by name.

I greatly regret that in a number of instances it proved impossible, in spite of sustained effort, to locate the copyright holders of certain materials quoted or reproduced in *Sober Men and True*. If any such will identify themselves to me, I will be happy to amend this omission in future printings or editions. In particular, I will welcome hearing from families that I was unable to contact who may wish to share additional information about the lives of their sailor-relatives who appear in these pages.

My friends Ira Dye and George Emery were good enough to read my manuscript and comment on it. Kenneth Hagan and Peter Karsten, the readers for Harvard University Press, made a number of fine suggestions that strengthened the book. *Sober Men and True* benefited from the excellent editorial eyes of David Lobenstine, Joyce Seltzer, and Christine Thorsteinsson of Harvard University Press—even if I was too stubborn to accept all of their wise recommendations. In preparing the photo essay I was particularly aided by David Lobenstine's expert guidance. *Sober Men and True* was not the manuscript that Joyce Seltzer solicited and was expecting from me, which makes me value all the more her resolute support of my writing over the past ten years and of the book that did finally arrive on her desk. Christine Hughes helped me by reading a set of the final proofs, a task an author could only inflict on a real friend.

Obermann Center colleague Jack D. Johnson unraveled Sonia's signature for me. Professor Dale C. Smith of the Uniformed Services University of the Health Sciences advised me on key medical points. Arnold Adelberg, professor of mathematics at Grinnell College, helped me sort out the long odds of crown and anchor; Jonathan Andelson, professor of anthropology, pointed the way to Victor Turner and rituals of status reversal; and Saadi Simawe, associate professor of English, translated Arabic street names in Alexandria for me. At the Grinnell College Libraries my colleagues Christina Coyle and Kevin Engel used their legendary information-finding skills to locate several pieces of essential data that were eluding me. My administrative assistant, Sharon Clayton, keeps my professional life in order, which enables me to find the time to pursue my research and writing. She also helped me proofread *Sober Men and True* not once but twice—and still said she liked the book!

My wife, Ann McKee, knows well my immense debt to her. Without Ann . . .

To each and all, my warmest thanks!

Index

Royal Navy is abbreviated RN

7/05⁴